CAMBODIA
& THE
VIETNAM WAR

CAMBODIA
& THE
VIETNAM WAR

Edited by Hal Kosut

FACTS ON FILE, INC.   NEW YORK

CAMBODIA
& THE
VIETNAM WAR

Library of Congress Catalog Card Number: 76-166436

ISBN 0-87196-208-X

9 8 7 6 5 4 3 2 1

PRINTED IN THE UNITED STATES OF AMERICA

N 106 CONTENTS

i

INTRODUCTION

CAMBODIA, ONE OF THE SMALLEST NATIONS of Southeast Asia, has played an increasingly major role in international politics because of the war in neighboring Vietnam.

The Vietnamese conflict has been raging with intensity since 1964, and Cambodia's borders were violated with increasing frequency by both sides. Major involvement of Cambodia in the Vietnam war finally took place in 1970. In an effort to cripple the operations of Communist Viet Cong and North Vietnamese troops operating in the border sanctuaries of Cambodia, U.S. and South Vietnamese forces launched a massive drive into Cambodia Apr. 29, 1970 and thereby transformed Cambodia into a major battle arena in the Indochina war.

In a prior development closely linked with the events leading to Cambodia's engulfment in the war, Prince Norodom Sihanouk, Cambodia's leading political figure for more than 2 decades, had been ousted Mar. 18 as Cambodian chief of state. At the time of his downfall, Sihanouk was on a trip to Moscow and Peking to solicit Soviet and Chinese Communist help in ridding Cambodia of the North Vietnamese and Viet Cong. Sihanouk was overthrown by a government he had appointed in Aug. 1969. This regime remained in office, with Gen. Lon Nol continuing as premier.

Prior to his ouster, Sihanouk had tried unsuccessfully, by military and political means, to force the withdrawal of the Communist troops from Cambodia. The Lon Nol government continued these efforts by proposing negotiations to bring about a peaceful withdrawal of the Communist forces from Cambodia. The North Vietnamese and Viet Cong, however, rejected these repeated offers.

At first, the Communists took measures to defend their base areas against Cambodian military pressure. But in early Apr. 1970 they began to move out of their sanctuaries along the Cambodian-South Vietnamese frontier and to penetrate deeper into Cambodian territory. Their apparent objective was to establish a solid Communist-held zone reaching to the port of Kompong Som on the Gulf of Siam and the sea along the

Cambodian-South Vietnamese frontier. This action plus their continued use of the border sanctuaries was regarded by the U.S. and South Vietnam as a threat to allied forces during a period when the policy of Vietnamization—of giving the South Vietnamese the chief role in the fighting—was proceeding in South Vietnam.

As a result of these developments, U.S. Pres. Richard M. Nixon announced Apr. 30 that the U.S. and South Vietnam were launching military operations into Communist-held territory in Cambodia for a period of exactly 2 months to protect U.S. and South Vietnamese military forces and the process of Vietnamization. The Cambodian government announced its approval of the U.S./South Vietnamese incursion as a means of preserving Cambodian sovereignty and neutrality.

The direct objective of the allied military operation was to capture Viet Cong/North Vietnamese stores and supplies, to disrupt Communist logistics and communications capabilities and to prevent the Viet Cong and North Vietnamese from building up their forces in these sanctuaries for attacks on U.S. and South Vietnamese forces. The American forces withdrew from Cambodia June 30 as scheduled, and Nixon said they had accomplished their mission. South Vietnamese troops remained, however, and fighting continued inside the Communist border sanctuaries and in other areas of Cambodia throughout the rest of 1970.

The American incursion into Cambodia precipitated widespread political repercussions in the U.S. The peace movement, in relative dormancy until then, was revitalized. University campuses were rocked by vociferous anti-war demonstrations. Congressional opposition was aroused. Fearing Presidential usurpation of Congress' foreign policy prerogatives, the Senate and House sought to restrict further actions by Nixon in Indochina without Congressional consent.

Following his dismissal from office, Sihanouk held a press conference in Peking May 5, 1970 and announced the formation of a Royal Government of National Union under the leadership of the National United Front of Kampuchea (Cambodia). The front was termed a liberation organization and was promised support by North Vietnam and other Communist nations. Sihanouk was proclaimed chief of state of this exile government, based in Peking, as well as chairman of the National United Front. Sihanouk's exile regime was recognized by Communist China, North Vietnam, Cuba and several other countries. Most nations, however, continued to recognize the Lon Nol regime as the only legitimate government of Cambodia.

This book is a journalistic record of the events that led to the U.S./South Vietnamese incursion into Cambodia, of the subsequent fighting that took place in Cambodia and of the political and diplomatic consequences of these operations. As with most INTERIM HISTORY books, this volume is based largely on material that appeared in FACTS ON FILE publications and is buttressed by information from State Department and various other governmental and press sources. Despite the controversial nature of the events recorded, every effort was made to keep this record as scrupulously free of bias as possible.

The Land & the People

Cambodia is a land of rice paddies and forest-covered hills and mountains on the Southeast Asian peninsula. Its area is about 66,000 square miles, approximately the size of Missouri. The level central part, formed by the basin of the Mekong River and the great lake of Tonle Sap, provides ideal conditions for rice cultivation. Along the 380-mile border with Thailand in the northwest runs a prominent and nearly continuous escarpment; a generally level plain is bounded with Laos to the northeast, South Vietnam to the east and forested hills and mountains to the southeast. The southwestern coastline on the Gulf of Thailand is irregular, fronted by many offshore islands, some of which are inhabited. The highest point in Cambodia, Phnom Aural in the western mountains, rises 5,741 feet above sea level.

The climate is like that of most other tropical monsoon-belt countries. The dry season extends from October to May. Annual rainfall at Pnompenh is approximately 58 inches. The temperature varies from about 68 degrees F. to 97 degrees F., and the humidity is consistently high.

Cambodia's population, estimated at close to 7 million, has a growth rate of 2.2% annually. The population density (about 104 persons per square mile) is low in comparison to other

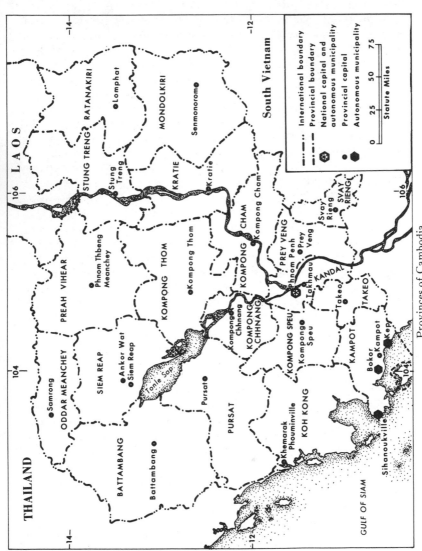

Provinces of Cambodia

Southeast Asian countries. Approximately 10% of the people live in Pnompenh.

Most of the people are ethnic Cambodians (Khmers). Cambodian society generally exhibits features common to other countries of Southeast Asia but is notably integrated and homogeneous. The Khmer majority, 85% of the population, is composed primarily of farmers living in small villages; there are few large landholders or tenant farmers. In recent years, however, the number of Khmers in the cities has increased sharply. With the expansion of the modern educational system, many Khmers are becoming active in business, government and other urban occupations.

Ethnic minorities consist of approximately 450,000 Chinese, 200,000 Vietnamese, 80,000 Cham-Malays (Moslems descended from the people of the ancient kingdom of Champa), 50,000 Khmer Loeu (hill tribesmen), 20,000 Thai and Lao, and 5,000 Europeans (mostly French). The small Burmese minority is important in the exploitation of gem deposits near Pailin. The Chinese community, important in trade and commerce, includes many of the pepper planters of the southwest. 75% of the Chinese speak the Teochiu dialect. The Vietnamese, many of whom migrated to Cambodia while the French ruled, are merchants, artisans and professional workers. About 25,000 Vietnamese fishermen live around the lake of Tonle Sap.

The common language is Khmer, and Theravada Buddhism is the national religion.

Cambodia's economy depends heavily on agriculture, stockraising and fishing, but efforts are being made to create an industrial base. Even though farms are small, methods primitive and productivity low, rice output is usually more than adequate. There is little pressure on land resources. Cambodia's balance of trade has generally been unfavorable despite the fact that imports are tightly restricted. (Most imports and exports were handled by a government foreign trade monopoly.) A relatively favorable foreign exchange position, however, has been maintained by the Cambodian government.

Brief History of Cambodia

Cambodia first appeared in recorded history as Chen-la, a vassal of the empire of Funan (*circa* 100-500 A.D.). Chen-la gradually won its freedom from Funan and overthrew the empire in the 6th century. (The name "Cambodia" was derived later from the name of an early Khmer ruler, Kambu Svayambhuva.) After a period of war, civil strife and foreign domination that followed the fall of Funan, Jayavarman II became king in 802, and his reign inaugurated the Khmer empire, which at its peak ruled not only Cambodia but also much of modern Thailand, Laos and South Vietnam. Cambodian power declined in the 14th century after the Thai sacked the imperial capital, Angkor, for the 2d time. Wars with Chams, Thai and Vietnamese reduced Cambodia to approximately its current borders by the beginning of the 19th century.

Cambodia struggled under increasing pressure from Thailand (Siam) and Vietnam until France appeared in the area. At the request of Cambodian King Ang Duong in 1863, France assumed a protectorate over Cambodia and prevented its division among its neighbors.

World War II turned France's attention elsewhere at a time, in the early 1940s when Japan had begun military moves aimed at the establishment of a "Greater East Asia Co-Prosperity Sphere." During this period Japan took *de facto* control of Cambodia. The Thai government had reached an accommodation with Japan, and it called on France to cede portions of northwestern Cambodia to Thailand. France refused, and Thai forces invaded Cambodia in Jan. 1941. After the Thais were defeated by the French, the Japanese intervened, and French authorities subsequently surrendered the northwestern provinces of Battambang and Siemreap to Thailand. Yet during most of World War II, until the spring of 1945, Japan permitted the Vichy French to continue nominal administrative control of Cambodia.

Allied forces occupied Pnompenh after the surrender of Japan ended World War II. Cambodia was recognized in Jan. 1946 as an autonomous kingdom within the French Union, and the 2 northwestern provinces were returned by Thailand. The Cambodian government also began negotiations to achieve an even greater degree of independence from France. In Feb. 1946 the French protectorate was replaced by a new arrangement, and in Nov. 1949 France and Cambodia signed an accord that made Cambodia an "Associated State" of the French Union.

In the early World War II year of 1941, when Norodom Sihanouk was 18, a crown council had elected him king. After the war Sihanouk persisted in attempts to obtain fuller independence for his country. Angered at what he denounced as French delays in granting more autonomy, Sihanouk began a public international and diplomatic campaign against French rule in June 1952. In June 1953, after traveling abroad to promote his cause, Sihanouk went into exile, refusing to return to Pnompenh until Cambodia was independent. The French government then announced July 4, 1953, that it was ready to "perfect" the independence and sovereignty of Cambodia (and the 2 other Indochinese states, Laos and Vietnam). Subsequent negotiations culminated Nov. 9, 1953, when the king announced Cambodia's attainment of full independence. Sihanouk abdicated in favor of his father in Mar. 1955 and resumed the title of prince. After the death of his father in 1960, Sihanouk assumed the title "chief of state" but allowed the throne to remain vacant.

After World War II France had faced a difficult military situation in Indochina. Vietnamese Communists began a rebellion for complete independence while France was trying to reestablish its control. In 1946 France accorded recognition to the Democratic Republic of Vietnam as a free state within the Indochinese Federation and French Union, and France agreed to withdraw its troops gradually from Vietnam. Fighting broke out, however. The 8-year conflict that followed spread to neighboring Cambodia and Laos. Viet Minh forces (purportedly a coalition of all anti-French Vietnamese groups) infiltrated into Cambodia from Vietnam in an effort to drive a wedge between French-supported areas in Indochina. The Cambodians, limited in their self-defense structure, relied almost entirely on French armed forces. The French were defeated May 7, 1954 by Viet Minh forces at Dienbienphu, North Vietnam. Pressure to end the Indochinese war had increased, and a Geneva conference was called to negotiate the peace terms.

The plenary sessions of the Geneva conference began May 8, 1954 with Cambodia, Laos and the State (later Republic) of (South) Vietnam participating along with France, Communist China, the U.S., the Democratic Republic of (North) Vietnam (the Viet Minh), the Soviet Union and Britain; the latter 2 countries served as co-chairmen. The Royal Cambodian delegation insisted that it was the only government that truly represented the Cambodian people, and it rejected a dissident Viet Minh-sponsored group that called itself the Free Cambodians ("Khmer Issarak").

The conference produced 4 documents known collectively as the "Geneva agreements of 1954": 3 separate cease-fire agreements covering Cambodia, Laos and Vietnam, respectively, and an unsigned final declaration. The Agreement on the Cessation of Hostilities in Cambodia of July 20, 1954 provided for a cease-fire, withdrawal of all foreign armed forces and military personnel, and the establishment of an International Control Commission (ICC)—representatives of Canada, India and Poland—to supervise its execution.

All conference participants, except the U.S. and the State of (South) Vietnam, associated themselves (by voice) with the final declaration. The U.S. delegate, State Undersecy. Walter Bedell Smith, stated that U.S. policy with regard to the Geneva agreements would be to refrain from the threat or the use of force to disturb the agreements and that the U.S. would view any renewal of aggression in violation of the agreements with grave concern and as seriously threatening international peace and security. The official Cambodian delegation agreed to the neutrality of the 3 Indochinese states, but it insisted on a provision in the cease-fire agreement that left the Cambodian government free to call for outside military assistance should the Viet Minh again threaten its territory or should others do so.

In a protocol to the Southeast Asia Collective Defense Treaty (the "Manila Pact"), which entered into force Feb. 19, 1955, the signatory states designated Cambodia, Laos and Vietnam as states to which Article IV of the treaty could apply at the invitation or with the consent of the country concerned. (Article IV provided for collective defense measures in case of armed attack.) In early 1956, while continuing Cambodia's posture of neutrality, Prince Sihanouk announced Cambodia's rejection of the Southeast Asia Treaty Organization (SEATO) "umbrella." In Sept. 1957 his government enacted a law to define neutrality as noncommitment to a military alliance or ideological bloc. It declared that Cambodia would abstain from such alliances and from aggressive actions.

Cambodia tried to hold to this commitment of neutrality as its neighboring countries of Laos and particularly South Vietnam came under increased Communist attack. The Vietnamese Communists in the late 1950s reactivated their insurgent apparatus in South Vietnam, and terrorism and guerrilla operations were intensified in the early 1960s. After a brief lull and the 14-nation Geneva conference on Laos of 1962, fighting again broke out in Laos in Apr. 1963. Sihanouk did not concede publicly that Cambodian provinces were being occupied by North Vietnamese army/Viet Cong troops until 1968, although their presence had been confirmed repeatedly by the mid-1960s.

Governmental Structure

After the Lon Nol government ousted Sihanouk as chief of state Mar. 18, 1970, it abolished the Cambodian monarchy and proclaimed the country the Khmer Republic Oct. 9, 1970. The Cambodian constitution, promulgated May 6, 1947, vested executive power in the Council of Ministers (cabinet), headed by a premier and responsible to the National Assembly. A revised constitution was drafted to reflect the change from monarchy to republic, and the Cambodian government said it would submit to a national referendum when security conditions permitted.

The Cambodian parliament is bicameral. The National Assembly (lower house), with 82 members, is elected by universal adult suffrage to a 4-year term. The Senate (upper house) has 24 members, who represent professional and regional interests and are elected by indirect suffrage. The National Assembly passes laws and sends them to the Senate; the Assembly can override any objection of the Senate by a vote of an absolute majority of the Assembly members.

The judicial system incorporates French juridical practices with traditional Cambodian forms. The constitution states that the separation of powers (executive, legislative and judicial) is alien to Cambodian tradition; these judicial powers are exercised in the name of the chief of state. In practice, however, with certain exceptions, separation does exist, and the power to interpret the constitution is assigned to the National Assembly, not the judiciary. There are 4 types of tribunals in criminal matters—the local courts (misdemeanors), courts of first instance (lesser offenses), criminal courts (felonies) and the Court of Review. Until independence, Cambodians and foreign nationals who violated French laws were tried by French courts under French law.

Administratively, Cambodia is divided into 20 Provinces *(khet),* the autonomous capital city, Pnompenh, and 5 other autonomous municipalities—Kirirom, Kep, Bokor, Pailin and Kompong Som. Pnompenh is administered by a governor assisted by an appointed municipal commission. Each provincial governor represents the central government and is responsible to the interior minister. The governors supervise the administrative subdivisions: districts *(srok),* townships *(sangkat,* or *khum)* and villages *(phum)* of the province. Since 1969 a number of sub-provinces *(anouckhet),* each incorporating 2 or 3 districts, have been created to improve administrative control, especially in remote or insurgent-plagued areas.

A Few Words About Sihanouk

Cambodia's outstanding 20th-century leader, the enigmatic Norodom Sihanouk, was born Oct. 31, 1922. The great-grandson of King Norodom and the grandson of King Sisowath, Sihanouk attended French schools in Saigon (Cochin China) and Paris before, at the age of 18, he was elected to the throne Apr. 26, 1941 by the Royal Council. (The royal title in Cambodia was not strictly hereditary; the king was either nominated by his predecessor or elected by the Royal Council.)

Sihanouk remained king during World War II when the Japanese forces ousted the French colonial rulers. When Japan granted independence to Cambodia in 1945, the king declared Cambodia independent of France. But in Jan. 1946 he and

France concluded an agreement that left the French in control of Cambodia's defense and foreign affairs. France gave Cambodia total independence Dec. 29, 1954 under the terms of the Geneva agreements ending the war in Indochina. Sihanouk then sought to change the electoral provisions of his country's 1947 constitution but was opposed by the International Control Commission supervising the Geneva accords. Sihanouk, therefore, abdicated Mar. 2, 1955 in favor of his father, Norodom Suramarit.

Sihanouk, however, continued to play a major role in shaping Cambodian policy. His first act was to organize a political party, the Popular Socialists, usually referred to as the Sangkum, which won an overwhelming majority in the Sept. 1955 elections. Cambodia, under his guidance, chose to follow a neutralist policy in international affairs and accepted aid from the U.S., the Colombo powers (Burma, Ceylon, India, Indonesia and Pakistan) and France as well as from the Communist bloc. During this period Sihanouk served as leader of the Sangkum and at times as premier.

Following the death of his father, King Norodom Suramarit, Apr. 3, 1960, Sihanouk assumed the office of chief of state. His policies received overwhelming support in a popular referendum held in June.

Sihanouk's rule during the following 10 years was marked by an unending struggle to maintain his country's neutrality, which was increasingly endangered by the Vietnamese war raging along Cambodia's borders. He was caught between the presence of North Vietnamese/Viet Cong on Cambodian soil using border sanctuaries and mounting U.S./South Vietnamese assaults on the Communist forces in those areas. Sihanouk's position was further complicated by the rising criticism of his domestic rule by his political foes. These factors led to his ouster as chief of state Mar. 18, 1970. Sihanouk established a government-in-exile in Peking in May with the asserted intention of eventually returning to his homeland to reassert political power.

GROWING INVOLVEMENT: 1962-9

Cambodia's embroilment in the Vietnamese conflict began in 1962 when its border regions were first entered in brief operations by South Vietnamese forces in hot pursuit of Viet Cong and North Vietnamese troops seeking sanctuary in Cambodian territory. In the ensuing years, these operations, joined by American forces, mounted in intensity as the Communists made wider use of Cambodia as a haven from allied air and ground strikes.

The seriousness of the increasing Communist use of Cambodian border regions was reflected in Dec. 1965 in an American command directive authorizing the pursuit of enemy forces from South Vietnam into Cambodia under certain circumstances.

Prince Norodom Sihanouk, Cambodian chief of state, insisted publicly that he was helpless to prevent the movement of Communist forces into and out of Cambodia. U.S. official and press sources, however, intimated strongly that Sihanouk was conniving at Communist military activity in Cambodia. This charge was vigorously denied by the Cambodian government.

The years 1962-9, leading up to Cambodia's direct involvement in the Vietnam war, were marked also by the intensification of the country's long-standing border dispute with South Vietnam. Cambodia and South Vietnam had competed for the Mekong Delta ricelands since the 17th century, when the Vietnamese had started moving down the coast and pushing the Khmer—or Cambodian—farmers inland. The southern border regions had never been defined clearly and remained undelineated after the French colonial government left Indochina in 1955. (Even after the downfall of Sihanouk in 1970 and South Vietnam's subsequent military cooperation in fighting the Communist intruders on its soil, the divergent

13

border claims and the bitterness surrounding them remained a source of friction between the 2 countries.)

The first incidents of South Vietnamese attacks on Cambodia's border areas in 1962 led to a Pnompenh decision the following year to sever diplomatic relations with Saigon. Cambodia's relations with the U.S. began to deteriorate in 1963, following an insulting statement allegedly made by the Cambodian government on Pres. John F. Kennedy's assassination. Both nations withdrew first their ambassadors. Sihanouk then severed ties with Washington in May 1965, after holding the U.S. responsible for an air strike on a Cambodian village the previous month. Efforts by both sides to reconcile their differences finally resulted in an agreement in June 1969 to restore diplomatic relations.

Pressured by stepped-up allied air and ground attacks on Viet Cong and North Vietnamese forces in the Cambodian border areas, and the resultant heavy civilian casualties, Sihanouk Nov. 25, 1963 issued an appeal for an international parley, similar to the 1954 Geneva conference, to safeguard his country's neutrality. Although Britain and the Soviet Union, as co-chairmen of the Geneva conference, favored such a meeting, the conference never materialized. Cambodia's plea for international assistance in keeping out of the Vietnam war was also directed at the UN Security Council, with which it filed frequent protests against allied attacks on its territory. The Council sought to settle the Cambodian-South Vietnamese border dispute by sending a commission to the region in 1964. The commission made several recommendations to deal with the problem. But both sides remained intransigent, and the proposals were never acted on.

Cambodia Cuts Ties with Saigon

Cambodia severed diplomatic relations with South Vietnam Aug. 27, 1963. The move was in protest against alleged border violations and South Vietnam's alleged persecution of South Vietnamese Buddhists. (Trade between the 2 countries was to be maintained despite the lack of diplomatic ties.) A resolution adopted by the Cambodian parliament Aug.

26 had accused Saigon of "multiple violations" of the Cambodian border. In one incident, a Vietnamese gunboat was said to have shelled a Cambodian village on the Gulf of Siam, killing one person. Thousands of Vietnamese residents of Cambodia demonstrated outside the Vietnamese embassy in Pnompenh when the severance of relations was announced. The demonstrators proclaimed their sympathy with their fellow Buddhists in South Vietnam and denounced the Saigon government of Pres. Ngo Dinh Diem.

Cambodia Seeks Neutrality Guarantee & Foreign Aid

2 factors—the increasing attacks on the Cambodian border by South Vietnamese forces pursuing Communist troops, and Pnompenh's deteriorating relations with Saigon and Washington—prompted Cambodia to issue a call Nov. 25, 1963 for the convening of an international conference to arrange for guarantees of Cambodia's independence and neutrality. The Pnompenh regime sought at the same time to strengthen its position by appealing for financial and moral support from France and Communist China.

Cambodia's call for a neutrality conference was directed at Britain and the USSR, co-chairmen of the 14-nation Geneva Conference of 1954, which had ended the Indochinese war and had led to the independence of the current 4 Indochinese states—North and South Vietnam, Laos and Cambodia. The Cambodian note suggested that a 9-nation meeting be held in Burma or Indonesia and be attended by representatives of Cambodia, Laos, South and North Vietnam, Communist China, the U.S. and France. All 9 nations (with Britain and the USSR as co-chairmen) had participated in the 1954 Geneva Conference. The Cambodian note reiterated previous charges by Sihanouk that South Vietnam, with the aid of the U.S., was threatening Cambodian security. Sihanouk Aug. 20, 1962 had proposed a similar international conference to guarantee Cambodia's borders.

Sihanouk promised Dec. 21 that the proposed conference would not be turned into a forum to attack policies of the U.S. and its Southeast Asian allies. The U.S. had accepted in principle the holding of such a meeting on the condition that its agenda be confined to discussion of Cambodia's neutrality. A government communique announcing Sihanouk's statement said that Cambodia had proposed the conference only "to obtain international recognition *de jure* of her neutrality." The communique suggested the formation of an international commission to guarantee Cambodia's neutrality.

Soviet Foreign Min. Andrei Gromyko had informed British Foreign Secy. R. A. Butler Dec. 17 that Moscow favored the proposed conference. Britain was reported Dec. 20 to have given its approval to the USSR and Cambodia.

Pressing his campaign for the international conference, Sihanouk warned the West Dec. 29 that if it refused to guarantee Cambodian neutrality, "we will be obliged to renounce our neutrality and negotiate a formal alliance with China." Sihanouk delivered his warning in a policy speech opening a 3-day "national congress." Sihanouk charged in the speech that the U.S. opposed Cambodian neutrality. "The American imperialists consider that we will not be independent unless we accept U.S. control of our national life," he said.

Sihanouk had announced Dec. 20 that his cancellation of U.S. economic and military aid Nov. 20 did not mean that his country was moving closer to Communist China. He emphasized that after the U.S. assistance was terminated, "France will continue to have a much more privileged position in Cambodia than anyone else."

Sihanouk announced that "France will continue to have administrative and military technicians here who are privy to the most secret affairs of this nation." He said that a French mission was due in Cambodia in Jan. 1964 and that "we will undoubtedly receive aid for our education system and long-term loans for our state enterprises." It had been reported Nov. 21 that Sihanouk had asked France to replace the U.S. assistance program. Agence France-Presse, the semi-official French news agency, said in Paris that Sihanouk had asked for French teachers to train engineers and technicians who had been instructed by departing Americans as part of the U.S. assistance mission. Sihanouk also was said to have asked France for military equipment in the form of trucks, armored cars and launches. Asserting that French Pres. Charles de Gaulle was concerned with the maintenance of Cambodia's as well as Vietnam's neutrality, Sihanouk said "no one can accuse him of practicing imperialism or neocolonialism here."

Aid from Communist sources had also been successfully solicited by Sihanouk. Chinese Communist Foreign Min. Chen Yi had promised Nov. 20 that Peking would provide Cambodia with "resolute support" in its "just and patriotic struggle against imperialism." Chen charged that Cambodia's "policy of peace and neutrality" was being "seriously threatened" by "increasingly frantic attacks and subversive activities" carried out by "U.S. imperialism" and Cambodian rebels operating from South Vietnam. A formal pledge of aid to Cambodia was made Nov. 21 in a Peking announcement that said the Chinese government would give Cambodia "all-out support" if it "encounter[ed] an armed invasion by the United States and its vassals." The announcement charged that the U.S. "and its vassals, the authorities of South Vietnam and Thailand," had increased "activities of flagrant aggression and subversion" against Cambodia, "seriously threatening its independence and security, the peace of Southeast Asia."

Sihanouk disclosed Nov. 22 that he had received a Chinese note pledging military, political and diplomatic backing in the event of "aggression" from South Vietnam or Thailand. Although acknowledging that Communist China was "Cambodia's best friend," Sihanouk said Cambodia had no intention of becoming Communist as long as its neutrality was not threatened. Denying that his government would become a Chinese satellite, Sihanouk called Peking "the explanation and cause of our survival" because a "balance of menaces" existed between China and hostile South Vietnamese and Thai troops who wanted to "kill" Cambodia.

(An agreement signed in Pnompenh Nov. 25 provided for the establishment of a regular airline between mainland China and Cambodia.)

Relations with U.S. Deteriorate

An alleged insulting statement by the Cambodian government on Pres. Kennedy's assassination Nov. 21, 1963 caused a deterioration in U.S.-Cambodian relations and led to the withdrawal of the 2 nations' ambassadors.

Reacting to a U.S. protest against the statement, Prince Sihanouk recalled Amb. Nong Kimny Dec. 12 and ordered the closing of the Cambodian embassy in Washington. U.S. Amb. Philip D. Sprouse was recalled to Washington for consultations Dec. 13.

The U.S. protest to Pnompenh, delivered by Sprouse, was based on a Cambodian communique broadcast by the government radio and picked up by U.S. monitors. The communique was said to have expressed rejoicing at the deaths of South Vietnamese Pres. Ngo Dinh Diem, Thai Premier Sarit Thanarat and "the great boss of these aggressors" (a phrase regarded by U.S. officials as an allusion to Kennedy). The Cambodian government Dec. 12 denied that any reference to Kennedy had been made in the broadcast. The Cambodian press service explained that in regard to Diem and Sarit the government communique had expressed satisfaction not for their deaths but for "the liberation from the menaces ... which they symbolized during their lives and from which peaceful Cambodia would have suffered during many years."

Sihanouk Dec. 14 ordered the recall of the Cambodian ambassador to Britain and the closing of the government's embassy in London. His action reportedly was the result of (a) British Amb. Peter Murray's protest about the alleged statement about Kennedy and (b) Britain's unfavorable response to Sihanouk's appeal for an international conference to guarantee Cambodia's neutrality.

Philippine Foreign Secy. Salvador P. Lopez announced Dec. 27 that the U.S. and Cambodia had accepted Pres. Diosdado Macapagal's offer to help resolve their dispute. The acceptance of Manila's mediation bid followed Philippine contacts that had started Dec. 23 with U.S. and Cambodian officials in Pnompenh and Manila. In accepting the Philippine offer, Sihanouk Dec. 26 repeated his previous demands that U.S.-Cambodian talks be contingent on (a) an apology by Charles W. Yost, U.S. delegate at the UN, for having charged that a Cambodian broadcast had expressed pleasure at Kennedy's assassination and (b) a formal withdrawal by U.S. Amb. Sprouse of his demand for an investigation of the broadcast. Sihanouk had first listed his demands as a condition for accepting a U.S. suggestion that ex-State Secy. Dean Acheson go to Pnompenh to discuss a possible U.S.-Cambodian reconciliation. The U.S. State Department Dec. 19 formally rejected Sihanouk's demands; it said it "obviously" had not expected that the proposed discussions "would be associated with conditions." The Cambodian government Dec. 24 then rejected the proposed Acheson mission.

Sihanouk discussed the U.S.-Cambodian dispute at a meeting with Macapagal in Manila Jan. 23-26, 1964. At the conclusion of the talks, Macapagal announced that Cambodia had accepted an undefined Philippine proposal to settle the feud and "bring about the restoration of normal relations between the 2 countries." The U.S. had accepted the plan previously. Sihanouk and Macapagal in Pnompenh Feb. 12 signed another joint communique. In it Cambodia thanked the Philippines for "bringing about settlement of certain misunderstandings" with the U.S.

Border Clashes Intensify

Cambodia's relations with the U.S. and South Vietnam grew worse rather than better in the mid-1960s as Viet Cong/North Vietnamese use of Cambodian sanctuaries brought increased cross-border attacks by U.S. and South Vietnamese forces on Communist military elements in Cambodian territory.

Prince Sihanouk asserted Feb. 11, 1964, that 5 Cambodian civilians had been killed in a South Vietnamese air strike Feb. 6 on the Cambodian village of Mong. He held the U.S. responsible for the attack. Sihanouk made the charge in disclosing that following the attack he had sent notes to the U.S., Britain and the Soviet Union; the notes repeated his previous demands for an international conference on Cambodia's neutrality. Charging that the U.S. was partially responsible because of its "overarming" of South Vietnam, Sihanouk said the conference would help prevent future attacks on Cambodian territory. Sihanouk warned in his notes to the 3 nations that if the U.S. remained "passive" to his plea for neutrality talks, "we would be compelled to modify our neutrality status and would have to consider assistance pacts with certain great friendly countries."

Cambodian and South Vietnamese officials met in Pnompenh Mar. 20 to discuss the border problem. But the negotiations were abandoned Mar. 23 because of tension caused by a South Vietnamese air and ground attack Mar. 19 on the Cambodian border village of Chantrea; 17 villagers were killed in the attack which was the most serious border crossing to date. (A Saigon dispatch Mar. 19 admitted that the Vietnamese unit had strayed into Cambodia in pursuit of Viet Cong guerrillas.) A joint communique issued in Pnompenh Mar. 23 said the Chantrea raid had created an "atmosphere" that was "not now favorable for negotiations." The conference had been requested by Sihanouk.

A Cambodian communique Mar. 20 had accused the U.S. and South Vietnam of joint participation in the Chantrea attack. The communique reiterated Cambodia's appeal for an international conference to assure Cambodia's neutrality. Detailing his charges concerning the assault on Chantrea, Sihanouk said Mar. 20 that 12 Vietnamese armored cars, accompanied by U.S. personnel, had penetrated 4 miles into Cambodia to attack Chantrea. A U.S.-made L-19 observation plane, shot down during the incident, crashed in South Vietnamese territory; a Vietnamese airman was killed and an American seriously injured.

The U.S. apologized for the Chantrea incident Mar. 21. In apparent reference to the L-19, a State Department statement said Cambodian planes might have shot down "an unarmed aircraft in South Vietnam's airspace." The statement attributed the village attack to faulty map reading. South Vietnamese Premier Nguyen Khanh Mar. 21 also apologized for the attack but charged that 2 Cambodian T-28 fighters were responsible for the shooting down of the L-19, which he said had crashed 2½ miles inside Vietnam. Huyn Van Cao, South Vietnam's chief negotiator in the Pnompenh border talks, visited Chantrea Mar. 21. Afterwards, he called the attack "a shameful mistake" and pledged compensation.

Sihanouk visited Chantrea Mar. 22. In a broadcast from the village, he declared that U.S. and Saigon apologies alone would not save the Cambodian-Vietnamese border talks. Charging that the U.S. was largely responsible for violations of Cambodian territory, Sihanouk warned that if the U.S., Britain and other interested countries did not agree by Mar. 30 (a deadline extended from Mar. 23) to attend a Cambodian neutrality conference, he would "go to Peking to discuss our problems with our good Chinese friends." Sihanouk expressed hope that Peking would help resolve Cambodia's frontier problems with "the ultimate masters of South Vietnam—that is, the government of North Vietnam." Sihanouk's explanation for extending the deadline was to give France and the Soviet Union, both of whom favored a neutrality conference, more time to exert pressure on nations reluctant to attend.

Cambodia Mar. 22 sent to Washington a protest demanding a formal apology for the Chantrea attack and payment for damages.

Prior to the receipt of the Cambodian protest, State Secy. Dean Rusk had sent Cambodian officials a note explaining the U.S.' version of the incident. Rusk's note, made public by the U.S. embassy in Pnompenh Mar. 23, said: "An American adviser was present with Vietnam ground forces" during the attack. "Following the bombing attack, about 4 Americans briefly landed with Vietnamese officers.... When it became clear ... that an error had been committed, the Vietnamese armed forces and the American personnel promptly withdrew." "No American personnel engaged in any firing or directly participated in the military action during the incidents."

In a letter to British Foreign Secy. R. A. Butler (made public Mar. 24), Sihanouk cited the Chantrea attack as further evidence of the need for a full-scale international meeting on Cambodia's neutrality. Sihanouk characterized Britain's reluctance to agree to such a conference as "ambiguous," "incomprehensible" and "stalling." Sihanouk rejected further bilateral talks with South Vietnam and withdrew his previous suggestion for a 4-power meeting of Cambodia, South Vietnam, the U.S. and Thailand. Sihanouk's note was in reply to a request by Butler for clarification of Sihanouk's various conference proposals.

London's preference for a 4-power conference on Cambodia was conveyed to the USSR Mar. 24 in a British note rejecting a request by Moscow (reported Mar. 23) to join it in calling a full-scale neutrality meeting. Asserting that there was no point in calling such a meeting until Thailand's and South Vietnam's participation was assured, the British appealed to Moscow to join Britain in issuing a plea to those 2 nations to join Cambodia and the U.S. in a discussion of the frontier problem.

The Chantrea incident was followed by further clashes on the South Vietnamese-Cambodian border in May and June 1964:

● Cambodian military authorities charged that South Vietnamese armored vehicles· had crossed 2 miles inside Cambodian territory May 7 and had raided the village of Taey, killing 6 persons.

● A South Vietnamese M-113 armored personnel carrier was destroyed May 8 by gunfire from a Cambodian M-24 tank after the M-113 had penetrated about ½ mile into Cambodian territory in pursuit of Viet Cong guerrillas. The AP reported that one Vietnamese soldier was killed and another wounded; both were turned over to Vietnamese authorities. The remaining M-113 occupants were captured. (The armored vehicle normally carried 15 soldiers and 4 operators.) At least 10 other Vietnamese armored vehicles involved in the anti-Viet Cong operation moved into the area but made no attempt to interfere with the Cambodian force. The action occurred near the Cambodian town of Chiphou, about 45 miles northwest of Saigon. According to witnesses, the Viet Cong troops fled unhindered through a Cambodian infantry unit, and the Cambodians then opened fire on the Vietnamese pursuers.

● The South Vietnamese Defense Ministry reported June 3 that Cambodian soldiers had killed 2 Vietnamese policemen June 2 near the Dinh Tien Hoang border post 85 miles north of Saigon.

A South Vietnamese government memo published May 27 accused Cambodia of provoking 95 border incidents and of violating Vietnamese airspace 9 times since Jan. 1963. Admitting that Vietnamese forces also had been responsible for some border violations, the Saigon memo said: "Responsibility is shared, and the errors are unavoidable. These errors will not end until confidence and friendship reign between the 2 countries."

Viet Cong Haven in Cambodia Reported   •

The *N.Y. Times* reported from Saigon May 20, 1964 that, according to Western intelligence sources, the Viet Cong were receiving haven and aid in Cambodia under a prearranged plan with Cambodian border unit commanders.

The sources said: The Viet Cong entered Cambodian territory freely to buy food and supplies. The Cambodians provided the guerrillas with safety in moving away from or into combat areas, and the Cambodians gave the Viet Cong intelligence reports about South Vietnamese troop strength and movements. The Viet Cong, in turn, disposed of their individual weapons on approaching Cambodian villages (except in combat) and conducted themselves in such a discreet manner that Cambodian authorities could disclaim awareness of their actual role. The U.S. and South Vietnam had been aware of this Cambodian-Viet Cong collusion but preferred not to raise the matter lest it jeopardize their efforts to reach a border agreement with Prince Norodom Sihanouk.

UN Mission Visits Border Areas

A 3-man UN Security Council commission visited the Cambodian-South Vietnamese border region June 26-July 14, 1964 to seek ways of ending the frontier clashes.

Reporting back to the Council July 28, the commission suggested: (a) Having the border clearly marked to avoid confusion; (b) appointing a top-level UN negotiator "approved by the 2 parties" to bring the South Vietnamese and Cambodian governments together to discuss the frontier problem; (c) urging the 2 governments to resume diplomatic relations; (d) sending teams of unarmed UN civilian observers to Cambodia to see if there were frontier incursions.

Cambodia had agreed to the UN observer plan. But South Vietnam had insisted, in a proposal unacceptable to Cambodia, that an international police force be established to keep the frontier under surveillance.

The report attributed much of the trouble to Cambodia's neutralism as contrasted with South Vietnam's pro-Western position.

In a message to the Security Council, made public July 29, Cambodia accused the U.S. and South Vietnam of conducting a chemical warfare campaign that had caused the deaths of 76 persons in 6 Cambodian villages. The message alleged that airplanes had dropped toxic powder on villages in the Dandaungpich area of Ratanakiri Province June 13 and 20 and July 9, 17, 20, 21, 22 and 23. It called the attacks "part of the chemical warfare that the United States-South Vietnamese forces had hitherto waged only in South Vietnam." It said the Cambodian government had protested to the U.S. and South Vietnamese governments and had appealed for help to the co-chairmen of the 1954 Geneva conference, Britain and the Soviet Union.

The U.S. Aug. 3 denied Cambodia's charges and told the Security Council that it would welcome an impartial investigation. South Vietnam also denied the charges Aug. 3.

U.S. Amb.-to-UN Adlai E. Stevenson criticized Cambodia Sept. 11 for refusing to cooperate with the UN commission's efforts to ease Cambodian-Vietnamese border tensions. In a memo to the Security Council, Stevenson praised the commission's July 28 report. Stevenson chided Pnompenh for not having submitted to the commission during its visit to Cambodia its charges that South Vietnamese planes had sprayed Cambodian villages with toxic chemicals. Cambodia repeated those charges in a memo handed to the Council Sept. 11. Terming the commission's proposals "strictly unacceptable," the Cambodian note said the UN group had no right to propose the resumption of Cambodian-Vietnamese diplomatic relations. In a note to the Council Aug. 28, South Vietnam had proposed the creation of a joint Cambodian-Vietnamese commission to investigate border incidents.

Cambodia Accused of Intervention

South Vietnamese Premier Nguyen Khanh accused Prince Sihanouk Sept. 19, 1964 of working with South Vietnam's enemies.

Khanh asserted that Sihanouk had sought to arrange talks between the Viet Cong and South Vietnamese neutralist exiles for the purpose of promoting a truce between the guerrillas and South Vietnamese forces. Khanh produced what he said was a facsimile of a letter Sihanouk reportedly had sent to ex-South Vietnamese Premier Tran Van Huu, head of the neutralist Committee for Peace & Revival for South Vietnam, which had its headquarters in Paris. The letter said that in response to

Huu's request, Sihanouk had invited Nguyen Huu Tho, head of the National Liberation Front (political arm of the Viet Cong), to send a representative to Pnompenh to confer with Huu's group. Tho, according to the letter, had sent a positive reply. Huu and the front were supporters of French Pres. Charles de Gaulle's proposal to end the South Vietnamese war and neutralize the country. Tho and other front leaders reportedly were in Cambodia.

Khanh called the letter evidence of Sihanouk's "positive connection with elements out to destroy" South Vietnam.

Border Clashes Increase

U.S. and South Vietnamese forces became increasingly involved in border clashes with Cambodia during September-October 1964:

● The South Vietnamese Defense Ministry charged that Cambodian mortars Sept. 5 had shelled South Vietnamese soldiers about 12 miles northwest of Hong Ngu to cover a retreating Viet Cong battalion that had been routed by a South Vietnamese force.

● The South Vietnamese Defense Ministry said Sept. 7 that a government soldier had been killed Sept. 6 when 10 Cambodian gunboats on a Mekong River tributary fired on a South Vietnamese post about one mile from the Cambodian frontier.

● Cambodia accused South Vietnam Sept. 6 of having launched a "major attack" the previous day near the Cambodian border town of Koh Rokar.

● A South Vietnamese communique Sept. 11 formally accused Cambodia of assisting the Viet Cong forces. Citing 2 instances, the communique said: Cambodian soldiers July 19 had machinegunned the Vietnamese border post of Cau Muong while it was being attacked by Viet Cong troops; the Cambodian border post of Banteai-Chakrey had fired on South Vietnamese troops Aug. 30 as they were pursuing 200 Viet Cong troops near the Cambodian border.

● Cambodia charged Oct. 21 that 3 South Vietnamese planes had bombed the village of Anlong Kres (one mile inside Cambodia) Oct. 20 and had killed 8 persons and wounded 8 others. A Cambodian protest filed with the UN Oct. 22 accused the U.S. of having participated in the attack with South

Vietnam. Prince Sihanouk protested the incident Oct. 24 in
notes to Soviet Foreign Min. Andrei Gromyko and British
Foreign Secy. Patrick Gordon Walker.

● A U.S. Army officer was captured Oct. 22 by Viet Cong
forces near the Cambodian border and was later found shot to
death. The officer, Capt. Herman Y. Towery of Georgetown,
S.C., was seized in Kien Phong Province, 80 miles west of
Saigon, by Communist troops who, reportedly, had come from
Cambodia. Towery was taken away in one of 8 sampans that
had engaged a similar fleet of Vietnamese boats. The officer's
body was reported Oct. 25 to have been found on South
Vietnamese territory 150 yards from the Cambodian border.

● A U.S. Air Force C-123 transport was shot down by ground
fire Oct. 24 near the Cambodian frontier as it was flying
supplies from Saigon to a Special Forces camp at Buprang, 100
miles north of the capital. 8 Americans aboard were killed. U.S.
authorities were not sure about whether the plane was hit by
Viet Cong or Cambodian ground fire. The Cambodian
government reported that its anti-aircraft guns had shot down
a twin-engine plane Oct. 24 over Cambodian territory. But
U.S. officials insisted that the C-123 was inside South Vietnam.
A U.S. spokesman in Saigon said Oct. 28 that the plane had
been hit by automatic weapon fire from the vicinity of the
Cambodian village of Dak Dam. He said that the unarmed
plane had accidentally penetrated Cambodian airspace because
of a "map-reading error" and bad weather. The U.S. official
said that U.S. helicopters, supporting rescue operations, had
attacked Dak Dam Oct. 25 in retaliation and had recovered the
bodies of 7 of the U.S. airmen during that operation. A
conflicting version of the incident was given Oct. 28 by Prince
Sihanouk and made public Oct. 29. Sihanouk said 2 U.S. planes,
and not one, had been shot down by Cambodian border guards
at Mondolkiri. (In support of its claim that the aircraft had
crashed on Cambodian territory, Cambodia was reported to
have brought the wreckage of a C-123 to Pnompenh Oct. 30 to
be exhibited during independence celebrations Nov. 9.)

A U.S. State Department statement Oct. 30 expressed
regret that U.S. "unarmed planes [had] inadvertently crossed
the Cambodian border." But it contended that this "in no way
... justified this precipitate action by the Cambodian forces

resulting in the loss of 8 American lives." The U.S. sent a formal protest to Cambodia Nov. 2.

U.S. and South Vietnamese leaders in Saigon admitted Oct. 28 that increased Viet Cong activity from Cambodian bases had precipitated U.S.-Vietnamese air action against Cambodian targets at least 5 times in the previous week.

U.S. officials in Washington reported Oct. 28 the receipt Oct. 26 of 4 Cambodian notes protesting recent border incidents. One related to the shooting down of the U.S. C-123, 2 referred to an alleged South Vietnamese air attack Oct. 28 on the Cambodian village of Anlong Kres in which 8 civilians were killed, and the 4th concerned the kidnaping and slaying of Capt. Towery. The note denied U.S. charges that a Cambodian fort had laid down covering fire to permit the Viet Cong to take Towery and 3 South Vietnamese prisoners back toward Cambodia. (The bodies of Towery and 2 of the Vietnamese were found on Vietnamese territory.)

A Cambodian communique issued Oct. 27 by Sihanouk warned that his government would sever diplomatic relations with the U.S. if there were further U.S.-supported Vietnamese attacks on the Cambodian frontier. Sihanouk threatened in the event of the "next aggression" to recognize North Vietnam and the National Liberation Front in South Vietnam. He warned that if Cambodia were attacked again its armed forces would carry out armed "reprisals regardless of the consequences."

Saigon accused Cambodia Oct. 27 of violations of South Vietnamese territory. Air Commodore Nguyen Cao Ky charged that in one of "several" raids 2 Cambodian planes had attacked a government outpost 50 miles west of Saigon Oct. 25. The Defense Ministry charged that in a joint operation Oct. 26 3 Cambodian planes and 100 boatloads of troops had crossed the border in the Kien Phong Province area and bombed and strafed the area.

34 dependents of U.S. embassy employes in Pnompenh were flown to Bangkok, Thailand Oct. 30 and Nov. 1. Their departure was a precautionary move taken against possible anti-U.S. demonstrations. Anti-U.S. feelings in Cambodia were pointed up in an article published Nov. 1 by the offical press agency AKP. Referring to an attack on Anlong Kres, Oct. 20, it said "the dead have fallen under the bullets and bombs of

modern barbarians ... [who came] from the mountains of Mississippi, Ohio or Missouri to exterminate a people who
would resist them."

Sihanouk Urges Indochina Stand Against U.S.

Prince Sihanouk appealed Nov. 9, 1964 to North and South
Vietnam and Laos to join Cambodia in a conference to
denounce U.S. policies in Southeast Asia. Speaking at
independence day anniversary ceremonies in Pnompenh,
Sihanouk said that "all the parties and patriotic movements" of
the 4 countries should meet and explain to the world that
Southeast Asia's peace "has been stolen from us by the
Americans." The meeting, Sihanouk said, would be "the best
method of compelling the United States to accept a peaceful
solution for our region and prevent war in South Vietnam from
degenerating into an international conflict that would sound
the death knell for humanity."

Sihanouk said Pres. Johnson would "probably never have
the courage to admit to his people that the population of South
Vietnam ... has overcome its 'fear of communism' and will
accept even communism provided the war stops." Sihanouk
upheld a remark made by Sen. Barry Goldwater (R., Ariz.)
during his election campaign that World War III already was
under way in South Vietnam. Sihanouk said that Goldwater
was the only U.S. statesman who had "the courage to renounce
the crazy enterprise" in South Vietnam.

Sihanouk appealed to French Pres. Charles de Gaulle to
help prevent the U.S. and South Vietnam from carrying out
"an action on a large scale against our country." Sihanouk
made his plea in a letter (reprinted Nov. 7 in Pnompenh's
French-language newspaper *Le Matin)* responding to one he
had received from de Gaulle Oct. 29. Asserting that he had
"information" that Washington and Saigon were "preparing"
such action, Sihanouk urged France to "stop the dangerous
evolution of a situation we neither created nor wanted."
Sihanouk thanked de Gaulle for his efforts "to convince certain
countries to accept the convocation" of another Geneva
conference to guarantee Cambodia's neutrality. (Sihanouk's
aides had explained that critical remarks made by the prince
Oct. 30 about France's position on a proposed Geneva

conference had been misinterpreted and that they represented no new policy toward Paris.)

The nations that had signed the 1954 Geneva conference agreement on Cambodia had been asked by the Soviet Union Nov. 4 to attend another such meeting. The Soviet news agency Tass said the appeal had been issued by Pres. Anastas I. Mikoyan and Premier Aleksei N. Kosygin in response to Sihanouk's request for Soviet support for Geneva talks "in connection with another air attack on Cambodian territory from South Vietnam...." This was an apparent reference to the South Vietnamese Oct. 20 air attack on the Cambodian border village of Anlong Kres.

U.S. & Cambodia Confer in New Delhi

In an effort to improve their deteriorating relations, the U.S. and Cambodia held a conference in New Delhi, India Dec. 8, 1964. The meeting, suggested by Washington, failed to resolve the differences.

The U.S. delegation was headed by Philip W. Bonsal, consultant to the State Department's Policy Planning Council. Pnompenh's delegation was led by Son Sann, privy councilor to Prince Sihanouk.

The Cambodian press agency Dec. 13 published these 5 demands it said Sann had submitted at the meeting: (1) A halt to U.S./South Vietnamese "aggression" against Cambodian border villages; (2) compensation to Cambodia for the loss of life and property in the frontier attacks; (3) International Control Commission supervision of the Cambodian-Vietnamese border; (4) an end to broadcasts by the exiled rebels' Khmer Serei radio; (5) the release by South Vietnam of Cambodians "arbitrarily" seized in border attacks.

The American proposal for the conference had been forwarded to Pnompenh by U.S. Charge d'Affaires Alf E. Bergesen Nov. 16 following a Cambodian threat to expel the remaining 33 personnel of the U.S. embassy. The embassy had been operating without an ambassador since Sihanouk had indefinitely postponed the acceptance of the credentials of Randolph A. Kidder, the new U.S. ambassador. (Kidder's appointment had been confirmed by the U.S. Senate July 8.)

The Cambodian press agency had reported Nov. 15 that
Sihanouk had called a special session of the National Assembly
for Nov. 16 to take action on the proposed embassy staff
ouster. Sihanouk had accused the U.S. officials of having given
American correspondents in Cambodia unfavorable
information about the country. The agency further charged
that the embassy officials were conducting secret activities
against Cambodia's major political movement—Sihanouk's
People's Socialist Community. (The agency said that U.S.
reporters would be barred from entering Cambodia and that
the "more guilty ones" in the country would be asked to leave.)

But National Assembly discussion of the U.S. embassy
case was indefinitely postponed. Sihanouk explained Nov. 17
that any future severance of U.S.-Cambodian diplomatic
relations would not "stop the killing of innocent Cambodian
villagers." He warned, however, that the question of U.S.
embassy personnel would be reopened if there were further
border incidents.

Soviets & Chinese Aid Pnompenh

A shipment of Soviet arms was formally accepted by
Cambodia Nov. 3, 1964 at Pnompenh airport. The equipment
included 2 MIG-17 fighter planes, 1,276 artillery pieces, 8 anti-
aircraft guns and other military supplies. In accepting the
arms, Prince Sihanouk asserted that Soviet, Chinese
Communist and French military aid received by Cambodia had
thwarted U.S./South Vietnamese plans for invading his
country. Sihanouk said Cambodia "remain[ed] favorable to
reconvening the Geneva conference, but we will not ask for it
anymore; likewise we will not beseech any country or
organization whatever." He said Cambodia was "determined to
render blow for blow" to resist "the murder of our women and
children."

Cambodia Oct. 31 had received a Chinese Communist
pledge of aid in its dispute with the U.S. and South Vietnam.
The assurance was made by Premier Chou En-lai and Liu
Shao-chi, head of state, in reply to a plea for assistance by
Sihanouk Oct. 26. The exchange of messages were made public
Nov. 2 by the Chinese news agency Hsinhua.

In his note, Sihanouk had complained about the Oct. 20 Anlong Kres attack. Sihanouk charged that "F-101 jet aircraft of the American forces" had bombed and strafed "a self-defense unit" in the village. He said this was "the first time the United States Air Force has committed an open act of war against Cambodia." Other remarks made by Sihanouk in his note: "It is impossible for us not to strike back, whatever the consequences"; "for the last time" Cambodia urged a new Geneva conference to "eliminate the danger menacing peace in Southeast Asia and the world"; "I believe that ... countries which firmly oppose United States imperialist provocations, like" Communist China, "would help Cambodia resist criminal acts of oppression."

Asserting that China was "indignant at the grave crimes recently committed by the armed forces of the United States and its puppets," Liu and Chou replied that "China cannot ignore any acts of aggression endangering" Cambodia's "security."

Cambodia Ends Relations with U.S.

Cambodia's dispute with the U.S. came to a head with an announcement by Prince Sihanouk May 3, 1965 that his government had ended diplomatic relations with Washington.

Sihanouk explained in a broadcast that Pnompenh had acted in retaliation for an Apr. 28 bombing-strafing attack by 4 South Vietnamese planes against 2 Cambodian border villages. In the attack one person had been killed and 3 wounded. One of the villages hit was Anlong Tras, 60 miles east of Pnompenh and 2 miles inside Cambodia.

Recalling his previous warnings that Cambodia would sever diplomatic ties with Washington if another Cambodian were killed in border incidents, Sihanouk asserted that "our warnings were not heeded."

Sihanouk also attributed Cambodia's decision to break relations with the U.S. to an Apr. 5 *Newsweek* article criticizing Queen Mother Kossamak. The magazine article had prompted a Cambodian mob attack on the U.S. embassy in Pnompenh Apr. 28.

Sihanouk said Cambodia favored maintaining consular relations with the U.S. He predicted that "diplomatic relations may be restored" "if the United States conducts itself correctly toward Cambodia."

The break in U.S.-Cambodian ties had been preceded by a Soviet proposal in Apr. 1965 for an international conference to secure Cambodia's neutrality. Cambodia opposed the plan, however, and the conference never took place.

U.S. approval of the plan had been expressed Apr. 25 by State Secy. Dean Rusk. Rusk said the proposal had been reviewed with Pres. Lyndon B. Johnson the previous week, "and at his direction we have informed a number of interested governments that if such a conference is called we will gladly participate." Rusk said that Amb.-at-Large W. Averell Harriman would be "our representative to the discussions."

British acceptance of the Soviet proposal was announced in the House of Commons Apr. 26 by Foreign Secy. Michael Stewart.

South Vietnamese Foreign Min. Tran Van Bo had said Apr. 23 that his government favored an international meeting on Cambodia. But he insisted that the talks be "strictly limited to the recognition and the guarantee of the neutrality and the territorial integrity of Cambodia."

Moscow Apr. 23 had renewed its appeal for talks on Cambodia. In a joint Soviet-Mongolian communique at the end of a week-long visit by Premier Yumzhagiin Tsedenbal, the 2 nations said they favored such a conference and a similar meeting on Laos.

Sihanouk Apr. 23 expressed opposition to any conference on Cambodia that would be used as an excuse to discuss Vietnam. In a further qualification, Sihanouk said Apr. 24 that he did not favor the inclusion of the U.S., Thailand and South Vietnam in the talks because, he held, their presence would inject the East-West dispute into the parley. Sihanouk said that since the U.S. was not party to the 1954 Geneva agreements it need not be invited to the proposed conference. Opposing having South Vietnam at the talks, Sihanouk said the Saigon regime "does not represent anything."

U.S. Allows Hot Pursuit into Cambodia

It was reported in Saigon Dec. 20, 1965 that U.S. military commanders in South Vietnam had been authorized to pursue North Vietnamese and Viet Cong troops into Cambodia under certain circumstances. The order followed repeated U.S. charges that the Communist troops were using Cambodian territory as bases for attacks in South Vietnam.

The U.S. State Department Dec. 21 confirmed the report and issued a statement justifying the legality of the proposed action. The statement, made by press officer Marshall Wright, said the U.S.' policy remained "to respect the sovereignty, the independence and territorial integrity of Cambodia and not to widen the war in Southeast Asia." But Wright said U.S. military commanders "throughout the world have authority to take those actions essential in the exercise of the inherent right of self-defense to protect their forces." Wright recalled that in UN Security Council debate May 21, 1964 on Cambodian-South Vietnamese border clashes, the late U.S. Amb. Adlai E. Stevenson had said that the frontier crisis was "deeply related to the fact that the leaders and armed forces of North Vietnam, supported by Communist China, ... [used] Cambodian territory as a passageway, a source of supply and sanctuary from counterattack."

Under the reported orders, U.S. troops could pursue Communist forces into Cambodia if the U.S. commanders believed that failure to do so would jeopardize the lives of their troops. The commanders also were given permission to order air strikes and artillery barrages against any North Vietnamese or Viet Cong troops in Cambodia.

In response to the allied hot-pursuit order, the Cambodian National Assembly warned the U.S. and South Vietnam Dec. 28 that Cambodia would employ military means to repel any U.S./South Vietnamese invasion of Cambodian territory. A Cambodian communique Dec. 26 had charged that U.S. and South Vietnamese troops were conducting operations on its territory "almost daily" and that Cambodian civilians were victims of air raids and skirmishes.

U.S. Raids in 1966 Hamper Peace Efforts

Washington's efforts to improve relations with Cambodia suffered a sharp setback in the summer of 1966 as Pnompenh assailed the U.S. for air strikes on Cambodian territory.

The official Cambodian news agency claimed Aug. 3 that 2 U.S. F-105 Thunderchief fighter-bombers had attacked the frontier village of Thlok Trach Aug. 2, killing at least 3 persons and wounding 9. The agency said that the village was inside Cambodia and that the bombings had occurred as representatives of the 3-nation International Control Commission (Poland, Canada and India) were on their way to the area to inspect damage inflicted in previous alleged U.S. air attacks July 31 on Thlok Trach and on another village, Anlong Trach. The agency said the ICC observers were accompanied by foreign correspondents and military attaches of several embassies in Pnompenh and that all had witnessed the Aug. 2 incident.

The Cambodian account of the Aug. 2 raid was confirmed by the Polish government Aug. 6. A Warsaw protest, published by the Polish press agency, claimed that U.S. Air Force F-105s, preceded by reconnaissance aircraft, had bombed and strafed Thlok Trach, "directly endangering the safety of the members of the commission." The protest insisted that Thlok Trach was inside Cambodia.

The ICC's Canadian observers partially supported the Polish government's version of the Aug. 2 attack, according to a report of the incident released by the Canadian External Affairs Department Aug. 8. The department said that the ICC observers had witnessed the strafing by planes but that none of the commissioners had been endangered. The department said Thlok Trach was on the Cambodian-South Vietnamese frontier, but it did not specify on which side of the border it was situated. The Canadian government Aug. 8 informed the U.S. State Department of its "concern" over the incident.

A spokesman at the U.S. embassy in Saigon acknowledged Aug. 12 that U.S. air attacks had occurred July 31 "in the vicinity of" a village called Thlok Trach and Aug. 2 at another point more than 900 yards east of the village. But the spokesman said that all "maps available to us show that the 2 targets are in South Vietnam." He said the U.S. regretted the "loss of any innocent lives" and the danger encountered by the ICC observers and the foreign representatives.

Prince Sihanouk Aug. 13 assailed the U.S. for its claim that Thlok Trach was in South Vietnam. Sihanouk complained that U.S. maps also falsely placed other Cambodian border villages and islands inside South Vietnam. Sihanouk declared that as a result of the U.S. position on the latest border incidents, he would refuse to meet in Pnompenh with U.S. Amb.-at-Large W. Averell Harriman. (The U.S. State Department had announced Aug. 2 that Harriman would go to Pnompenh in September to confer with Sihanouk on U.S.-Cambodian diplomatic relations, severed by Cambodia in May 1965.) Sihanouk said that in order for him to meet with Harriman, the U.S. "must first recognize that Cambodia is a country that has a border."

The State Department conceded Aug. 16 that the ICC observers' visit to Thlok Trach Aug. 2 had "clearly indicated that the area in question is under the administration" of the Cambodian government. The statement reiterated the previous U.S. contention that "the maps available to us show the area in question to be on the Vietnamese side of the border, and these maps include a Cambodian map of recent date." The statement expressed "regrets" at "any loss of Cambodian life and property and any intrusion into Cambodian territory which may have occurred in connection with these incidents."

The South Vietnamese government Aug. 17 said it regretted the attack on Thlok Trach, but it affirmed that a 1964 Cambodian map supported South Vietnam's claim to the village.

Further explaining his reasons for cancelling Harriman's visit to Pnompenh, Sihanouk said Aug. 19 that U.S. air raids on Cambodian territory would have continued during the ambassador's stay and that this "would have provoked grave reaction among the people, which the government would have had to put down." Sihanouk said that the South Vietnamese government had repeatedly rejected his proposals for clear demarcation of the border and that he was, instead, working out a frontier accord with the Viet Cong's National Liberation Front.

The State Department reported Aug. 25 that Sihanouk had formally informed the U.S. government of his refusal to meet with Harriman.

Further U.S. air strikes on Cambodia were reported by Pnompenh in September:

● A Cambodian government statement Sept. 9 said that 2 helicopters bearing U.S. markings had machinegunned the Cambodian border village of Sramar Sept. 7, killing one person and wounding 2.

● A Cambodian statement Sept. 22 claimed that 2 U.S. helicopters had fired 8 rockets Sept. 21 at a Cambodian army post near Snoul, about 20 miles west of the Cambodian-South Vietnamese frontier. The report said one soldier had been killed and 4 wounded.

The U.S. State Department Sept. 23 expressed regret for "any violation of Cambodian territory or any loss of life or property that might have occurred." A department statement Oct. 14 had acknowledged that, "due to a pilot error," 2 U.S. helicopters had "strayed across the border and fired on Cambodian territory." The department note said that "compensation ... is being offered" by the South Vietnamese government. U.S. officials explained that Saigon would pay for the loss of life or property because U.S. forces involved in the Sept. 21 attack had been acting on South Vietnamese request. The department promised that in the future, "much more care would be exercised by pilots when they know they are near the Cambodian border."

Sihanouk charged Sept. 24 that the helicopter attack near Snoul had pointed up the U.S.' "threatening" attitude. Sihanouk warned that U.S.-Cambodian relations could not be improved unless the U.S. stopped bombing Cambodian territory and "recognize[d] our territorial integrity and our frontiers."

Cambodia filed a protest with the UN Security Council Sept. 30; it called the helicopter raid near Snoul "a despicable act of aggression."

Cambodia accused the U.S. and South Vietnam Jan. 1, 1967 of a new attack. It charged in a communique that allied air and ground elements had assaulted the Cambodian border village of Ba Thu (95 miles from Pnompenh) Dec. 30, 1966. 2 Cambodians were reported killed, 12 wounded and 12 kidnaped.

According to the report: about 50 helicopters flew over the village, while 2 F-105 jets attacked Ba Thu with bombs and machineguns; after the 10-minute assault, 42 helicopters landed in Ba Thu, and South Vietnamese and U.S. troops got out and fired on the villagers. U.S. authorities in Saigon and Washington denied any knowledge of the incident.

Another allied incursion was claimed by the Cambodian government Feb. 5, 1967. It charged that 100 U.S. and South Vietnamese troops had crossed the border Feb. 2 and had attacked the village of Svayngong. The statement claimed that 2 Cambodians were killed and 6 wounded.

Although there were no further allied ground strikes into Cambodia during the remainder of 1967, the border question remained a sensitive item amid persistent reports of a North Vietnamese/Viet Cong buildup in Cambodia, denials by Cambodia that it was providing sanctuary to the Communist forces and U.S. assurances that it had no intentions of expanding the Vietnam war into that country.

Sihanouk Scores U.S. Policy

Prince Sihanouk Nov. 4 and 8, 1967 criticized U.S. policy in Vietnam and reiterated demands for U.S. recognition of Cambodia's borders as the price for the re-establishment of U.S.-Cambodian diplomatic relations.

In his Nov. 4 statement, Sihanouk said that even if U.S.-Cambodian ties were restored, "I would continue to disapprove of American policy in Vietnam and continue to give moral and diplomatic support to North Vietnam and the National Liberation Front." Except for some Communist troops who might be "pushed" into Cambodia during the course of the fighting, Sihanouk denied that Cambodian territory was being used as a sanctuary for Viet Cong and North Vietnamese soldiers. He also denied that Cambodia was supplying military equipment to those forces. In demanding American recognition of his country's frontiers, Sihanouk condemned U.S. incursions into Cambodia during clashes in the area with Communist troops.

Sihanouk Nov. 4 described the U.S. as the aggressor in South Vietnam because, he said, it opposed the wishes of the majority of the people of Vietnam. Asserting that the U.S. could not win the war, Sihanouk urged Pres. Lyndon B. Johnson to disavow the Saigon regime, end the bombing of North Vietnam, withdraw American troops and then enter into peace negotiations with Hanoi and the NLF (National Liberation Front). U.S. policy was destroying the forces in Southeast Asia that could serve as a barrier to Chinese Communist expansion, "if such a thing exists," Sihanouk warned.

Sihanouk Nov. 8 renewed demands that the U.S. recognize Cambodia's borders and pledge no further frontier incursions. Sihanouk assailed the U.S. as a neocolonialist invader of "our Indochina."

Communist Base Operations Reported

U.S. press reports in Nov. 1967 claimed that Viet Cong and North Vietnamese troops were using Cambodian territory as a base of operations against the allies in South Vietnam and that the Cambodian port of Sihanoukville, on the Gulf of Siam, was being used to ship supplies to Communist forces in South Vietnam. The accounts told of a "new military complex constructed by the Viet Cong in Cambodia."

The Cambodian government Nov. 21 denounced the reports as "grotesque and a challenge to good sense." The statement denied that there were North Vietnamese or Viet Cong in Cambodia.

Prince Sihanouk declared Nov. 22 that if there were Viet Cong soldiers in Cambodia, "it is the fault of the Americans." Sihanouk warned that "if the escalation of the war comes" to Cambodia, "we will do like our North Vietnamese brothers, and we will resist all aggression."

In retaliation for U.S. press reports on alleged Cambodian aid to the Communist war effort, Sihanouk said Nov. 24 that "from now on the door of Cambodia is hermetically sealed to all American journalists." Sihanouk asked: "If we were in collusion with the Viet Cong, why did we permit American journalists the freedom to investigate?"

Cambodia denied Nov. 29 that Sihanoukville was used to funnel supplies for the Communists. The government said: Cambodia remained neutral; if the U.S. wanted "to stop the sending of arms and equipment to the Vietnamese patriots, it would be logical that military reprisals be made against powers and countries which furnish them, that is Russia, China and all the Socialist countries."

Gen. William C. Westmoreland, commander of U.S. forces in Vietnam, said Nov. 29, on his return to Saigon from a 2-week visit to Washington, that he was convinced the Viet Cong and North Vietnamese were "taking advantage of the eastern border area of Cambodia, with or without the consent" of the Cambodian government.

The report of a Viet Cong base in Cambodia had been filed from Pnompenh Nov. 19 and 20 by AP correspondents George McArthur and Horst Faas. They had visited the alleged Communist camp with UPI correspondents and had photographed the site. According to their dispatches: An abandoned Viet Cong camp site was found 4 miles inside Cambodia on the South Vietnamese border opposite War Zone C, about 70 miles northwest of Saigon. Military records written in Vietnamese indicated that the camp had been used for several months since February by possibly several hundred men and that it had been evacuated several days before the AP correspondents got there. A heavily traveled road from the camp led to the Vietnamese border and crossed it 9 miles from Locninh, where allied and North Vietnamese forces had fought Oct. 29-Nov. 3.

Cambodian Premier Son Sann said his government would investigate. He said: "It is impossible that the camp was used for any long period of time. It was not a sanctuary." Son Sann conceded that some Communist troops had crossed into Cambodia, but he said his government had always insisted that they leave as soon as the intrusions were discovered.

A N.Y. Times report from Washington Nov. 23 said U.S. military authorities in Saigon and Washington had expressed concern about reports that large ammunition shipments were reaching Viet Cong and North Vietnamese forces in South Vietnam through Cambodia. The ammunition reportedly arrived at the Cambodian port of Sihanoukville, was transshipped from there to Pnompenh and then moved into

South Vietnam. According to U.S. intelligence reports, large rice shipments, bought in Pnompenh for the Vietnamese Communists, were moved toward the Vietnamese border by Cambodian army trucks, possibly without government authorization but by corrupt Cambodian officers. The U.S. naval command was ordered to study the feasibility of quarantining the Cambodian coast to interdict strategic supplies for Communist forces. A U.S. State Department official said Nov. 29, however, that "we do not contemplate initiating any quarantine of the Cambodian coastline."

The *Times'* Nov. 23 dispatch quoted an American official as saying: Sihanouk "may not know the full extent of the North Vietnamese activities in his remote border areas and wouldn't be able to do much with his 40,000-man army even if he wanted to. But he could very well control what moves through his port. And if military intelligence can come up with convincing proof of arms traffic, we think Sihanouk could make no reasonable excuse for not controlling it."

The State Department disclosed Dec. 26 that the U.S. government had sent to Cambodia Dec. 4 a note reassuring the Pnompenh regime that it had "no hostile intentions toward Cambodia or Cambodian territory." The note was aimed at countering speculation that the Johnson Administration was considering extending the Vietnam war into Cambodia to flush out Viet Cong or North Vietnamese forces allegedly using Cambodian territory as a base of operations. The State Department said: Washington's note had sought "to provide the Cambodian government with information which would enable it to move toward a solution of a problem which we believe should be of concern to the Cambodian government as well as the United States"; the U.S. "continues to respect the neutrality, sovereignty and territorial integrity of Cambodia."

The U.S. had decided to announce the dispatch of its Dec. 4 note after Cambodia broadcast the text of its reply, sent the previous week. Asserting that its territory was not being used as a base for Communist forces involved in the Vietnam war, the Cambodian note had stated that the U.S. was seeking to justify military action against Cambodia by raising "groundless" charges of a Viet Cong/North Vietnamese presence in Cambodia. The statement added: "The United States tries to present as legitimate the right she gives herself to militarily intervene in all the Indochinese countries in order to smother with unprecedented brutality the aspirations of their people to complete independence and territorial integrity." Cambodia charged that U.S. and South Vietnamese forces had committed "flagrant violations" of international law through "daily incursions" into Cambodian territory for "purposes of sabotage and assassination."

Cambodia warned the U.S. Dec. 21 and 26 that it would fight if American forces invaded Cambodia. The Dec. 26 statement said Cambodia would enlist the support of friendly nations to help it resist any incursion.

South Vietnamese officials stated that they favored "hot pursuit" of Communist forces into Cambodia if necessary. Pres. Nguyen Van Thieu had said Dec. 2 that he "advocate[d] for the South Vietnamese forces the power to pursue and attack inside Cambodia during battles with the Viet Cong." Foreign Min. Tran Van Do said in Paris Dec. 26: "We would be obliged to do so [pursue Communist forces into Cambodia] if the enemy troops use Cambodian territory as a sanctuary and cross the frontier to attack our troops. But we have no intention of invading Cambodia.... For our defense we are obliged to follow the enemy if he crosses the frontier. We have responsibilities toward our troops and toward our allies."

The U.S. State Department Dec. 11 had reaffirmed American willingness to assist the International Control Commission for Cambodia in becoming more effective "as a means of protecting the integrity and neutrality of Cambodia in view of the reported use of its territory by Communist forces.

Sihanouk Threatens to Seek Communist Aid

Sihanouk again warned Dec. 27, 1967 that if U.S. troops invaded Cambodia in search of North Vietnamese and Viet Cong forces, his government would "ask [Communist] China, Russia and other anti-imperialistic powers for new military aid." "In the event we are unable to contain the successive waves of the aggressor, we will call on 'volunteers' from certain friendly nations, in the first place China, North Korea and Cuba," Sihanouk said. He also threatened to appeal to the UN Security Council and General Assembly to consider "the illegal occupation of Indochina, killing of its peoples and the aggression against non-Communist Cambodia" by the U.S.

In an interview appearing in the *Washington Post* Dec. 29, Sihanouk said that "if limited combat breaks out between American and Vietnam forces" in uninhabited areas of Cambodia, "it goes without saying that we would not intervene militarily." Sihanouk explained that Cambodia would shun retaliation in this instance because "on the one hand we lack sufficient and rapid means of transport and on the other hand because this would constitute a double violation of our territorial integrity and our neutrality. In that case we would protest to both parties involved." But Cambodian forces would respond with an all-out attack "if serious incursions or bombings are committed against our border regions inhabited by Cambodians," Sihanouk said.

Sihanouk, in effect, invited Pres. Johnson to send an emissary to Pnompenh to discuss the tense Cambodian border situation. Sihanouk conceded that "small units" of Communist forces had entered Cambodia "under pressure from American forces," but he held that they had "withdrawn to their territory within a few hours at the request" of Cambodian military authorities. But Sihanouk continued to deny the presence of any North Vietnamese/Viet Cong base or large Communist force in Cambodia.

Sihanouk reiterated his hope that the International Control Commission in Cambodia would be strengthened to curb border incidents. He "welcome[d] the delivery by the United States to the ICC of all means that would permit it to accomplish its mission better." Sihanouk expressed regret that the Soviet Union, as co-chairman of the 1954 Geneva Conference, and Poland, as one of the 3 members on the ICC, had opposed expanding the commission's activities.

Sihanouk's warning of appeals for outside aid followed a *N.Y. Times* dispatch from Washington Dec. 13 that the Johnson Administration was considering giving American field commanders in Vietnam permission to carry out "hot pursuit" of the enemy into Cambodia. But the American officials insisted that they had no intentions of ordering an outright attack against Cambodia.

The State Department Dec. 13 reaffirmed the policy of "self-defense," first announced in Dec. 1965, which gave field commanders authority to protect their troops in border regions. The U.S.' increasing concern over the Cambodian border was reflected in the recent battles fought with Communist troops in that sector at Dakto and Locninh in South Vietnam.

The Soviet Union had warned the U.S. Dec. 10 against extending the Vietnam war to Cambodia and Laos. The official news agency Tass said American "officials and the United States military command" had urged a blockade of the Cambodian coast or an invasion of Cambodia. It said other American plans called for sending U. S. troops into southern Laos to link Thailand with South Vietnam. Tass added: "In this way, by pursuing the piratic line to further aggravation of the war in Vietnam, the United States' aggressive circles are by all indications preparing to spread the fire of that war to other countries of Southeast Asia."

The Soviet statement insisted on strict observance of the Geneva agreements guaranteeing the independence and neutrality of Cambodia and Laos. It warned that American "attempts to cause further aggravation of the situation in Southeast Asia will be strongly rebuffed by the peace-loving states of the world, and the United States will naturally bear the complete responsibility for the consequence of its actions."

U.S. Denies Plans to Expand War

The U.S. Dec. 27, 1967 again disavowed any intentions of expanding the Vietnam war, and it reiterated its concern over alleged military pressures by Communist forces in Cambodia as well as in Thailand and Laos. (A State Department statement said pro-Communist Pathet Lao and North Vietnamese forces in Laos had started a drive that appeared to be more intense than the usual annual dry-season foraging activities. Communist military operations along Thailand's border with Laos, "in a measured way, seems greater than in the past," the statement said.)

The State Department Dec. 27 released the note it had sent to Cambodia Dec. 4 on alleged Communist use of Cambodian territory as a sanctuary and Cambodia's reply of Dec. 24. "The root cause of incidents affecting Cambodian territory is the

Viet Cong and North Vietnamese presence in the frontier region and their use of Cambodian territory in violation of the neutrality of Cambodia," the U.S. note said. It expressed support of previous Cambodian suggestions to strengthen the International Control Commission (ICC) "so that it could more effectively monitor the border areas between Cambodia and South Vietnam" and carry out a surveillance of Sihanoukville, through which war equipment reportedly was being transshipped to Communist forces fighting in Vietnam. The U.S. note cited "evidence" of North Vietnamese/Viet Cong activity on Cambodian soil, but the alleged incidents were not made public.

The Cambodian reply to the American note expressed regret over "the deterioration of its relations" with the U.S. "and stresses that the responsibility of it lies with the U.S. government, which has refused to recognize the present frontiers of Cambodia, continues its aggressive acts against Khmer territory and encouraged a propaganda compaign hostile" to Cambodia. Denying American charges of North Vietnamese/Viet Cong presence in Cambodia, Pnompenh reaffirmed in its note "that no foreign armed forces are implanted" on Cambodian soil. "The only evidence recognized by the ICC in Cambodia and many groups of international investigators were the incursions in ground and air attacks on Khmer territory by the U.S., South Vietnamese and Thai forces," the note charged.

U.S. Mission Seeks to Ease Tensions

U.S. Amb.-to-India Chester Bowles began talks with Cambodian officials in Pnompenh Jan. 9, 1968 on the strained relations between the U.S. and Cambodia. The major topic on the agenda was the possible "hot pursuit" by U.S. and allied forces into Cambodia to attack Viet Cong or North Vietnamese troops suspected of using Cambodian territory as sanctuary. The 2 nations Jan. 12 announced agreement on means of preventing Cambodia from becoming involved in the Vietnam war.

At the Pnompenh conference, Bowles met with Prince Sihanouk, who had proposed the talks Dec. 29, 1967, and with Premier Son Sann. The conferees said in the communique in which they announced their agreement:

● Bowles "renewed American assurances of respect for Cambodian sovereignty, neutrality and territorial integrity. He expressed hope that ... the International Control Commission would avert violations of Cambodian territory and neutrality by forces operating in Vietnam. Moreover, he declared that the ... United States ... is prepared to provide material assistance to the International Control Commission to enable it to increase its ability to perform its mission."

● Sihanouk expressed "the desire to keep the war in Vietnam away from his borders" and to have Cambodia's territory and neutrality "respected by all countries, including the belligerents in Vietnam." Cambodia, therefore, was "exerting every effort to have the present frontiers of the kingdom recognized and respected."

● Bowles emphasized that the U.S. intended not to violate Cambodian territory and to "do everything possible to avoid acts of aggression against Cambodia as well as incidents and accidents which may cause losses and damage to the inhabitants of Cambodia."

● Sihanouk reiterated his 1961 suggestion that the ICC be strengthened "by the creation of mobile teams and by the establishment of fixed posts at various points in the country" "so that it may be able, within the framework of its competence as defined by the Geneva agreements of 1954, to investigate, confirm and report all incidents as well as all foreign infiltrations on Cambodian territory."

On returning to New Delhi later Jan. 12, Bowles said he had not given Cambodia assurances against accidental intrusions. "'Hot pursuit' is not our intention and should never be necessary," Bowles asserted. "We said flatly that 'hot pursuit' was not an issue. The whole issue was how he [Sihanouk] and we would cooperate to prevent Cambodia's neutrality from being infringed upon by anybody."

The Cambodian news agency reported Jan. 12 that Sihanouk would dispatch Cambodian troops "to request the Viet Cong to leave Cambodian territory" on receipt of evidence of infiltration. The U.S. would "inform Cambodia of all information she possesses of Communist Vietnamese infiltration [to] enable Cambodia to perform its duties as a neutral country," the agency said.

In commenting on the U.S.-Cambodian agreement, Asst. State Secy. (for Far Eastern affairs) William P. Bundy said in Washington Jan. 12 that Bowles had emphasized to Sihanouk that the U.S. maintained the right to self-defense, including the right to pursue Communist troops who might be launching attacks from Cambodia. "When you have a situation where Viet Cong and North Vietnamese troops are there [in Cambodia], there may arise a situation where American forces are faced with the necessity of taking action in what is called the right of defending yourself."

The 1954 Geneva agreements establishing the 3-nation International Control Commission, had not made clear whether ICC decisions required unanimous or only majority vote. Therefore, implementation of the U.S.-Cambodian agreement to expand ICC surveillance powers remained questionable. The Cambodian news agency reported that Sihanouk had been informed Jan. 11 by Soviet Amb.-to-Cambodia Sergei M. Kudryautsev and M. Mylicki, head of the Polish mission to the ICC, that widening the commission's authority required not only unanimous ICC consent but also the approval of all the participants of the Geneva conference. The Soviet Union and Poland opposed granting the ICC wider powers in Cambodia. The U.S. held that ICC actions could be decided by a 2-vote majority.

An Indian government spokesman in New Delhi had noted Jan. 4 that the ICC's military components had been withdrawn from Cambodia and that it therefore was impossible for the ICC to supervise the border with South Vietnam. Meeting with Indian Prime Min. Indira Gandhi in New Delhi Jan. 1, Bowles had suggested that India take the lead in strengthening the ICC in Cambodia. Mrs. Gandhi reportedly told Bowles that her government would not commit itself until it consulted with Cambodia.

In an interview published in the *N.Y. Times* Jan. 6, Sihanouk had said of Bowles' then impending visit: If Bowles brought U.S. "recognition of our present borders, we shall immediately re-establish diplomatic relations with the United States. If he does not, ... Mr. Bowles' mission will at least permit, if Mr. Johnson is willing to prevent aggression against our country, a reduction in tension between the United States and Cambodia." Sihanouk reiterated his support of proposals to expand ICC powers to carry out surveillance of the Cambodian-South Vietnamese borders. But he noted that the Soviet Union, co-chairman of the Geneva Conference, and Poland opposed such expansion.

If U.S. forces invaded Cambodia, Pnompenh would first call on Communist China for "material aid," Sihanouk warned. "If American pressure became too strong," he said, his government would appeal for Communist Chinese "volunteer combatants to be placed under Khmer [Cambodian] command [and] who would be subject to repatriation at any time." Sihanouk ruled out a request for Communist volunteer soldiers from North or South Vietnam because "we have learned from experience through the previous Viet Minh occupation, after the departure of the French in 1953."

(British concern over the "hot pursuit" issue was reflected in a note sent to the Cambodian government Jan. 12. The note said London respected Cambodia's frontiers. Japan Jan. 12 sent Pnompenh a similar note expressing the view that it planned to recognize "the inviolability" of Cambodia's frontiers. Cambodia had warned Tokyo that unless it recognized its borders by Jan. 15, it faced the prospect of a break in Cambodian-Japanese diplomatic relations.)

Communists Warn U.S. Against Invasion

Communist China, North Vietnam and the Soviet Union warned the U.S. during Jan. 1968 not to attempt an invasion of Cambodia.

Peking asserted Jan. 3 that it would "not look on with folded arms" if U.S. troops entered Cambodia in pursuit of Communist troops.

North Vietnam was reported Jan. 12 to have promised to come to Cambodia's aid in the event of U.S. aggression against Cambodia. The pledge was made in a joint Cambodian-North Vietnamese communique on 9 days of talks Cambodian Foreign Min. Prince Norodom Phurissara had held in Hanoi with North Vietnamese officials. Phurissara had left Hanoi Jan. 8 after conferring with North Vietnamese Pres. Ho Chi

Minh, Foreign Min. Nguyen Duy Trinh and Premier Pham Van Dong. The joint communique assailed the U.S. for fighting a "war of aggression" in South Vietnam and a "war of destruction" against North Vietnam for the purpose of transforming the area into American "neo-colonies and military bases." In the communique, Cambodia pledged "resolute support" of the South Vietnamese National Liberation Front.

The Soviet Union warned the U.S. Jan 12 that Moscow would "not remain indifferent" to U.S. "attempts to violate Cambodia's territorial integrity, whatever the pretexts." The text of the Soviet note was made public Jan. 18 in Washington and Moscow. A similar warning had been delivered orally by Soviet Charge d'Affaires Yuri N. Chernyakov Jan. 12 to U.S. Amb.-at-Large Averell Harriman in Washington. The USSR said in its note: American claims of Viet Cong/North Vietnamese use of Cambodian territory were a pretext "to justify the spreading of military actions to . . . Cambodia and Laos, which is now being prepared." "Special anxiety is evoked by calls by American military leaders for actions that would mean a violation of the sovereignty and territorial integrity of Cambodia and Laos, up to and including a direct incursion of ground forces into . . . neutral Cambodia." U.S. calls for the strengthening of the International Control Commission (ICC) in Cambodia were "an attempt to find an excuse for hostile actions against that country and justify such actions in advance."

In disclosing the contents of the Soviet note, the State Department said Jan. 18 that Harriman had asked Chernyakov whether the Soviet Union had discussed with Hanoi the question of Viet Cong/North Vietnamese operations in Cambodia. The department again appealed to the Soviets to "turn their attention and influence to efforts to strengthen the International Control Commission and to assure the neutrality and territorial integrity of Cambodia."

A similar plea to the Soviets had been issued by the State Department Jan. 17 because of fears that Prince Sihanouk might have been changing his mind about his previous appeals for widening ICC surveillance powers. Sihanouk was quoted as having said at a news conference Jan. 16 that, when he had met with the Soviet ambassador to Cambodia, he had informed the

Russian envoy "that I am not interested in a strengthening of the ICC personnel or power or otherwise and that I am interested precisely in what has been done by the Soviet Union to dissuade the Americans from launching aggression on us." The Soviet ambassador, Sihanouk stated, had "brought me the good news that the Soviet Union had taken further steps in Washington and New York and even in Moscow to persuade the Americans to fully respect Cambodia and its borders and to refrain from crossing them." Soviet support of Cambodia's cause, Sihanouk said, was "worth all the helicopters in the world that can be given to the ICC. It is the best deterrent possible to halt the aggression of the inveterate U.S. warmakers."

Sihanouk Charges U.S. Violates Agreement

Prince Sihanouk charged Jan. 17, 1968 that the U.S. had violated its Jan. 12 pledge to respect Cambodia's borders. Speaking at a dinner in honor of Yugoslav Pres. Tito, who had arrived in Cambodia that day for a 6-day state visit, Sihanouk said that U.S. government statements made after the accord had been announced had (a) "cynically" proclaimed that "America is not bound by promises just made by the representative of Pres. Johnson [Amb. Chester Bowles]" and (b) affirmed the U.S.' "right to launch military operations up to 16 kilometers [10 miles] inside our territory."

The U.S. State Department Jan. 18 denied that "any responsible United States official" had said that U.S. troops would, if necessary, push 10 miles into Cambodia. American assurances to respect Cambodia's borders were also conveyed Jan. 18 to Cambodian Premier Son Sann by the ambassador of Australia, which represented U.S. interests in Pnompenh.

Sihanouk's accusation against the U.S. was followed by a Cambodian government charge Jan. 19 that a combined U.S.-South Vietnamese force had clashed with Pnompenh's troops Jan. 18. The statement said the fighting had occurred after the allied force penetrated 200 yards into Cambodian territory in Preyveng Province. According to the Pnompenh report: 3 government soldiers had been killed and one seriously wounded in the allied attack on a government outpost at Peam Momtea; the allied force, supported by 4 fighter-bombers and a spotter reconnaissance plane, fled after 40 minutes. In a further report on the incident, the Cambodian government said Jan. 21 that abandoned equipment of the "American-South Vietnamese" force found on the battlefield, later shown to the ICC, included paratroop commando scarves, a U.S. officer's helmet, weapons and radio sets. 15 of the attackers were killed and "several" wounded, according to the report.

The U.S. State Department Jan. 22 described the Jan. 18 thrust into Cambodia as inadvertent. The statement said: "The [border] crossing took place without hostile intent. It was not planned. It occurred in the heat of battle ... [in] an attempt by the U.S. and ARVN [Army of the Republic of Vietnam, or South Vietnamese] forces to protect themselves." The Viet Cong force had been bombarded by allied guns in a Vietnamese village and then had fled across a river into Cambodia. The allied patrol crossed into Cambodia after being fired on by the guerrillas from Cambodia, and 2 U.S. and 4 South Vietnamese soldiers were killed in the operation. The department expressed "regrets" for any casualties that may have been suffered by Cambodians.

The Cambodian ambassador to the UN, Huot Sambath, said in New York Jan. 22 that he had filed 851 protests against U.S./South Vietnamese air, land and sea intrusions of Cambodian territory during May 1-Oct. 31, 1967. Sambath said 25 Cambodians had been killed and 49 wounded in that period.

Cambodia claimed Feb. 3 that a U.S.-South Vietnamese force Feb. 2 had attacked a Cambodian government post in Takeo Province (adjacent to South Vietnam's Chudoc Province), killing one Cambodian soldier and wounding 5 others.

Sporadic border clashes continued through the remainder of 1968. 2 of them involved naval incidents on the Mekong River and one of its tributaries. *Among developments involving alleged violations of Cambodia's borders:*

● Prince Sihanouk June 10 released 2 U.S. Army soldiers who had been captured May 25 aboard a Philippine tug intercepted on the Mekong River one mile inside Cambodia. 8 Filipino crewmen had been freed June 8. The U.S. had protested the detention of the Americans, claiming the boat had penetrated Cambodian territory inadvertently.

● Cambodia protested to the U.S. and South Vietnam June 8
against what it charged were a series of fresh violations of
Cambodia's borders. A protest June 5 had charged that 2
Cambodians had been killed and 4 wounded in U.S.-South
Vietnamese air raids on villages the previous week. The most
recent attack allegedly had occurred June 2.

● U.S. and South Vietnamese air attacks on Cambodian
territory were charged by the Pnompenh government in July.
A Cambodian note to the UN Security Council July 8 claimed
that 2 U.S. helicopters June 29 had raided a rice field 600 yards
inside Cambodia, killing 14 peasants and wounding 4. A
Cambodian statement July 17 said that U.S. and South
Vietnamese planes had bombed the Cambodian village of
Prasot July 10 and that one person was killed and 2 wounded.
Prince Sihanouk urged UN Secy. Gen. U Thant to require the
Americans to "put an end to their criminal aggression against
peaceful and neutral Cambodia."

● A U.S. patrol boat was seized on a Mekong River tributary
by Cambodian forces July 17 after the craft, according to the
State Department, had "inadvertently intruded" into
Cambodian territory "as a result of a navigational error." 11
U.S. soldiers and one South Vietnamese were aboard. (They
were released Dec. 19.) The State Department said that the
patrol vessel had been on a "routine supply mission" between
Vungtau and Binhthuy when it strayed into Cambodia. The
department disclosed July 19 that it had apologized to the
Cambodian government for the intrusion. But a Cambodian
note July 22 rejected the American version of the incident. In
first disclosing the incident July 19, Prince Sihanouk had
warned that the 11 Americans would be tried "according to
Cambodian law" unless the U.S. offered a tractor or bulldozer
for the return of each man seized.

● Cambodia charged that U.S. helicopter gunships Nov. 6 had
fired on the Cambodian village of Preytoul, killing one person
and wounding 23 others.

● The Cambodian government charged Nov. 17 that U.S. and
South Vietnamese patrol boats had shelled the Cambodian
village of Prekkoeus in Kampot Province Nov. 16. It reported
12 civilians killed and 12 wounded. Pnompenh said the allied
boats had fired from the South Vietnamese side of the
Gianthanh River above the village.

● Prince Sihanouk had asserted Nov. 11 that as a result of
allied border attacks in the previous 5 days, he was forced to
reconsider his position on the status of the 11 U.S. servicemen
captured by Cambodian forces July 17. Rejecting a conciliatory
note in which State Secy. Dean Rusk had requested the release
of the Americans, Sihanouk told newsmen: "I cannot examine
any possibility of liberating the prisoners for the moment." "If
I get something from Pres. Johnson directly, I will re-examine
the situation." Sihanouk had said Nov. 7 that he would free the
U.S. captives if Pres. Johnson "sends me a cablegram,
promising that the military will do their best to refrain from
bombing our villages along the Cambodian border." In
announcing the release of the 11 Americans Dec. 19, Sihanouk
said they were set free "without any condition" as "a gift to the
United States." But Cambodia would keep the landing craft "as
a small indemnity to Cambodia," he added. The U.S. State
Department confirmed Dec. 19 that there had "not been any
exchange of any material or goods for persons involved in the
matter."

At another news conference held later Dec. 19, Sihanouk
announced the release of a U.S. helicopter gunner, who had
been taken when he fell or jumped into Cambodia from his
aircraft Nov. 27. The crewman remained hospitalized in
Pnompenh with a leg injury suffered in the fall, but he was
returned to allied authorities later on his recovery.

(Cambodia Mar. 11, 1969 freed 4 U.S. airmen who had
been captured by Viet Cong in South Vietnam Feb. 12. The
airmen had been taken prisoner after their observation plane
was shot down near the Cambodian-Vietnamese border. The
Viet Cong turned them over to Cambodia. The account of their
capture was confirmed by the airmen when they arrived in
Bangkok, Thailand Mar. 12. Pres. Richard M. Nixon had asked
for the men's release in a letter sent Mar. 9 to Prince Sihanouk.)

Cambodia Admits Red Use of Bases in Cambodia

U.S. officials in Washington quoted Cambodian leaders
Oct. 4, 1968 as publicly admitting for the first time that Viet
Cong and North Vietnamese forces were using Cambodian
territory for attacks on South Vietnam. The wider employment
of Cambodia as a Communist sanctuary and staging area—

with alleged Cambodian complicity—had been indicated in intelligence reports made public in Saigon Sept. 28.

The U.S. officials said that Prince Sihanouk had conceded in a recent speech that "though having accepted recognition of our frontiers, the Vietnamese Reds have sent their troops to [the provinces of] Ratanakiri and Mondolkiri," bordering South Vietnam. "Many of them [Vietnamese Communist forces] have come to live on our territory," Sihanouk reported. U.S. military officials had said that the 2 provinces were used as Communist supply routes into South Vietnam.

A report broadcast Oct. 3 by Cambodian State Secy. for National Security Sosthene Fernandez (monitored by U.S. sources) complained that "despite efforts of [Svayrieng] provincial authorities to repel them, armed [Communist] Vietnamese are continuing to install themselves on Khmer [Cambodian] territory near the frontier." "The Vietnamese are becoming increasingly hostile to the local people and authorities," he said. Svayrieng Province jutted into South Vietnamese territory close to Saigon.

Heretofore, Cambodian officials had denied U.S. charges that Viet Cong and North Vietnamese forces operated on Cambodian soil. Sihanouk had acknowledged several times that Viet Cong forces might have intruded briefly but had insisted that they had left when Cambodian authorities asked them to leave. (By Oct. 16, 1969 Sihanouk charged publicly that 40,000 Viet Cong and North Vietnamese troops were occupying 7 Cambodian provinces bordering South Vietnam.)

According to intelligence reports disclosed to newsmen in Saigon Sept. 28: Viet Cong/North Vietnamese military activity "in the area of Cambodia closest to Saigon" had "increased 3-fold" since Nov. 1967. "They now have munitions, workshops, hospital huts, prisoner-of-war camps, supply depots and training centers in the area." New weapons and ammunition for Communist troops were being transported over Cambodian highways in trucks sometimes driven by Cambodian military personnel.

The intelligence sources also reported:

● One of the Communists' major base camps in Cambodia was located at Ba Thu, 35 miles west of Saigon. It served as a center for outfitting and retraining Viet Cong/North Vietnamese units. The 30th Viet Cong Battalion had crossed the

Cambodian border into the Ba Thu area in May. Several hundred houses, cafes, and refreshment stands had been built there by Viet Cong sympathizers recruited from Hau Nghia Province in South Vietnam. The battalion had reassembled around Ba Thu May 9 and had marched to another area to exchange old weapons for Sovietmade AK47 rifles, mortars and rockets shipped from the Cambodian villages of Ph Senta and Ph Trapeang Run.

● A Viet Cong administrative headquarters had been established in Cambodia. Its function was to coordinate political activities in several provinces near Saigon and along the Cambodian border.

● A Cambodian major commanding a 40-man Cambodian unit operating from an outpost north of Ba Thu had been paid in money and ammunition for trucking military supplies twice a month to the Ba Thu area.

A Communist military presence in Cambodia was further evidenced by a Saigon report of a clash across the border Sept. 20. Lt. Gen. Do Cao Tri, commander of South Vietnam's III Corps, reported Sept. 24 that government howitzers had fired on Viet Cong mortars inside Cambodia after the enemy guns had shelled South Vietnamese troops in covering the retreat of a fleeing Viet Cong force. The enemy unit had sought to overrun a government outpost at Phuoctan, 2 miles from the Cambodian border.

UN Gets Cambodian Complaint Against Allies

The UN Secretariat received documented complaints in which the Cambodian government charged Jan. 31 and Feb. 1, 1969 that U.S. and South Vietnamese forces had killed and wounded civilians in Cambodian territory Dec. 14, 1968 and in 3 raids in Nov. 1968. The earlier attacks had been protested previously by the Cambodian government Nov. 17, 1968.

The Secretariat Feb. 1 issued as a Security Council document a Cambodian letter containing photos of the bodies of 7 persons identified as slain in the Dec. 14 attack (in which a truck had been ambushed). It quoted 2 survivors as saying that some of the wounded had been shot to death and that the truck was looted by the attackers, who left in "5 United States helicopters," summoned by radio by "whites speaking in loud voices." The document listed 3 incidents in November in which 16 civilians reportedly had been killed and 29 wounded. 23 civilians, including 8 children and 5 women, were injured Nov. 6 in a helicopter gunship attack at Preytoul in Svayrieng Province. One of the wounded later died. 3 Cambodian provincial guards were killed by allied fire Nov. 15 about 110 yards inside the Cambodian border at Bosman, in Svayrieng Province. The most serious incident was said to have occurred Nov. 16, when 3 armed motorboats fired into the village of Bat Naleak in Kampot Province. 3 children and 9 women were slain; 7 persons were wounded.

Accompanying the documents was a magazine edited by Prince Sihanouk with the same photos and editorial comment. The editorial said: "The world must be aware of the savagery of the assassins." "Why, to satisfy what principles, for what military requirements were these citizens of a neutral and peaceful country selected as victims by these murderers of the American Army?"

A Cambodian note handed to the UN Security Council Apr. 18 called on the Council to demand that the U.S. "immediately halt its military operations" on Cambodian territory. The note said that it was "particularly significant" that U.S. Defense Secy. Melvin Laird had commented, during a recent trip to South Vietnam, "that the purpose of all these frontier crossings was to ensure the security of U.S. troops, thus opening the door to invasion of any country on the mere pretext of maintaining security." Laird had made the statement Mar. 10 in commenting on a brief incursion of U.S. troops into Laos reported during an operation against Viet Cong and North Vietnamese forces.

In a separate note to the Security Council Apr. 18, Cambodia charged that U.S. and South Vietnamese troops had killed one Cambodian villager and wounded 2 others in 4 border incidents between Mar. 17 and 25. A Cambodian communique Apr. 14 claimed that allied helicopters and armored vehicles had killed 2 civilians in raids against Cambodian villages in Svayrieng Province Apr. 5.

South Vietnam called on the International Control Commission Apr. 18 to ask Cambodia to stop North Vietnam from using its territory for attacks on South Vietnam. In the note to the ICC, South Vietnam charged that North

Vietnamese troops had attacked the South Vietnamese border
province of Kientuong from Cambodia.

Cambodia Charges Defoliation Raids

The U.S. State Department disclosed June 4, 1969 that
Cambodia had filed a protest with the U.S. government
charging that American and South Vietnamese planes had
defoliated Cambodian crops near the South Vietnamese
frontier. The missions, carried out between Apr. 18 and May
14, destroyed millions of dollars worth of crops, according to
the Cambodians.

The State Department said June 4 that U.S. planes
"engaged in defoliation operations in the Republic of Vietnam
approached no closer than 5 kilometers [3 miles] from the
Cambodian border." The department said the U.S. had asked
the Pnompenh government June 2 to permit American
observers to enter Cambodia to investigate possible crop
damage. Cambodia agreed to the request.

Huot Sambath, Cambodian delegate to the UN, was
reported June 4 to have charged in a letter to Secy. Gen. U
Thant that U.S. and South Vietnamese planes had destroyed
about 37,000 acres of Cambodian rubber plantations and
hundreds of acres of fruit crops. Sambath estimated the
damage at about $7.7 million. In a letter to the UN Security
Council May 7, Sambath had said that Cambodian police Apr.
28 had shot down 2 U.S. helicopters over Cambodian territory
and that several other U.S. helicopters had violated Cambodian
airspace to rescue survivors. The Cambodian letter denounced
"the disgraceful tactics" used by U.S. forces "and by certain
United States newspapers which represent Cambodian posts
and troops as foreign encampments in order to justify
aggression and bombing against Cambodia."

The N.Y. Times reported May 8 that Nixon
Administration sources had disclosed that U.S. B-52 bombers
had raided several Viet Cong and North Vietnamese supply
dumps in Cambodia for the first time in previous weeks, but
Cambodia did not protest. The Times report said that
Cambodian authorities had often provided U.S. and South
Vietnamese military officials at the border with information on

Viet Cong/North Vietnamese troop movements into South Vietnam from Cambodia.

Following further U.S. air strikes on North Vietnamese positions in Cambodia in November, the Pnompenh government warned Nov. 22 that these raids jeopardized U.S.-Cambodian relations. Huot Sambath said air strikes Nov. 16-18 had killed 27 Cambodians and wounded many others. A Pnompenh communique Nov. 25 claimed that U.S. planes had deliberately attacked a Cambodian post at Dak Dam in Mondolkiri Province Nov. 16-17. The U.S. apologized for the strikes.

U.S. & Cambodia Agree to Restore Ties

The State Department disclosed June 11, 1969 that the U.S. and Cambodia had agreed in principle to re-establish diplomatic relations, suspended since May 3, 1965. After administrative arrangements had been worked out, officials said, the 2 countries would resume relations on the level of charges d'affaires.

The agreement to restore diplomatic relations followed an earlier exchange of notes between Prince Sihanouk and Pres. Nixon. In one of his previous notes the Cambodian chief of state had reversed an earlier decision to resume ties with Washington.

During the earlier exchange, Nixon had declared in a message delivered to Sihanouk Apr. 16: "In conformity with the UN Charter, the U.S. recognizes and respects the sovereignty, independence, neutrality and territorial integrity of the kingdom of Cambodia within its present frontiers."

In response to Nixon's note, Sihanouk later Apr. 16 thanked the President "for this gesture of justice and fairness." He reported that he was ready to resume diplomatic relations with the U.S. Shanouk said: "We have lost much in the past 4 years through not having direct contact with the Americans. The significance of relations is that they will permit the settlement, in a certain measure," of the incidents arising from intrusions into Cambodia of U.S. and South Vietnamese troops pursuing Communist forces. The resumption of relations, Sihanouk said, would permit Pnompenh "to play a new card

since Asian Communists are already attacking us before the
end of the Vietnam war."

In reply to Sihanouk's statement, the U.S. State
Department said Apr. 16: "Of course, we are interested in
establishing and maintaining diplomatic relations on a
mutually satisfactory basis with Cambodia and welcome
indications that Cambodia shares this view." The U.S. was
"prepared to engage in discussions for this purpose."

Sihanouk Apr. 30 withdrew his assent to the resuming of
diplomatic relations with the U.S. because the U.S. had failed
to mention its stand on disposition of a group of offshore
islands, including Dao Phu Duoc, claimed by both Cambodia
and South Vietnam. The key phrase in the Apr. 16 U.S. note
with which Sihanouk took issue was its recognition of
Cambodia's sovereignty "within its present boundaries." The
State Department had declined to specify what the U.S.
regarded as Cambodia's current frontier.

The U.S. delivered another note to Pnompenh May 22. In
its May 22 message, the U.S. asserted that "no statements had
been made by or on behalf of the U.S. government
contradicting, expanding or expressing reservations" to the
Apr. 16 note.

Sihanouk accepted Washington's explanation and reversed
his Apr. 30 decision against recognition.

Despite the reversal of Sihanouk's decision, continued
exacerbation of relations between the 2 countries forestalled an
actual exchange of ambassadors. Diplomatic ties were not
resumed formally until after Sihanouk's ouster in 1970. (A U.S.
ambassador presented his credentials in Pnompenh Sept. 15,
1970.)

Viet Cong Mission Gets Embassy Status

The Cambodian Foreign Ministry announced May 9, 1969
that it had agreed to raise diplomatic relations with the
National Liberation Front, the political arm of South
Vietnam's Viet Cong, to the embassy level. The NLF had
maintained a diplomatic mission in Pnompenh for years.

SIHANOUK'S OUSTER—INCREASING TENSION:

MARCH – MAY 1970

The precarious neutrality that Cambodian Chief of State Norodom Sihanouk had sought to preserve over the years was finally shattered in 1970 by his ouster in a coup d'etat and by the subsequent direct involvement of Cambodia in the Vietnam war several weeks later.

Rightwing political foes of Sihanouk, led by his premier, Lon Nol, deposed the chief of state Mar. 18 while he was traveling abroad. They accused Sihanouk of "absolute despotism," and they held him responsible for the continued use of Cambodian border sanctuaries by Viet Cong and North Vietnamese troops and for the resultant allied retaliatory attacks on those areas. (In 1969, as a result of economic trouble accompanying Sihanouk's nationalization policies and the Communist troop encroachment, Sihanouk had appointed a new cabinet headed by Lon Nol.)

Following his overthrow Sihanouk went to Peking, where he received the support of Communist China and established a government-in-exile. Later in March there were several demonstrations by Sihanouk supporters demanding his return. These took place in Cambodian provinces bordering South Vietnam; they were short-lived, and Sihanouk's successors appeared firmly entrenched.

Sihanouk's downfall had been preceded by a deepening crisis centered on his government's heightened policy of trying to rid the country of the Viet Cong and North Vietnamese. The continued presence of the Communist forces in Cambodia had precipitated violent anti-Communist demonstrations earlier in March in Pnompenh and elsewhere. Targets of the attacks, reputedly government-sponsored, included the Viet Cong and North Vietnamese embassies in the capital as well as shops owned by Vietnamese residents. Cambodian-Communist talks to take up the entire controversy were held Mar. 16, but they collapsed immediately. The talks were followed by an acceleration of the fighting inside Cambodia. The Communists expanded their operations deeper inside Cambodia as the U.S.

*and South Vietnamese forces intensified their attacks on the
border sanctuaries amid reports of actual South Vietnamese
thrusts into Cambodia.*   ~

Cambodia Demands Communist Withdrawal

Cambodia began talks Mar. 16, 1970 with Viet Cong and
North Vietnamese representatives in a demand for the removal
of an estimated 40,000-60,000 Communist troops operating in
Cambodia. The Communist delegates in turn demanded
compensation for the damage done to their embassies in
Pnompenh Mar. 11 by 20,000 Cambodians demonstrating
against the presence of North Vietnamese and Viet Cong
troops in their country.

The meeting, held at an undisclosed location in Cambodia,
had been proposed by Hanoi Mar. 14 after the Mar. 11
demonstrations and similar outbursts in Pnompenh the
following 2 days.

The Viet Cong and North Vietnamese embassies were
sacked and burned by the rioters. The demonstrators rempaged
through Pnompenh's streets Mar. 11-13, attacking Vietnamese
shops and homes. (An estimated 500,000 Vietnamese lived in
Cambodia.) The violent disturbances had been preceded by an
anti-Communist demonstration Mar. 7 in Svayrieng Province
bordering South Vietnam.

The attack on the embassies was followed by Cambodian
notes of apology Mar. 12 and a demand that the Viet Cong and
North Vietnamese troops be withdrawn from the country by
Mar. 15. The notes, issued by Premier Lon Nol, asserted that
the presence of these forces and their continued infiltration into
the country were "contrary to the vital interests of the
Cambodian people." The Mar. 15 deadline passed with no
apparent exodus of the Communist troops.

(A Cambodian army spokesman said Mar. 13 that there
had been 164 skirmishes between Cambodian border forces and
the Viet Cong since Jan. 1. The latest incident was said to have
occurred Mar. 13 when Cambodian troops fought briefly with
300 Viet Cong in Svayrieng Province, forcing the infiltrators
back into South Vietnam. No casualties were reported.)

Hanoi's proposal for the meeting with Cambodia was hailed Mar. 15 by the North Vietnamese Communist Party newspaper *Nhan Dan*. The Communist journal charged that Cambodian-North Vietnamese relations were complicated by "the aggression by the U.S. imperialists in South Vietnam and their schemes to abolish the independence" of Cambodia. Cambodian and Communist officials met Mar. 16 but the talks were broken off the same day when the Communist delegation refused to discuss anything until the Cambodians promised compensation for damage done to their embassies in Pnompenh.

Prince Norodom Sihanouk, in Europe since January for medical treatment, had declared in Paris Mar. 11 that the attack on the Communist embassies was a rightist plot "organized by personalities aiming to destroy . . . the friendship of Cambodia with the Socialist camp and throw our country into the arms of an imperialist capitalist power." Sihanouk, on his way home, stopped off in Moscow Mar. 14-16 to discuss the crisis with Soviet officials. Following meetings with Soviet Premier Aleksei N. Kosygin and Pres. Nikolai V. Podgorny, Moscow said in a statement issued Mar. 16 that the USSR "again confirmed its respect for the neutrality and territorial integrity of Cambodia within her present borders." The statement said U.S. and South Vietnamese "aggression" and "provocations" were "the main reason for the aggravation of the situation in Indochina and in Southeast Asia as a whole."

Military Rightists Oust Sihanouk

While Prince Sihanouk was traveling abroad, he was ousted as Cambodian chief of state in a bloodless *coup d'etat* carried out in Pnompenh Mar. 18 by Lt. Gen. Lon Nol, premier and defense minister, and First Deputy Premier Prince Sisowath Sirik Matak, a cousin of Sihanouk's. Sihanouk, in Peking on a scheduled stopover, announced Mar. 23 that he would form a "national union government"-in-exile and a "national liberation army" to restore his authority. The Cambodian National Assembly voted Mar. 20 to arrest Sihanouk and press charges of treason against him if he attempted to return to the country.

Sihanouk's overthrow was announced in a communique issued by the coup leaders and broadcast Mar. 18 by Pnompenh radio. It said: "Following the political crisis provoked by Prince Norodom Sihanouk in the past few days, the National Assembly and the Royal Council in joint session, in accordance with the constitution of the kingdom, withdrew their confidence from Sihanouk." The statement said Sihanouk would be replaced by National Assembly Pres. Cheng Heng, who would serve until the election of a permanent chief of state. (Cheng was officially sworn in Mar. 21.) The "political crisis" referred to were the public demonstrations in Pnompenh against the presence of Viet Cong and North Vietnamese troops in Cambodia.

The National Assembly Mar. 19 granted what it called "full power" to Premier Lon Nol and declared a state of emergency. By suspending 4 articles of the constitution, it permitted arbitrary arrest, and it banned public assembly.

A warning of a possible attempt by Sihanouk to mount a countercoup was made in an order to the armed forces Mar. 20. The statement, issued in the name of the high command, said it was "the duty of our army to crush by means of arms all actions that Prince Norodom Sihanouk may be planning in an attempt to misuse the legal standing that he lost ... in consequence of the vote of the 2 houses." The order specified that Sihanouk had ceased to be commander-in-chief of the armed forces and that these duties had been taken over by Cheng Heng.

A news blackout imposed at the start of the uprising was lifted Mar. 19. Pnompenh's airport, which had been shut, was reopened Mar. 23.

The new government Mar. 23 officially exiled Sihanouk, his family and other prominent figures connected with his rule. Those exiled included Penn Nouth, his former premier and currently his personal aide, Gen. Nhiek Tioulong, a former head of the army, and Pomme Peang, mother of Princess Monique, Sihanouk's wife.

A number of high-ranking officials were purged by the coup leaders. They included Col. Oum Mannorine, secretary at the Interior Ministry in charge of ground defense, Maj. Buor Horl, chief of the Pnompenh police force, and Foreign Min. Prince Norodom Phurissara.

Background of the Coup

Sihanouk's attempt to steer Cambodia on a neutral course and his alleged personal excesses had met with growing opposition in some circles in Cambodia.

Sihanouk ran afoul of the military as a result of his efforts to maintain the country's neutrality in the face of use of Cambodian territory by Viet Cong and North Vietnamese forces seeking to escape U.S. firepower in the fighting in neighboring South Vietnam. Cambodian military authorities had charged that although Sihanouk had made speeches condemning the Vietnamese Communists, he had pressured the military to release all Viet Cong troops captured by Cambodian soldiers. Premier Lon Nol was said to have insisted on a tougher stand against the Viet Cong.

Prince Sirik Matak was said to have opposed Sihanouk because of the chief of state's insistence on the nationalization of Cambodia's few industries, the alleged wastefulness in the use of limited investment capital and his alleged tolerance of widespread corruption. A number of National Assembly deputies were said to have accused Sihanouk of dictatorial rule and nepotism and to have protested his building of government-owned gambling casinos. In National Assembly speeches Mar. 18, several legislators accused Sihanouk of supplying arms to the Viet Cong and of financial and moral corruption.

North Vietnam and the Viet Cong accused the U.S. of instigating the coup against Sihanouk and pledged support to the deposed Cambodian chief of state. A statement broadcast by Hanoi radio Mar. 21 said the uprising was "the end result of a process of sabotage, subversion and aggressive activities carried out by the U.S. imperialists against the independence and the policy of peace and neutrality" in Cambodia. North Vietnam's backing of Sihanouk was broadcast Mar. 22. The statement said: "We are determined to support the just struggle that Sihanouk and the Cambodian people are waging" against the new government in Pnompenh.

The Soviet Communist Party newspaper *Pravda* Mar. 22 attributed the crisis in Cambodia to "military fever born of American aggression."

South Vietnamese support of the new government of Cambodia was expressed Mar. 24 by Vice Pres. Nguyen Cao Ky in a note to Cheng Heng, interim chief of state. Ky said he hoped the 2 countries would cooperate closely in their struggle against the Communists.

The U.S. continued to recognize Cambodia despite Sihanouk's ouster, the State Department said Mar. 19. "Our position is that the question of recognition does not arise," department spokesman Carl A. Bartch said. He added: "Constitutional reasons" in Cambodia made it unnecessary for Washington to take action on diplomatic recognition.

Premier Lon Nol and Deputy Premier Sirik Matak assured foreign governments Mar. 19 that Sihanouk's ouster would cause no change in Cambodia's policy of "independence, sovereignty, peace, strict neutrality and territorial integrity." Stressing their desire to maintain Cambodia's neutrality, the new leaders Mar. 22 urged Britain and the Soviet Union, co-chairmen of the 1954 Geneva conference, to reactivate the International Control Commission (ICC) in Cambodia to "help put a stop in a peaceful way to the occupation of its national territories" by Viet Cong and North Vietnamese forces. (Sihanouk had ordered the removal of the ICC in 1969 on the ground that Cambodia could not afford the cost of its operations.)

Cambodian Chief of State Cheng Heng accused Sihanouk Mar. 24 of "absolute despotism." He vowed that his government would "accomplish the total evacuation of our territory of Viet Cong and North Vietnamese" troops. Cheng spoke at the 15th anniversary meeting of Sangkum, the political movement founded by Sihanouk. At the meeting, the movement elected a new central committee, which in turn chose National Assembly Pres. In Tam as president of the Sangkum. In Tam had been instrumental Mar. 18 in pushing through a resolution in a joint session of the National Assembly ousting Sihanouk.

Sihanouk's Reaction & Plans

Sihanouk had been in Moscow, concluding a 5-day meeting with Soviet leaders, when he received news of his dismissal. He had conferred Mar. 17 with Soviet Communist Party Gen. Secy. Leonid Brezhnev, and he flew to Peking Mar. 18.

Sihanouk said in his first public statement on the coup, issued in the Communist Chinese capital Mar. 20, that his ouster was "absolutely illegal." He said there was no provision in the Cambodian constitution "allowing parliament and the government to depose the head of state, who is implicitly appointed for life." Sihanouk said he could only be dismissed "by the nation as a whole," and he called for a referendum under International Control Commission auspices to determine who should rule Cambodia. Sihanouk attributed the "turbulence" in his country to the coup leaders and the U.S. Central Intelligence Agency.

Sihanouk and his aides had conferred with Chinese leaders on the Cambodians' arrival in Peking Mar. 19 and again Mar. 20. According to Hsinhua, the Chinese Communist press agency, the discussions were held on a lower diplomatic level. Participating were Deputy Premier Li Hsien-nien and Wu Fa-hsien for China, and Sihanouk and 2 advisers, Penn Nouth and Gen. Ngo Hou.

Sihanouk said Mar. 22 that the Soviet Union and Communist China had granted his request to live in exile alternately in Moscow and Peking.

A statement issued by Sihanouk's aides Mar. 23 said he would form a "national union government" and "a national liberation army" to rescue Cambodia from the "dictatorship of the pro-imperialist revolutionaries" who had seized power and for the "struggle against the American imperialists, their masters." The struggle, the statement said, would be waged with the aid of the forces of "the fraternal countries. Sihanouk, "as legal chief of state," proclaimed the dissolution of the new Cambodian government of Premier Lon Nol and Cheng Heng, accusing them of "high treason," the statement said.

In a statement issued in Peking Mar. 24, Sihanouk called on his supporters in Cambodia and Europe to join in his fight to oust the coup leaders. Sihanouk urged his followers in Cambodia "to go underground to fight the enemy." He promised them arms to carry "the flag of revolt against the reactionary clique" then ruling Cambodia with "their masters, the American imperialists." Sihanouk's statement was an elaboration of the declaration, issued the previous day, which had proclaimed his plans to form "a national union government" and "a national liberation army."

In his Mar. 24 statement, Sihanouk insisted that he remained the "legal chief of state." He charged that the "group of traitors and renegades" who had seized power had established a "dictatorship" that was leading Cambodia toward "anarchy and war provoked" by the U.S. Sihanouk promised to resign from office after the defeat of the "imperialists and their lackeys."

Prince Souphanouvong, leader of the pro-Communist Pathet Lao rebels in Laos, expressed support for Sihanouk Mar. 24.

Sihanouk had appealed to UN Secy. Gen. U Thant Apr. 1 to withhold recognition of the Lon Nol regime on the ground that his ouster was unconstitutional. He urged that Cambodia's UN seat be left vacant until its people made their own decision in "their current struggle for the return of our state to constitutional legality and peace." Sihanouk said the UN should not interfere in Cambodian affairs and, instead, should get the U.S. to withdraw its forces from the Indochina peninsula.

Sihanouk's appeal for non-interference was echoed by a Hanoi broadcast Apr. 2. The North Vietnamese statement expressed opposition to either a UN or International Control Commission presence in Cambodia because it would constitute *"de facto* recognition" of the new Pnompenh regime.

Sihanouk Supporters Riot

Violent demonstrations of anti-coup marchers demanding the return of Sihanouk, allegedly instigated by the Viet Cong, were staged Mar. 26-29 in Cambodian provinces along the South Vietnamese frontier. The government Mar. 27 imposed a 6 p.m.-to-6 a.m. curfew in Pnompenh, closed the capital's airport and intensified precautionary military measures throughout the country. (The airport was reopened Mar. 30 as the tensions eased.) The riots were the first open manifestation of opposition to the leaders who had deposed Sihanouk.

The most violent demonstration occurred Mar. 26 in Kompong Cham, 35 miles northeast of Pnompenh. Some 10,000 persons rioted, sacking an official building and destroying documents. Dozens of persons were killed or wounded. Among those slain were 2 National Assembly deputies. More than a thousand demonstrators were held. After the rioting, the demonstrators commandeered trucks and cars in an attempt to drive on Pnompenh. A 15-vehicle convoy from Kampong Cham was stopped by police on a bridge leading into the capital. Shots were exchanged but no casualties were reported. Another protest column from Svayrieng Province was also halted about 20 miles from Pnompenh.

Many of those arrested in Kampong Cham were Vietnamese. A North Vietnamese protest Mar. 29 charged that their seizure was illegal.

Government troops Mar. 29 killed 9 persons and wounded 7 in breaking up a pro-Sihanouk demonstration in Angtassom in Takeo Province, 40 miles south-southwest of Pnompenh. Before they were dispersed, about 700 demonstrators broke into a government building, ransacked it and burned its files. Other demonstrations took place throughout provinces along the Mekong Delta bordering South Vietnam.

During another pro-Sihanouk demonstration, police Apr. 1 fired into a mob in Phom Phnom Preyslek, 50 miles south of the capital, and killed 30 persons. Similar demonstrations, previously reported in Takeo Province Mar. 29-30, were said to have been suppressed by troops who shot and killed 109 persons.

(The Lon Nol government Apr. 2 released 486 political prisoners jailed by Sihanouk when he had been in power.)

Sihanouk Rallies Asian Communist Support

Prince Sihanouk initiated a high-level meeting of Communist leaders from North and South Vietnam and Laos at a secret site in Communist China Apr. 24-25. The conferees pledged cooperation in their struggle against U.S. and other forces that opposed them in Indochina.

At the meeting, disclosed by Hanoi radio Apr. 27, Sihanouk headed a delegation of 7 Cambodian supporters. The other delegations were led by Premier Pham Van Dong of North Vietnam, Prince Souphanouvong of the pro-Communist

Pathet Lao of Laos and Nguyen Huu Tho, president of the Presidium of the Central Committee of the South Vietnamese National Liberation Front.

A declaration adopted by the parley assailed the U.S. as an "imperialist aggressor" determined to prolong and widen the war in Indochina. It called on the people of Vietnam, Cambodia and Laos to "step up the fight against the common enemy— American imperialism and its lackeys in the 3 countries—until total victory." The text of the declaration, released by Hsinhua, condemned all attempts by the U.S., "its agents and other Asian reactionaries to misuse the name of the United Nations or any organization or any international or Asian conference to legitimize the illegal power of the Lon Nol-Sirik Matek reactionaries and interfere in Cambodia."

(The declaration also supported the Pathet Lao's proposals for peace in Laos, which had been rejected by the Vientiane government Apr. 9. The plan, submitted Mar. 22, had called for an immediate end to U.S. air attacks in Laos as a precondition for negotiations to end the fighting there. Laotian Premier Souvanna Phouma's Apr. 9 response had proposed instead that peace talks with the Pathet Lao be preceded by a cease-fire and the immediate supervised withdrawal of all foreign troops from Laos. Souvanna's omission of any reference to the American bombing in effect rejected the Pathet Lao demand for an unconditional halt in the raids. Souvanna took issue with Pathet Lao proposals that failed to say anything about the "60,000 North Vietnamese soldiers who had come to Laos at the request of a single political party to aid its revolution."

(A Pathet Lao broadcast Apr. 14 denounced Souvanna's proposals as "an act of propaganda" designed "to dupe the people" and pave the way for intensified fighting.)

Communist China played a major role at the meeting, according to official reports from Peking and Hanoi Apr. 30. Premier Chou En-lai flew from Peking to the conference site Apr. 25 to give a banquet for the delegates. In a speech at the dinner, Chou assailed the "U.S. imperialists" for believing that the Cambodian rightists who had deposed Sihanouk could "place Cambodia under their sway and thwart the resistance of the Vietnamese people and thereby materialize their foolish ambition of occupying Indochina as a whole." Chou pledged that China would "fight shoulder to shoulder" with "the 3 fraternal Indochinese people," who would "win victory together."

An official Chinese statement Apr. 28 expressed support for the declaration adopted by the conferees. The Peking statement said China would "always provide a powerful backing of the Indochinese people in their war against United States aggression and for national salvation."

Soviet Premier Aleksei N. Kosygin indorsed the aims of the conference. In a message sent to the participants Apr. 29, Kosygin expressed confidence that the parley would bring about "a further strengthening of the united anti-imperialist front of the peoples of Indochina."

Sihanouk Forms Government-in-Exile

Sihanouk announced the formation of his government-in-exile in Peking May 5. The regime was promptly recognized by Communist China as the "sole legal" government of Cambodia. China May 6 then severed diplomatic relations with the Cambodian government of Lon Nol, as did North Vietnam and North Korea. (Soviet Premier Kosygin expressed support for the Sihanouk government in a telegram sent to the prince May 10, but he avoided the subject of recognition of his exile regime. Moscow continued to maintain diplomatic relations with the Pnompenh government of Lon Nol.)

In a proclamation announcing his new government, Sihanouk declared that it was prepared "to make all sacrifices for achieving final victory over the American imperialists and their [Cambodian] lackeys," Lon Nol and his first deputy premier, Prince Sisowath Sirik Matak. The exile government's foreign policy would be one of "national independence, peace, neutrality and non-alignment," the proclamation said. The exile government, according to the statement, would combat "the American imperialists" and overthrow "the dictatorship of their valets headed by Lon Nol-Sirik Matak." After total victory, the proclamation said, the exile regime would construct an "independent, peaceful, neutral, democratic and prosperous Cambodia."

The exile government was proclaimed under the leadership of the National United Front of Kampuchea, a recently formed Cambodian political group headed by Sihanouk. Sihanouk said the front included Communists. The principal members of Sihanouk's cabinet were Penn Nouth, premier, and Sarim Chhak, foreign minister. Penn Nouth had served as Sihanouk's political adviser since the prince's ouster. The other ministers were: Chau Seng, charged with special missions; Chan Youran, popular education and youth; Ngo Hou, religious and social affairs; Thiounn Mumm, economy and finance; Khieu Samphan, national defense; Maj. Gen. Duong Sam Ol, military equipment and armament; Hu Nim, information and propaganda; Huot Sambath, former ambassador to the UN, telecommunications and reconstruction; Hou Youn, communal reforms and cooperatives; and Chea San, justice and judicial reforms.

Chinese recognition of the government-in-exile was extended in a letter sent by Foreign Min. Chou En-lai to Sihanouk. It said Peking simultaneously "severs all diplomatic relations already long severed with the Lon Nol-Sirik Matak rightist traitorous clique and will withdraw the Chinese diplomatic mission, personnel and experts from Pnompenh." In a reply to Chou May 7, Sihanouk lauded China as Cambodia's "No. 1 friend" because it was the first to recognize his new government.

Diplomatic recognition of the Sihanouk government was reported May 6 to have been extended by North Vietnam, North Korea, Rumania, Yugoslavia, Cuba, Syria, Iraq, Albania, the Pathet Lao and the Viet Cong.

At rallies reported May 8 to have been held throughout China, participants hailed Sihanouk's government and pledged full support to him and all the Indochinese people in their struggle against the U.S. The Chinese news agency Hsinhua reported that Premier-in-exile Penn Nouth had sent a message May 6 to U.S. Sen. Mike Mansfield (D., Mont.), urging him to use his influence as Senate majority leader to make "the great American people understand that they are being dangerously dragged by their President into a war spreading to the whole of Indochina." Penn Nouth was said to have expressed thanks to Mansfield and other U.S. Senators for opposing Pres. Nixon's move into Cambodia.

MILITARY THREAT INTENSIFIES:

MARCH-APRIL 1970

The ouster of Prince Norodom Sihanouk as Cambodian chief of state Mar. 18, 1970 was followed in 2 days by a sharp intensification of military activity by all sides in Cambodia. The heightened fighting turned out to be the prelude to a massive movement of South Vietnamese and U.S. forces into Cambodia Apr. 29-May 1.

South Vietnamese troops and U.S. planes stepped up their attacks on Viet Cong/North Vietnamese forces operating in the Cambodian border sanctuaries in March, but Saigon and Washington officially denied any allied military incursion in Cambodia. Cambodia also denied persistent reports that it was cooperating with the allied military moves. As allied forces mounted their assaults on Communist positions along the South Vietnamese border, the Viet Cong and North Vietnamese pushed deeper into Cambodia and became increasingly involved in heavy clashes with Pnompenh's troops. The expanded Communist military activity was concentrated in a Svayrieng Province sector known as "the Parrot's Beak," an area in the southeast that jutted into Viet Cong-controlled sections of South Vietnam. Cambodia called on UN Secy. Gen. U Thant Mar. 30 to get the Communists to withdraw.

The discovery in mid-Apr. 1970 of the massacred bodies of Vietnamese civilian residents of Cambodia served as a further reminder of the underlying distrust between the Cambodian and South Vietnamese governments. It was never definitively determined whether the slain men and women were targets of Cambodian animosity or unintended victims of war. Other incidents of widespread shootings of Vietnamese civilians by Cambodian troops also were reported. These incidents led to the repatriation to South Vietnam of about 80,000 Vietnamese residing in the border areas of Cambodia.

71

Allies Attack Communist Sanctuaries

South Vietnamese fighter-bombers Mar. 20 and 23, 1970 attacked Viet Cong and North Vietnamese positions a few miles inside Cambodia across from Anphu district in South Vietnam's Chaudoc Province. The air raids were reported by Saigon sources Mar. 25. Both air strikes were said to have been requested by the Cambodian area commander during meetings with the Anphu district chief, Lt. Col. Truong Dinh Chat. It was reported Mar. 25 that South Vietnamese howitzers in Anphu had provided close combat support for Cambodian units on at least 4 occasions since Mar. 16.

U.S. fighter-bombers attacked North Vietnamese gun positions in Cambodia Mar. 24 after they had fired on South Vietnamese rangers operating in the northern part of South Vietnam's Plain of Reeds, about 65 miles west of Saigon. A U.S. command spokesman said the attack was the 5th air strike in Cambodia since Jan. 1 by American forces in exercise of their "inherent right of self-defense." The government operation in the Plain of Reeds Mar. 19-25 had resulted in the deaths of 152 enemy and 30 South Vietnamese troops.

Cambodian troops Mar. 20 battled Viet Cong soldiers for 2 hours inside Cambodia with the aid of an American spotter plane and South Vietnamese artillery inside South Vietnam. The action was the first coordinated allied-Cambodian effort against Communist forces. It was the most determined Cambodian drive so far to clear the border areas of Viet Cong. The fighting began when a 150-man Viet Cong company attacked a Cambodian outpost about 10 miles north of the South Vietnamese district capital of Anphu in Chaudoc Province. South Vietnamese howitzers in Anphu fired on the Communist attackers after receiving a radioed request for aid from the Cambodian commander. The shelling forced the Viet Cong to withdraw. The Cambodian commander later requested allied aerial observation as his troops were about to make a sweep of the area in search of the enemy force. A U.S. spotter plane sighted enemy movement, and the Anphu howitzers shelled the area again on the Cambodians' request.

Allied involvement in the fighting on the side of the Cambodians followed reports that South Vietnamese district officials in Chaudoc Province had been instructed Mar. 18 by Col. Tran Van Hui, province chief, to provide all possible aid to the Cambodians short of troops in operations against Communist forces. The U.S. command in Saigon Mar. 19 directed its military advisers in the border districts to attempt to establish radio communications with Cambodian commanders on the opposite side of the frontier. Maj. Gen. Nguyen Viet Thanh, commander of South Vietnam's IV Corps area, which took in Chaudoc Province, had authorized his commanders earlier Mar. 20 to provide forward artillery spotters for the Cambodians if they requested it.

South Vietnamese troops carried out their first major ground operation in Cambodia Mar. 27-28. A ranger battalion, supported by artillery and advance air strikes, penetrated 2 miles into Kandal Province in a sweep of a known Viet Cong sanctuary Mar. 27. U.S. helicopter gunships supported the assault, attacking targets inside Cambodia. One U.S. observer helicopter was hit by antiaircraft, but it landed safely in South Vietnam. The South Vietnamese killed 53 enemy troops of a force of 300. 3 rangers were reported killed. The engagement was fought 10 miles northeast of Anphu. The battle strategy was said to have been planned at meetings of Col. Chat and Cambodian military commanders Mar. 23.

South Vietnamese rangers crossed into Cambodia again Mar. 28 in an attempt to trap 2 Viet Cong battalions on the edge of Paknam Forest in Kandal Province. American helicopters supported the operation but remained over South Vietnam. 2 battalions of Cambodian troops were said to have served as a blocking force to prevent the Viet Cong from escaping north, but they did not actually engage in the fighting.

U.S. authorities in Washington had said Mar. 27 that American air support of the South Vietnamese operation in Cambodia that day had occurred without their prior knowledge or consent. The officials reaffirmed the U.S. policy of not widening the war in Vietnam but said that incursions or firing into Cambodia would continue for self-defense purposes. These rules had been reiterated to South Vietnamese authorities, the officials said.

South Vietnamese and U.S. military authorities in Saigon Mar. 28 flatly denied that their forces had participated in the fighting in Cambodia the previous day. An unnamed ranking South Vietnamese officer, however, confirmed the operation. "This involves delicate diplomatic matters between our country and Cambodia, so officially, we cannot admit it," he said.

U.S. sources in Saigon said Mar. 28 that American advisers and commanders had been ordered in a classified directive the previous week not to participate in any ground crossings into Cambodia planned by South Vietnam. But the directive did not prohibit the Americans from taking part in actually planning such operations.

Col. Ernest Terrell Jr., the senior American adviser in Kein Tuong Province, accompanying South Vietnamese officers, met inside Cambodia Mar. 28 with a Cambodian commander. The meeting took place a few miles from the South Vietnamese frontier, 6 miles north of the provincial capital of Moc Hao. Terrell said he was under orders "to encourage meetings between Vietnamese and Cambodians."

A White House statement Mar. 28 said the U.S. government was "not aware" of American ground incursions into Cambodia and could not confirm whether U.S. helicopter gunships had flown into that country. American forces were permitted to cross into Cambodia in response to enemy threats, at the discretion of field commanders, the statement said. Presidential Press Secy. Ronald Ziegler said this policy was only a restatement of previous Defense Department rulings already in force along the border.

Premier Lon Nol denied Mar. 30 that South Vietnamese, U.S. and Cambodian officers had been consulting each other on action against Vietnamese Communist forces in Cambodia.

A Pnompenh communique Mar. 29 charged the Viet Cong with "flagrant violations of Cambodian territory" and listed a series of incidents to support its allegations. The statement said Viet Cong troops had been sighted Mar. 28 near the vital road center of Neak Luong, 40 miles southeast of the capital. *According to the communique:*

● Viet Cong forces Mar. 27 had seized 2 members of the national police force, a paramilitary organization, 12 miles inside Cambodia at Peamchor in Preyveng Province. One man had been released.

● A "sizable" Communist force Mar. 27 had attacked a government unit 2 miles inside the frontier near Prekchrieu in Kratie Province, killing 2 Cambodians and wounding 8. 6 were missing.

● A 3,000-man Communist force occupied Svayandong, 5 miles from the border in Preyveng Province, posing a threat to the military post at Preah Shach in the same area.

● The government post of Ankgen, 5 miles from the border, was assaulted by a Communist unit, which surrounded a government platoon garrisoned there.

● Other Communist troops were sighted near Tukmeas in the southernmost border province of Kampot, 12 miles inside Cambodia, and near Po Tassuy in Takeo Province, about 6 miles from the frontier.

An accompanying statement issued by Premier Lon Nol appealed to the "Socialist Vietnamese leaders" to halt their attacks. It said: "Why do you want to invade our country? Why are you helping the same Sihanouk whom in your subversive propaganda you used to accuse as a tyrant, a reactionary and a lackey of the imperialists?"

A government statement Mar. 27 had charged that the Viet Cong had "implanted their troops on Cambodian soil, that they had indoctrinated, trained and armed" Cambodian rebels fighting the government, and that at Prince Sihanouk's behest they were increasing their attacks on Cambodian territory.

Lon Nol disclosed Mar. 30 that he had instructed the Cambodian mission to the UN to ask the Security Council to send observers to verify Pnompenh's charges of Communist troop incursions into Cambodia. U Thant said after meeting with Or Kosalak, the acting head of the Cambodian delegation, that he would "look into the matter."

The government disclosed Mar. 31 that it had renewed its appeal to Britain and the Soviet Union, co-chairmen of the 1954 Geneva Conference, to return the International Control Commission (ICC) to Cambodia to investigate Cambodia's charges of North Vietnamese and Viet Cong military incursions. The appeal had been filed with the British and Soviet embassies Mar. 22. It charged that the Communist troops "not only refused to withdraw from Cambodian territory but now attacked openly Cambodian posts and defense forces inside Cambodia." Britain responded favorably to the Cambodian request and called on the Soviet Union Mar. 26 to cooperate in recalling the ICC to Cambodia.

Meanwhile, Cambodia carried out mobilization measures to cope with what the government considered a growing Communist military threat. Reservists and veterans were recalled to military service, and the government said that all other men between the ages of 18 and 45 would be called on to volunteer for military duty. Sandbags were placed around police and military installations in Pnompenh.

Foreign diplomats in Pnompenh had reported Mar. 25 that the government had closed the port of Sihanoukville to ships carrying arms for the Viet Cong. The port was a vital supply funnel for the Communists in their operations against South Vietnam.

Cambodia Scores All Foreign Incursions

The Cambodian government Apr. 1 denounced all foreign incursions into its territory—Communist, U.S. and South Vietnamese. The statement, made amid reports of fresh Viet Cong attacks on Cambodian troops, was followed Apr. 5 by the 3d major South Vietnamese ground strike against Communist sanctuaries in Cambodia.

The Pnompenh communique assailed the American policy of "hot pursuit," which authorized U.S. and South Vietnamese forces to cross into Cambodia to attack Communist soldiers. "Faithful to its policy of strict neutrality, Cambodia will not in fact accept the right of pursuit to be exercised on its territory," the communique said. The statement added that the government "intends also to protest against all violations of Cambodian territory by foreign forces, whatever camp they come from."

The U.S. government responded to the Pnompenh communique by stating Apr. 1 that "all governments ought to respect Cambodia's desire for neutrality." The statement was issued following a discussion of the latest Southeast Asian developments by Pres. Nixon and State Secy. William P. Rogers.

The Pnompenh communique reported that "several thousand Viet Cong and North Vietnamese" had entered Cambodia Mar. 31 in the Snoul region in Kratie Province and had attacked a detachment of Cambodian soldiers, inflicting heavy casualties. Pnompenh filed a complaint with the UN Security Council Apr. 1.

Another Cambodian government communique told Apr. 2 of a "massive attack" the previous night by about 100 Viet Cong soldiers against a civil defense post at Phum Kampo, 5 miles from the Vietnamese border and 12 miles from the provincial capital of Svayrieng.

Cambodian forces were reported Apr. 9 to have evacuated the Parrot's Beak following Communist attacks Apr. 6-7 on Chiphou, near the eastern end of Svayrieng Province. About 30,000 civilians also were removed from the area. Most of those remaining were Vietnamese who were not permitted to flee westward. Cambodian government losses in the Chiphou battle were placed at 20 killed, 30 wounded and 30 missing. Communist casualties were listed at 40 dead.

Cambodian troops abandoned Chiphou and the border post of Brevet Apr. 9, withdrawing to the town of Svayrieng and to Prasot to the west. Fighting broke out between Svayrieng and Prasot Apr. 9. It was reported that a government ambush killed 300 Viet Cong soldiers Apr. 10. Prasot came under Communist· attack later in the day, and Cambodian sources said 89 Vietnamese civilians caught in the crossfire had been killed. Other sources placed the death toll between 90 and 100. The victims, including women and children, were in a barbed-wire compound where they had been placed by Cambodian authorities Apr. 8 as suspected Viet Cong sympathizers. ABC correspondent Steve Bell quoted refugees as saying that the Cambodian soldiers had told the Vietnamese to run when the Viet Cong approached, then had opened fire. Cambodian artillery in Svayrieng pounded the Viet Cong and prevented them from overrunning Prasot.

(The Viet Cong were reported to have seized 8 foreign newsmen Apr. 5, 6 and 8 near a Communist roadblock near Chiphou. The correspondents included 2 Americans, 2 Japanese and 2 Frenchmen. The Americans were identified as Sean Flynn, 29, son of the late actor Errol Flynn, and Dana Stone, a free-lance photographer for CBS.)

Saigon sources reported Apr. 8 that South Vietnamese forces were cooperating with the Cambodians in the fighting in Svayrieng Province. South Vietnamese helicopter gunships were said to have flown 5 miles inside Cambodia in the previous 24 hours and to have killed an estimated 150 Communist troops. Cambodian authorities Apr. 10 cut off the flow of Vietnamese refugees into South Vietnam. An estimated 200-500 were said to have fled Cambodia in the past several days. A 6 p.m.-to-6 a.m. curfew was imposed on Pnompenh's 120,000 Vietnamese residents Apr. 11. The action was taken to curb an increase in "subversive activities," government authorities said.

Vietnamese Communist forces continued to press their advance deeper into Cambodia. By Apr. 20 they had reached to within 15 miles of Pnompenh. Meanwhile, South Vietnamese troops carried out major thrusts into Cambodia Apr. 9-20 to strike at Viet Cong and North Vietnamese forces along the Vietnamese frontier. One of the operations was conducted jointly with Cambodian troops. But a Cambodian military spokesman admitted Apr. 17 that the Viet Cong were in virtual control of 3 Cambodian provinces. (The Cambodian areas he reported under Viet Cong control were the provinces of Ratankiri and Mondolkiri in the northeast and Svayrieng in the Parrot's Beak to the south.)

The Communist threat to Pnompenh was heightened with the capture Apr. 19 of Saang, 15 miles south of the capital. The village was occupied after Cambodian troops had fled. Cambodian reinforcements established a defensive line just north of Saang. The Communists' action directly south of Pnompenh represented a shift from their previous area of major operations in the southeast sector in the Parrot's Beak.

A Pnompenh official reported Apr. 19 that the Communists had blown up railroad tracks south of Takeo, about 50 miles south of the capital. He said 5 more of the country's 17 provinces were half occupied by the Communist forces—Kampot, Kandal, Preyveng, Takeo and Kompong Cham.

Communist troops had raided Takeo Apr. 15 but were repulsed with a loss of 6 killed, a military spokesman reported the following day. Enemy soldiers also were said to have raided the town of Mareng, south of Pnompenh, and to have kidnaped a district chief, his deputy and 8 militiamen.

The South Vietnamese government continued to deny that its forces were making ground strikes into Cambodia despite persistent reports to the contrary. Among the major actions reportedly taken by Saigon's troops:

● South Vietnamese soldiers, supported by armored vehicles and artillery, conducted a sweep against Communist forces inside Cambodia opposite South Vietnam's Chaudoc Province Apr. 9-10. U.S. military advisers were said to have witnessed the operation and to have participated in its planning from a command post atop a mountain overlooking Cambodia. Allied artillery and helicopter gunships struck suspected Viet Cong and North Vietnamese positions, setting fields afire.

● South Vietnamese troops, accompanied by a token force of 100 Cambodians, reportedly pushed at least a mile into Cambodia Apr. 14, destroying a North Vietnamese base and killing 179 of the enemy. The battle, involving 2,000 government troops, was said to have erupted 5 hours after the North Vietnamese attacked a nearby South Vietnamese border post and were repulsed. This apparently was the first instance of Cambodians joining South Vietnamese in a large operation. Heretofore, the Cambodians were reported to have served only as a blocking force in South Vietnamese actions against Communist troops in Cambodia. Saigon insisted that the battle took place ½ mile inside South Vietnam. Government losses were listed as 7 killed.

● A South Vietnamese incursion into Cambodia was observed Apr. 16 by CBS correspondent Gary Sheppard. He said he had filmed a line of trucks crossing on the highway connecting Pnompenh and Saigon.

● Saigon sources reported Apr. 18 that government troops fighting 2 operations in Cambodia earlier in the week had smashed 2 Communist bases, killing 450 enemy soldiers and seizing huge munitions stockpiles. South Vietnamese losses were put at 13 killed and 104 wounded. A South Vietnamese government communique issued Apr. 18 repeated the assertion that the operations had taken place in South Vietnam.

● Further South Vietnamese ground strikes into Cambodia were said to have occurred Apr. 18 and 20. In the latter operation, 2,000 government soldiers attacked across the border from the western Mekong Delta, about 55 miles west of Saigon, killing 144 North Vietnamese and Viet Cong. 20 government troops were reported killed. The attackers, supported by bombers and artillery, were said to have driven at least 2 miles into Svayrieng Province. A Saigon communique Apr. 20 mentioned the action but placed it just inside South Vietnam. Premier Lon Nol had issued a world appeal Apr. 14 for arms to help his forces combat "an escalation of systematic acts of aggression" launched by Viet Cong and North Vietnamese troops against eastern Cambodia. In a broadcast statement, the premier said the Pnompenh government "has the duty to inform the nation that in view of the gravity of the present situation, it finds it necessary to accept all unconditional foreign aid, wherever it may come from, for the salvation of the nation."

Cambodians Recapture Saang

Cambodian soldiers recaptured Saang Apr. 23. The village, 15 miles south of Pnompenh, had been abandoned by the Viet Cong.

In the Cambodian counterattack, Cambodian forces using U.S.-made T-28 aircraft had strafed enemy troops Apr. 20 along the Bassac River.

Cambodian troops Apr. 21 forced Vietnamese civilians to march through Saang in order to draw Viet Cong fire. At least 2 of the Vietnamese civilians were reported wounded, and 10 were listed as missing. The commander in the area, Gen. Sosthene Fernandez, told newsmen that the move "was a good way to discover where the Viets have their automatic weapons. This exercise now gave us a good reading for our 105-mm. cannon." Sosthene Fernandez said Apr. 22 that the plan had been conceived by Premier Lon Nol. Cambodian officers said the Vietnamese had volunteered for the mission. But a participant in the march said the civilians had been rounded up in 4 villages and were brought to Saang by truck.

After the capture of Saang, major action shifted to Angtassom, 40 miles south of Pnompenh, where Vietnamese Communist forces fought their way into the center of the town Apr. 24 after 2 days of heavy clashes. Cambodia claimed Apr. 26 that its forces had counterattacked and recaptured the village following fierce hand-to-hand fighting. 4 government battalions were said to have pushed the Viet Cong about ½ mile to the south. Newsmen, however, reported that Viet Cong forces still occupied the roads leading into Angtassom. A Communist roadblock had been set up Apr. 24 about 500 yards north of the village, cutting off Pnompenh from Kampot, a port on the south coast. The government withdrew its claim Apr. 27 and admitted that its forces had not cleared Communist troops from Angtassom.

In an action south of Pnompenh, the Viet Cong Apr. 26 reportedly occupied the district capital of Tani, several miles south of Angtassom, and set up an administration there. The provincial capital of Takeo, 6 miles south of Angtassom, continued to come under Communist harassment and was hit by recoilless rifle fire Apr. 25. Communist forces Apr. 24 had staged a terrorist raid on Kep, a coastal resort town, setting several buildings afire and killing 3 civilians. The raid was carried out from Communist-held offshore islands.

The Pnompenh government was reported Apr. 24 to have asked U.S. military commanders to send B-52 bombers to attack a Viet Cong headquarters at Mimot, about 100 miles northeast of Pnompenh. But State Department officials in Washington said Apr. 25 that no such request had been received.

About 5,000 South Vietnamese troops were reported to have crossed back into South Vietnam Apr. 24 following a 4-day operation against Communist forces about 2 miles inside Cambodia. The drive, which had been launched from the Mekong Delta west of Saigon, was reported to have resulted in the killing of 245 North Vietnamese and Viet Cong. Saigon's losses were said to have totaled 28 dead and 127 wounded.

Brig. Gen. Srey Saman, Cambodian army chief of staff, said Apr. 24 that "about 3,500" Cambodians had been killed, wounded or had "disappeared" in a month of fighting the Vietnamese Communists. (Srey issued the statement in Paris, where he had conferred for 2 days with Cambodian ambassadors from Europe, Africa and the Americas.)

Vietnamese Civilians Massacred

The bodies of hundreds of Vietnamese civilian residents of Cambodia, suspected victims of a mass killing, floated down the

Mekong River in the southeastern part of the country Apr. 11-17. Another 100 Vietnamese civilians were reported slain in a Cambodian government compound in Takeo Apr. 16.

The first bodies were sighted in the Mekong Apr. 11 at a ferry landing at Neak Leung, 36 miles southeast of Pnompenh. A police official at Neak Leung reported counting 400 bodies Apr. 15. Other sources said as many as 1,000 bodies had been seen in the river. Most of the victims were men. Many had their hands tied behind their backs.

A Reuters dispatch Apr. 17 quoted witnesses as saying that the Vietnamese had been shot to death on Tachhor, a small island in the Mekong 4 miles upstream from Neak Leung. According to the witnesses, farmers and fishermen nearby, the shootings had started on the island Apr. 10 after the arrival from the direction of Pnompenh of a passenger boat containing about 100 Cambodians and Vietnamese escorted by Cambodian soldiers. The disembarkation from boats followed by the shooting of the civilians continued for 5 successive nights, the reports said.

The Cambodian Information Ministry asserted Apr. 14 that the killings were "not the result of collective assassination perpetrated by Cambodian armed forces." The ministry said the civilians had been caught inside their detention camp "between the firing of the Viet Cong invaders and the Cambodian forces defending" the village of Prasot. The statement noted that the Viet Cong had frequently "used Vietnamese residents of Cambodia as auxiliaries of their aggression."

Cambodian Information Min. Trinh Heanh reiterated Apr. 16 that the corpses sighted in the Mekong River "were victims of a battle" between the Viet Cong and Cambodian troops. He said the dead included Cambodians and Vietnamese civilians who had been thrown into the river by the Viet Cong after the fighting.

An apparent contradiction of the government's version of the incident was contained in a statement issued Apr. 16 by Lt. Col. Kim Eng Kouroudeth, chief of army intelligence. He assumed that the victims might have been slain by Cambodian civilians aroused by the alleged collusion between Vietnamese residents of Cambodia and the Viet Cong and North

Vietnamese forces that had invaded the country. Kim said he had ordered an investigation.

The Pnompenh government reportedly had been fomenting a campaign against both the Vietnamese residents of Cambodia and the Vietnamese Communist invaders since the ouster of Prince Norodom Sihanouk. The Cambodians and the Annamese of Vietnam had been traditional enemies. Government planes Apr. 11 had dropped leaflets on Pnompenh recalling a historic massacre "when the Khmers [Cambodians] once rose up and killed all Annamese on Cambodian territory in one night."

A Cambodian government statement Apr. 19 denied that a campaign was in progress against Vietnamese civilians in the country. It said the drive was directed only at Viet Cong and North Vietnamese invaders and not "against the peaceful Vietnamese ... as long as they do not seek to trouble public order."

The South Vietnamese government had said Apr. 15 that it was asking the Pnompenh government to permit a "people's delegation" from charitable agencies to enter Cambodia to investigate the alleged massacre of Vietnamese civilians. South Vietnamese Foreign Min. Tran Van Lam said at a news conference Apr. 17 that his government was asking Pnompenh to receive an official mission to arrange for the repatriation of 50,000 Vietnamese. Lam said 1,467 Vietnamese refugees had been registered by South Vietnamese border officials since Mar. 18. He said several times that number had probably crossed into South Vietnam without authorization.

A U.S. government statement Apr. 17 said that "we consider the massacre of innocent civilians to be abhorrent and to be actions that warrant condemnation."

An earlier mass slaying of Vietnamese in Prasot had been reported Apr. 10. The Associated Press said Apr. 15 that available evidence showed that the killings had been perpetrated by Cambodian troops. Reports of the number of the victims varied from 73 to 100. At least 7 more Vietnamese were shot to death by Cambodian troops Apr. 11 just south of Kompong Trabek, near the border west of Prasot.

In the incident at Takeo, about 150 Vietnamese civilians, herded under detention into a school building Apr. 13, were fired on by Cambodian soldiers Apr. 16. About 100, including perhaps 30 children, were killed. The account of the slaughter was related to foreign newsmen who visited the scene Apr. 17 by some of the 50 survivors. The survivors said they had given no provocation and did not know why the shootings took place. Soldiers on guard at the school, who did not contradict the account of the slayings, indicated that the killings were in reprisal for a Viet Cong attack on Takeo Apr. 15.

Commenting on the alleged massacre, Premier Lon Nol expressed regret Apr. 20, but he said it was difficult to distinguish between Vietnamese citizens who were Viet Cong and those who were not. Lon Nol charged Apr. 23 that Vietnamese civilians had fired on Cambodian troops. "So it is quite normal that the reaction of Cambodian troops, who feel themselves betrayed, is difficult to control," he said.

The South Vietnamese House of Representatives Apr. 20 appealed to "all nations in the world and all international organizations" to intervene to protect the lives of Vietnamese residing in Cambodia. The French government was specifically urged to require Cambodia to "prevent renewed massacres of Vietnamese." The latter plea was made by Pham Dang Lam, head of the Saigon delegation to the Paris peace talks.

Cambodia assured Saigon Apr. 27 that it would take all measures necessary to protect the lives of Vietnamese civilians residing in Cambodia. The assurances were given to a South Vietnamese Foreign Ministry official, Pham Huy Ty, during talks with Cambodian Foreign Min. Yem Sambaur in Pnompenh. Yem Sambaur attributed these "horrible crimes" to Viet Cong forces and said that Cambodian officials were victims of the atrocities as well. Ty reported that the foreign minister had also responded favorably to Saigon's proposal to repatriate to South Vietnam any of the Vietnamese who wished to leave.

More than 200 Vietnamese refugees arrived in Saigon Apr. 27 from Cambodia at the start of an organized airlift. Another group of refugees had flown to Saigon Apr. 26 aboard a plane carrying a 5-man South Vietnamese delegation that had discussed the repatriation plan that day with Cambodian officials in Pnompenh. Cambodia had agreed Apr. 23 to receive the delegation. It did so following 2 weeks of discussion with the South Vietnamese government. The negotiations had been assisted by Australians and Japanese. Saigon's evacuation plan had been disclosed Apr. 17 by Foreign Min. Tran Van Lam. Lam said the proposal had been made because of "a situation of panic" among the Vietnamese in Cambodia.

A massive repatriation of South Vietnamese was started May 10, and about 50,000-80,000 were removed from Cambodia by the time Saigon decided to suspend the program May 22. The halt was ordered because measures adopted by the Pnompenh government provided greater security for the Vietnamese residents in Cambodia, according to Pham Huy Ty. The decision to stop the flow of repatriates also had been prompted by political opposition in Saigon against adding to the already large refugee population in South Vietnam.

Lt. Gen. Do Cao Tri, commander of South Vietnamese troops in Cambodia, warned May 22 that "if the Cambodians should continue to mistreat our compatriots, then our army will have an appropriate action." South Vietnamese State Min. Pham Quang Dan, chairman of a committee to aid Vietnamese repatriates, said Saigon's policy "is to transfer Vietnamese from dangerous to safe areas in Cambodia. Repatriation to Vietnam will be the exception from now on."

U.S. Munitions Ship Seized by Mutineers

A 7,500-ton U.S. freighter, the *Columbia Eagle,* bound for Sattahip, Thailand with munitions for the U.S. Air Force, was seized by 2 armed crewmen Mar. 14 in the Gulf of Siam and was forced to sail to Cambodian waters. The mutiny was described as a protest against the U.S. war effort in Vietnam. The ship was finally released by Cambodia Apr. 8.

24 of the ship's 39 crewmen were set adrift in 2 lifeboats by the mutineers and were picked up within hours of the mutiny by another American munitions ship en route to Sattahip. The *Columbia Eagle,* with $1/3$ of its crew still aboard, was anchored by the mutineers near a small island 5 miles from the Cambodian port of Sihanoukville and 4 miles from the Cambodian naval base of Ream. The Cambodian government advised the U.S. Mar. 16 that it planned to grant political asylum to the 2 mutineers, Clyde W. McKay Jr., 25, of

Escondido, Calif. and Alvin Glatkowski, 20, of Long Beach, Calif. The U.S. asked Cambodia to return the ship, its cargo and 13 crewmen, including the captain, Donald A. Swann, 51, of Portland, Ore., to American jurisdiction.

As the *Columbia Eagle* had sailed into Cambodian waters, the U.S. Coast Guard cutter *Mellon* had followed it. The crew of the *Mellon* had been told in a message from the *Columbia Eagle's* radio officer that armed men were seizing the ship. The *Mellon* was ordered Mar. 15 to bring the freighter out by force. The order, issued by Adm. John Hyland, commander of the Pacific Fleet, was rescinded within minutes, however, by Adm. John S. McCaine, commander in chief, Pacific. The U.S. State Department said Mar. 17 that the recapture of the vessel was only a "contingency" plan "among a number of other options." 5 U.S. ships were off Sihanoukville in international waters and were to remain there to offer "contingency assistance," the State Department said.

In a radio message sent from his ship Mar. 16, Capt. Swann said he had been warned by McKay and Glatkowski that "this was the first in a series of such mutinies" aimed to "impede the war effort in Vietnam." Sen. Mark O. Hatfield (R, Ore.) said Defense Department officials had told him that Navy authorities concluded that the capture of the *Columbia Eagle* was an antiwar protest. (The freighter carried 750- and 500-pound bombs and other munitions for use by U.S. Air Force planes in Thailand in bombing missions against Communist targets in Laos and South Vietnam. It had taken on its cargo at Long Beach, Calif. and San Francisco.)

Crewmen aboard the freighter that picked up the 24 *Columbia Eagle* crewmen provided this account of the vessel's seizure: While steaming up the Gulf of Siam, 100 miles off Cambodia, Capt. Swann, under threat by a gunman, ordered the ship abandoned because of an impending bomb explosion. The gunman told Swann that he was taking the ship to neutralist Cambodia to ask for political asylum and would blow up the vessel if the asylum request were refused. The 24 crewmen, some thinking that a boat drill was in progress, were hustled into 2 lifeboats, which were ordered cast off after they were lowered. The *Columbia Eagle* was then headed for Cambodia with the remaining crewmen aboard.

The *Columbia Eagle* was released by Cambodia Apr. 8. The ship arrived in Subic Bay, the Philippines, Apr. 13 with the remaining 13 of its crew members and its cargo. A U.S.-Cambodian agreement on the release of the vessel had been announced by the State Department Mar. 31.

Capt. Swann, on arriving in Subic Bay, filed mutiny charges against McKay and Glatkowski, who were in Pnompenh awaiting a decision on their application for political asylum in Cambodia. McKay had said in an interview Mar. 25 that he and his companion were supporters of the militant Students for a Democratic Society in the U.S. and that their seizure of the ship was "an SDS plot more than anything else." McKay, who opposed the Vietnam war, said he and Glatkowski were not SDS members, but "we support the groups we believe in if we hold similar ideas and have common enemies."

ALLIED CAMPAIGN IN CAMBODIA:

APRIL-JUNE 1970

More than 20,000 U.S. and South Vietnamese troops began a massive drive into Cambodia Apr. 29 and May 1, 1970 with the avowed aim of smashing the Viet Cong/North Vietnamese border sanctuaries in Cambodia. U.S. Pres. Nixon announced the action in a TV address to the American people. The President pledged that once the allied objectives were achieved, American forces would be pulled out. Nixon fulfilled that pledge, and American troops were removed from Cambodia June 29. South Vietnamese forces remained, however, and continued to fight on through the remainder of 1970, with no indication as to when they would conclude their operations. During the period after the American withdrawal, Cambodian troops became increasingly involved in heavy clashes with North Vietnamese forces deep inside Cambodia, around Pnompenh and in the north-central area.

The allied drive into Cambodia was concentrated in 2 areas—the "Parrot's Beak," about 33 miles from Saigon, and the "Fishhook" area, about 50 miles north of the South Vietnamese capital. Saigon military spokesmen May 14 confirmed that South Vietnamese forces had carried out 4 "unannounced operations" into Cambodia prior to the massive thrust into the Parrot's Beak Apr. 29. The spokesmen said government troops, accompanied by U.S. advisers, had pushed into the Beak Mar. 20 and Apr. 13, 20 and 29. Some of these operations had been reported previously in the Western press but had been denied at the time by Saigon.

The operations against the Communists were widened in May as allied troops opened new fronts in the Parrot's Beak, in the Fishhook and in other sectors, including the region opposite South Vietnam's Central Highlands south of the Sesan area and in the Mekong Delta. Additional U.S. and South Vietnamese troops were brought into Cambodia to handle the expanded operations, and by the time the fighting was at its height, American forces in Cambodia had risen to a peak of 23,000 men and South Vietnamese strength there to 40,000.

The presence of increasing numbers of South Vietnamese troops in Cambodia exacerbated the traditional animosities between Cambodians and Vietnamese. Pnompenh expressed fears that South Vietnam would use the struggle against the North Vietnamese and Viet Cong in Cambodia as a pretext to promote expansionist designs against Cambodia. The Cambodians also accused South Vietnamese troops of mistreating Cambodian civilians.

Nixon Announces U.S. Move into Cambodia

The U.S. offensive into Cambodia was announced by Pres. Nixon in a special TV address Apr. 30 while the thrust was under way. The American phase of the allied incursion, involving several thousand U.S. soldiers in the Fishhook area 50 miles northwest of Saigon, was described by Nixon as an attempt to destroy a "key control center" for the enemy and its "headquarters for the entire Communist military operation in South Vietnam."

Nixon asserted that the attack was "not an invasion of Cambodia" since the areas were "completely occupied and controlled by North Vietnamese forces." The U.S. purpose, he continued, was not to occupy the areas. Once the enemy was driven out and his military supplies destroyed, Nixon said, "we will withdraw." Nixon said the move was made "to protect our men who are in Vietnam and to guarantee the continued success of our withdrawal and Vietnamization program."

The text of Nixon's address:

Good evening my fellow Americans.

10 days ago, in my report to the nation on Vietnam, I announced a decision to withdraw an additional 150,000 Americans from Vietnam over the next year. I said then that I was making that decision despite our concern over increased enemy activity in Laos, in Cambodia and in South Vietnam. At that time, I warned that if I concluded that increased enemy activity in any of these areas endangered the lives of Americans remaining in Vietnam, I would not hesitate to take strong and effective measures to deal with that situation.

Despite that warning, North Vietnam has increased its military aggression in all these areas, and particularly in Cambodia.

After full consultation with the National Security Council, Amb. [Ellsworth] Bunker, Gen. [Creighton W.] Abrams and my other advisers, I have concluded that the actions of the enemy in the last 10 days clearly endanger the lives of Americans who are in Vietnam now and would constitute an unacceptable risk to those who will be there after withdrawal of another 150,000.

To protect our men who are in Vietnam and to guarantee the continued success of our withdrawal and Vietnamization programs, I have concluded that the time has come for action.

Tonight, I shall describe the actions of the enemy, the actions I have ordered to deal with that situation and the reasons for my decision.

Cambodia, a small country of 7 million people, has been a neutral nation since the Geneva agreement of 1954—an agreement, incidentally, which was signed by the government of North Vietnam.

American policy since then has been to scrupulously respect the neutrality of the Cambodian people. We have maintained a skeleton diplomatic mission of fewer than 15 in Cambodia's capital, and that only since last August. For the previous 4 years, from 1965 to 1969, we did not have any diplomatic mission whatever in Cambodia. And for the past 5 years, we have provided no military assistance whatever and no economic assistance to Cambodia.

North Vietnam, however, has not respected that neutrality.

For the past 5 years—as indicated on this map that you see here—North Vietnam has occupied military sanctuaries all along the Cambodian frontier with South Vietnam. Some of these extend up to 20 miles into Cambodia. The sanctuaries are in red and, as you note, they are on both sides of the border. They are used for hit-and-run attacks on American and South Vietnamese forces in South Vietnam.

These Communist occupied territories contain major base camps, training sites, logistics facilities, weapons and ammunition factories, air strips and prisoner-of-war compounds.

For 5 years, neither the United States nor South Vietnam has moved against these enemy sanctuaries because we did not wish to violate the territory of a neutral nation. Even after the Vietnamese Communists began to expand these sanctuaries 4 weeks ago, we counseled patience to our South Vietnamese allies and imposed restraints on our own commanders.

In contrast to our policy, the enemy in the past 2 weeks has stepped up his guerrilla actions, and he is concentrating his main forces in these sanctuaries that you see on this map where they are building up to launch massive attacks on our forces and those of South Vietnam.

North Vietnam in the last 2 weeks has stripped away all pretense of respecting the sovereignty or the neutrality of Cambodia. Thousands of their soldiers are invading the country from the sanctuaries; they are encircling the capital of Pnompenh. Coming from these sanctuaries, as you see here, they have moved into Cambodia and are encircling the capital.

Cambodia, as a result of this, has sent out a call to the United States, to a number of other nations, for assistance. Because if this enemy effort succeeds, Cambodia would become a vast enemy staging area and a springboard for attacks on South Vietnam along 600 miles of frontier—a refuge where enemy troops could return from combat without fear of retaliation.

North Vietnamese men and supplies could then be poured into that country, jeopardizing not only the lives of our own men but the people of South Vietnam as well.

Now confronted with this situation, we have 3 options.

First, we can do nothing. Well, the ultimate result of that course of action is clear. Unless we indulge in wishful thinking, the lives of Americans remaining in Vietnam after our next withdrawal of 150,000 would be gravely threatened.

Let us go to the map again. Here is South Vietnam. Here is North Vietnam. North Vietnam already occupies this part of Laos. If North Vietnam also occupied this whole band in Cambodia, or the entire country, it would mean that South Vietnam was completely outflanked and the forces of Americans in this area, as well as the South Vietnamese, would be in an untenable military position.

Our 2d choice is to provide massive military assistance to Cambodia itself. Now unfortunately, while we deeply sympathize with the plight of 7 million Cambodians whose country is being invaded, massive amounts of military assistance could not be rapidly and effectively utilized by the small Cambodian army against the immediate threat. With other nations, we shall do our best to provide the small arms and other equipment which the Cambodian army of 40,000 needs and can use for its defense. But the aid we will provide will be limited to the purpose of enabling Cambodia to defend its neutrality and not for the purpose of making it an active belligerent on one side or the other.

Our 3d choice is to go to the heart of the trouble. That means cleaning out major North Vietnamese and Viet Cong-occupied territories, these sanctuaries which serve as bases for attacks on both Cambodia and American and South Vietnamese forces in South Vietnam. Some of these, incidentally, are as close to Saigon as Baltimore is to Washington. This one, for example, is called the Parrot's Beak. It is only 33 miles from Saigon.

Now faced with these 3 options, this is the decision I have made: In cooperation with the armed forces of South Vietnam, attacks are being launched this week to clean out major enemy sanctuaries on the Cambodian-Vietnam border.

A major responsibility for the ground operations is being assumed by South Vietnamese forces. For example, the attacks in several areas, including the Parrot's Beak that I referred to a moment ago, are exclusively South Vietnamese ground operations under South Vietnamese command with the United States providing air and logistical support.

There is one area, however, immediately above Parrot's Beak, where I have concluded that a combined American and South Vietnamese operation is necessary. Tonight, American and South Vietnamese units will attack the headquarters for the entire Communist military operation in South Vietnam. This key control center has been occupied by the North Vietnamese and Viet Cong for 5 years in blatant violation of Cambodia's neutrality.

This is not an invasion of Cambodia. The areas in which these attacks will be launched are completely occupied and controlled by North Vietnamese forces. Our purpose is not to occupy the areas. Once enemy forces are driven out of these sanctuaries and once their military supplies are destroyed, we will withdraw.

These actions are in no way directed at the security interests of any nation. Any government that chooses to use these actions as a pretext for harming relations with the United States will be doing so on its own responsibility and on its own initiative, and we will draw the appropriate conclusions.

Now let me give you the reasons for my decision:

A majority of the American people, a majority of you listening to me, are for the withdrawal of our forces from Vietnam. The action I have taken tonight is indispensable for the continuing success of that withdrawal program.

A majority of the American people want to end this war rather than to have it drag on interminably. The action I have taken tonight will serve that purpose.

A majority of the American people want to keep the casualties of our brave men in Vietnam at an absolute minimum. The action I take tonight is essential if we are to accomplish that goal.

We take this action not for the purpose of expanding the war into Cambodia but for the purpose of ending the war in Vietnam and winning the just peace we all desire. We have made, and we will continue to make, every possible effort to end this war through negotiation at the conference table rather than through more fighting on the battlefield.

Let us look again at the record. We have stopped the bombing of North Vietnam. We have cut air operations by over 20%. We have announced withdrawal of over 250,000 of our men. We have offered to withdraw all of our men if they will withdraw theirs. We have offered to negotiate all issues with only one condition—and that is that the future of South Vietnam be determined not by North Vietnam, not by the United States, but by the people of South Vietnam themselves.

The answer of the enemy has been intransigence at the conference table, belligerence in Hanoi, massive military aggression in Laos and Cambodia and stepped-up attacks in South Vietnam designed to increase American casualties.

This attitude has become intolerable. We will not react to this threat to American lives merely by plaintive diplomatic protests. If we did, the credibility of the United States would be destroyed in every area of the world where only the power of the United States deters aggression.

Tonight, I again warn the North Vietnamese that if they continue to escalate the fighting when the United States is withdrawing its forces, I shall meet my responsibility as commander-in-chief of our armed forces to take the action I consider necessary to defend the security of our American men.

The action that I have announced tonight puts the leaders of North Vietnam on notice that we will be patient in working for peace, we will be conciliatory at the conference table, but we will not be humiliated. We will not be defeated. We will not allow American men by the thousands to be killed by an enemy from privileged sanctuaries.

The time came long ago to end this war through peaceful negotiations. We stand ready for those negotiations. We have made major efforts, many of which must remain secret. I say tonight that all the offers and approaches made previously remain on the conference table whenever Hanoi is ready to negotiate seriously.

But if the enemy response to our most conciliatory offers for peaceful negotiation continues to be to increase its attacks and humiliate and defeat us, we shall react accordingly.

My fellow Americans, we live in an age of anarchy both abroad and at home. We see mindless attacks on all the great institutions which have been created by free civilizations in the last 500 years. Even here in the United States, great universities are being systematically destroyed. Small nations all over the world find themselves under attack from within and from without.

If, when the chips are down, the world's most powerful nation, the United States of America, acts like a pitiful, helpless giant, the forces of totalitarianism and anarchy will threaten free nations and free institutions throughout the world.

It is not our power but our will and character that is being tested tonight. The question all Americans must ask and answer tonight is this: Does the richest and strongest nation in the history of the world have the character to meet a direct challenge by a group which rejects every effort to win a just peace, ignores our warning, tramples on solemn agreements, violates the neutrality of an unarmed people and uses our prisoners as hostages?

If we fail to meet this challenge, all other nations will be on notice that despite its overwhelming power the United States, when a real crisis comes, will be found wanting.

During my campaign for the Presidency, I pledged to bring Americans home from Vietnam. They are coming home.

I promised to end this war. I shall keep that promise.

I promised to win a just peace. I shall keep that promise.

We shall avoid a wider war. But we are also determined to put an end to this war.

In this room, Woodrow Wilson made the great decisions which led to victory in World War I. Franklin Roosevelt made the decisions which led to our victory in World War II. Dwight D. Eisenhower made decisions which ended the war in Korea and avoided war in the Middle East. John F. Kennedy, in his finest hour, made the great decision which removed Soviet nuclear missiles from Cuba and the Western Hemisphere.

I have noted that there has been a great deal of discussion with regard to this decision that I have made, and I should point out that I do not contend that it is in the same magnitude as these decisions that I have just mentioned. But between those decisions and this decision there is a difference that is very fundamental. In those decisions, the American people were not assailed by counsels of doubt and defeat from some of the most widely known opinion leaders of the nation.

I have noted, for example, that a Republican Senator has said that this action I have taken means that my party has lost all chance of winning the November elections. And others are saying today that this move against enemy sanctuaries will make me a one-term President.

No one is more aware than I am of the political consequences of the action I have taken. It is tempting to take the easy political path: to blame this war on previous administrations and to bring all of our men home immediately, regardless of the consequences, even though that would mean defeat for the United States; to desert 18 million South Vietnamese people, who have put their trust in us and to expose them to the same slaughter and savagery which the leaders of North Vietnam inflicted on hundreds of thousands of North Vietnamese who chose freedom when the Communists took over North Vietnam in 1954; to get peace at any price now, even though I know that a peace of humiliation for the United States would lead to a bigger war or surrender later.

I have rejected all political considerations in making this decision.

Whether my party gains in November is nothing compared to the lives of 400,000 brave Americans fighting for our country and for the cause of peace and freedom in Vietnam. Whether I may be a one-term President is insignificant compared to whether by our failure to act in this crisis the United States proves itself to be unworthy to lead the forces of freedom in this critical period in world history. I would rather be a one-term President and do what I believe is right than to be a 2-term President at the cost of seeing America become a 2d-rate power and to see this nation accept the first defeat in its proud 190-year history.

I realize that in this war there are honest and deep differences in this country about whether we should have become involved, that there are differences as to how the war should have been conducted. But the decision I announce tonight transcends those differences.

For the lives of American men are involved. The opportunity for 150,000 Americans to come home in the next 12 months is involved. The future of 18 million people in South Vietnam and 7 million people in Cambodia is involved. The possibility of winning a just peace in Vietnam and in the Pacific is at stake.

It is customary to conclude a speech from the White House by asking support for the President of the United States. Tonight, I depart from that precedent. What I ask is far more important. I ask for your support for our brave men fighting tonight halfway around the world—not for territory—not for glory—but so that their younger brothers and their sons and your sons can have a chance to grow up in a world of peace and freedom and justice.

Thank you and good night.

At a news conference May 8, Nixon pledged that American troops would be withdrawn from Cambodia by mid-June. The specific pullout date was subsequently set at June 30.

U.S. & South Vietnam Start 2-Pronged Drive

The controversial allied military campaign in Cambodia started when more than 20,000 U.S. and South Vietnamese troops began a 2-pointed drive into Cambodia Apr. 29 and May 1 in an effort to destroy Communist sanctuaries along the border. The Americans were under orders to penetrate no deeper than 30-35 kilometers (18.6-21.7 miles). The South Vietnamese were under no such restrictions.

The U.S./South Vietnamese campaign against the North Vietnamese and Viet Cong bases in the eastern border regions of Cambodia concentrated in the Parrot's Beak and the Fishhook area. By May 4 neither of the 2 allied columns was reported to have made any substantial contact with the enemy. Cambodian residents in both areas reported that thousands of Communist soldiers had fled to the west before the invasion began. Allied forces in both operations uncovered large caches of small arms, food and medical supplies.

The Fishhook operation, launched May 1, involved about 8,000 Americans and more than 2,000 South Vietnamese soldiers. It penetrated 20 miles into Cambodia. About 1,500 U.S. reinforcements were brought into the area May 4. Hundreds of helicopters, tanks and armored cars took part in what was described as the largest allied war effort in two years.

The attack in the Parrot's Beak started initially Apr. 29 with 6,000 South Vietnamese soldiers supported by U.S. warplanes and artillery and accompanied by American advisers. The force penetrated 24 miles to the vicinity of Prasot. A statement issued Apr. 29 by the South Vietnamese Defense Ministry said the Parrot's Beak operation represented "an indispensable and efficient measure to save the lives" of the South Vietnamese people, its soldiers and allies. The operation also was "a necessary measure in the framework of the policy" of giving the South Vietnamese forces greater responsibility in waging the war, the ministry said.

Military spokesmen in Saigon reported May 14 that up until then 641 enemy soldiers had been killed in the Fishhook operation and that 118 persons had been detained; the latter consisted mostly of women, children and old men. Most of the enemy fatalities were inflicted by aerial and artillery strikes. American casualties were listed as 10 killed and 35 wounded. South Vietnamese losses in both operations were put at 95 killed and 400 wounded.

The principal target of the Fishhook drive was the Viet Cong/North Vietnamese base known as the Central Office for South Vietnam (COSVN), described as the control center for all Communist military and political operations in South Vietnam. It was believed to be a mobile headquarters, including hospital, sleeping and working quarters for top commanders and an advance communications network. Allied troops May 4 reached the site of what was described as the largest North Vietnamese base area discovered thus far. The stronghold was identified on tactical maps as "The City." It was located near the northwestern tip of South Vietnam's Binhlong Province. An allied reconnaissance force May 3 had penetrated to the north and west about 30 miles inside Cambodia. In one of the few direct actions that day, U.S. helicopter gunships and bombers destroyed part of the rubber plantation town of Mimot after enemy gunners reportedly shot at American helicopters from the village. Mimot had been captured by Communist troops Apr. 28 after 3 days of encirclement.

Cambodian forces also became embroiled in the fighting against Communist troops. While allied soldiers pressed their drive along the eastern border region, Communist forces launched heavy attacks on Cambodian targets in the area around Pnompenh. Viet Cong and North Vietnamese units May 4 cut the Pnompenh-Saigon highway at a point 29 miles from the capital. Communist troops the previous day had attacked and partly occupied Neak Luong, a key Mekong River crossing point 35 miles southeast of Pnompenh.

Beleaguered Cambodian troops were reinforced by the arrival of 2,000 Cambodian mercenaries who had been flown to Pnompenh from South Vietnam May 2-3. The men had served with U.S. Special Forces and had been requested by Premier Lon Nol in a message to Pres. Nixon Apr. 20.

North Vietnam Hit by Biggest U.S. Raid Since '68

As the allied thrust into Cambodia gathered momentum, American planes in a parallel action conducted large-scale bombing raids over 2 North Vietnamese provinces May 1-2. The raids were the heaviest since the bombing halt declared by the U.S. in Nov. 1968. They were acknowledged in Washington May 2 after a Hanoi radio broadcast had charged that more than 100 U.S. planes had struck "yesterday and today" in Quangbinh and Nghean Provinces, killing or wounding "many civilians, including 20 children." The broadcast said 2 planes had been shot down.

Washington sources said the raids by 128 fighter-bombers were "protective reaction" against antiaircraft guns to defend unarmed reconnaissance aircraft.

Defense Secy. Melvin R. Laird had warned earlier May 2 that bombing of North Vietnam would be resumed if Hanoi reacted to the Cambodian thrusts by moving troops across the demilitarized zone (DMZ) into South Vietnam. He also indicated that the Cambodian border with South Vietnam would be subject to air and ground attacks and that air raids were being conducted against 3 such areas. (Senate Republican Leader Hugh Scott [Pa.] commented later that Laird was not necessarily stating Nixon Administration policy with regard to a resumption of the bombing of North Vietnam.)

The description of the attacks as "protective reaction" was supported by Vice Pres. Spiro T. Agnew and State Secy. William P. Rogers May 3 in hastily arranged TV appearances. Rogers, on a CBS documentary on the Cambodian crisis, said that the raids were "not a new policy at all" and that attacks to protect reconnaissance flights were "part of the arrangement made with North Vietnam when we stopped the bombing." He and Agnew, who appeared on CBS' "Face the Nation" program, said the North Vietnam bombing and the thrusts into Cambodia were limited operations and did not represent an escalation of the Vietnam war. Both cited the 8-week time limit for the Cambodia operation. Agnew added that "we have other troops on standby that can be sent in there because we don't intend to take forever to complete this operation, and we are going to send what force is necessary to do it." Agnew also claimed that the U.S. action in Cambodia was undertaken to counter an attempt by the Communist forces to extend their sanctuaries and establish new supply lines to the sea.

Democratic National Chairman Lawrence F. O'Brien May 3 rejected the Administration's defense of the military incursion into Cambodia. He charged that North Vietnam air strikes combined "with the invasion of Cambodia means, in effect, that the American policy of disengagement has ended."

The Defense Department announced May 4 it had "terminated" the large-scale air raids. It acknowledged that the raids, involving 50-100 planes in 3 strikes, were larger in scope than any since the 1968 halt in the bombing of North Vietnam. It said "logistics support" facilities had been struck in addition to the antiaircraft gun and missile sites. The raids had been carried out near Barthelemy Pass, about 240 miles north of the

DMZ, and near Bankarai Pass and another area immediately
north of the DMZ.

The department's spokesman, Assistant Defense Secy.
Daniel Z. Henkin, acknowledged that authorization for the
raids had come from Washington. (White House Press Secy.
Ronald L. Ziegler said May 4 Pres. Nixon had "approved the
overall policy of protective reaction." The President reportedly
had authorized at least one such bombing raid after his
Cambodia speech Apr. 30.)

Henkin disclosed May 5 that a 4th protective reaction raid
had been conducted by 75-90 planes against air defense targets
near Mugia Pass about 75 miles north of the DMZ along the
Laotian border. Apologizing to newsmen, Henkin indicated
that Laird also had been unaware of the 4th raid until that time
but had cited it during the White House briefings of
Congressional committees. Henkin disputed reports from
Hanoi that 13 planes had been shot down during the 4 raids, but
he withheld details pending rescue operations.

The Pentagon had said May 4 that during the 18-month
bombing halt period, 60 missions, including the recent ones, had
been conducted and that 9 jets and one helicopter had been shot
down over North Vietnam. An additional plane was downed in
the current raids.

Allies Expand Operations

U.S. and South Vietnamese troops extended their military
operations against Communist sanctuaries in Cambodia by
opening 6 new fronts May 5-9. This raised to 8 the number of
separate attacks launched since the initial allied thrusts across
the border. Allied operations were further widened May 9 by a
naval blockade of a 100-mile stretch of the Cambodian coast. In
another action, a flotilla of 140 U.S. and South Vietnamese
boats pushed into Cambodia on the Mekong River May 9 in a
move to secure the banks of the stream and to aid in the
repatriation of Vietnamese civilians. The South Vietnamese
section of the fleet arrived in Pnompenh May 11, while U.S.
ships and advisers halted their advance 40 miles downriver.

A White House report May 9 called the allied military sweep a success. It announced that U.S. and South Vietnamese forces had captured more Communist ammunition than the North Vietnamese and Viet Cong had fired in the January-April period. A White House list of casualties after 9 days of operations said 60 Americans and 184 South Vietnamese had been killed. Communist fatalities were put at 3,740, and 1,041 of the enemy were said to have been captured.

Allied command headquarters in Saigon reported May 9 that captured Communist equipment and supplies thus far totaled 6,757 rifles, 1,232 heavy machine guns, rocket launchers and other weapons, 865 tons of ammunition, 1,653 tons of rice, 12 tons of medical supplies and 130 trucks.

The 3d major allied incursion into Cambodia was carried out May 5 in the Sesan area of Ratanakiri Province, about 200 miles north of the Fishhook area. U.S. and South Vietnamese troops were airlifted into the area, 50 miles south of Laos. Originally a force of 6,000 men was prepared for this invasion, but bad weather and heavy enemy fire limited the landing to 500 men. The scope of the operation was expanded May 6 with the airlifting of 2,000 more American troops into the sector. Heavy enemy fire was encountered as 3 U.S. battalions penetrated 3-10 miles inside Cambodia. The target of this drive was described as a Communist supply center and headquarters for the North Vietnamese troops operating against U.S. Special Forces camps in South Vietnam.

In the Fishhook area to the south, U.S. forces May 5 captured Snoul after a squadron of nearly 100 tanks of the 11th Armored Cavalry Regiment and jet planes virtually leveled the village, which had been held by the North Vietnamese. The town was about 20 miles from the tip of the Fishhook.

3 new fronts were opened May 6 as American troops pushed into Cambodia northeast of the Fishhook and between the Fishhook and the Parrot's Beak, where South Vietnamese troops had been operating since Apr. 29. One American spearhead, involving soldiers of the 25th Infantry Division, moved across the border from South Vietnam's Tayninh Province, 60 miles north of Saigon. Another force, troops of the First Cavalry Division (Airmobile), was airlifted into jungles 23 miles north of Phocbinh.

South Vietnam May 7 announced the withdrawal of 10,000 of its troops from the Parrot's Beak after successfully completing its mission there. This action reduced the number of allied troops in Cambodia to 40,000 men, including 20,000-25,000 Americans. The first U.S. troops, totaling 800 men, moved into the Parrot's Beak May 8. Their mission was to watch for a possible renewal of Communist activity there. Previously, the only U.S. forces in the Parrot's Beak had been 40 advisers who had accompanied the original South Vietnamese thrust into the area.

The opening of a new American front in the Parrot's Beak was followed by another U.S. operation into Cambodia, announced by the American high command May 9. Elements of the 25th Division pushed into an area west of the Fishhook to join the search for enemy supplies and bases.

The White House May 7 had announced the capture by U.S. forces that day of an abandoned major Communist base in the Fishhook. A Defense Department statement said, however, that "there is no verification from the field that this is part of COSVN," the Central Office for South Vietnam, assumed to be the control center for all Communist military operations in South Vietnam. The latest stronghold, described as "the most sophisticated base complex" yet uncovered in Cambodia, was said to have consisted of 400-500 huts, a large bunker and a "hugh cache" of equipment.

The U.S. command in Saigon reported May 10 that 9 U.S. helicopters had been lost in Cambodia the previous week. 7 were shot down by enemy fire, and 2 others crashed.

In fighting between Cambodian and Communist forces, about 2,000 government troops May 7 had recaptured Kokithom and advanced to within 4 miles of the Neak Luong ferry crossing seized by the Viet Cong May 2. Kokithom, about 25 miles south of Pnompenh, had been occupied by the Viet Cong May 4. A government spokesman reported the Viet Cong capture of Senomorom and Kratie, 170 and 100 miles northeast of the Cambodian capital.

The launching May 9 of the U.S.-South Vietnamese naval blockade off a 100-mile stretch of the Cambodian coast was disclosed May 12 by South Vietnamese Vice Pres. Nguyen Cao Ky. The American command in Saigon confirmed that its naval forces were participating in the action, aimed at preventing North Vietnamese and Viet Cong boats from landing supplies on Cambodian beaches, stretching from the principal port of Kompong Som (formerly Sihanoukville) to the South Vietnamese border. The ships involved included heavily armed U.S. coastal patrol boats and South Vietnamese junks equipped with heavy machine guns.

Ky said the blockade had been discussed in advance by senior South Vietnamese and Cambodian military officers and the 2 governments. Citing previous joint military cooperation, Ky disclosed that his government had been providing air support for the Cambodians fighting on the western side of the Mekong River in the previous 2 days. He said this aerial assistance had enabled the Cambodians to recapture Takeo, which had been taken by the Communists 2 weeks before.

The bulk of the allied ships that sailed up the Mekong River had assembled May 9 at the Neak Luong ferry crossing, recaptured from Communist forces by South Vietnamese troops earlier in the day. The fleet consisted of 30 U.S. river gunboats and 110 South Vietnamese craft. The South Vietnamese vessels carried 1,400 government sailors and 1,800 marines, about 600 of whom had landed outside Neak Luong to clear suspected enemy positions. This phase of the operation was assisted by U.S. jet fighters and helicopter gunships. The American vessels moved no further north than Neak Luong in compliance with the U.S. policy of limiting the American penetration of Cambodia to 21.7 miles. 47 South Vietnamese vessels arrived in the heart of Pnompenh May 11. The remaining fleet had returned to South Vietnam with several thousand Vietnamese refugees picked up along the banks of the Mekong since the convoy had started upstream earlier in the week.

The military and humanitarian aspects of the Mekong operation had been hastily combined after South Vietnamese Foreign Min. Tran Van Lam had inadvertently revealed publicly May 7 that a fleet would be sailing up the river to rescue Vietnamese refugees. Lam was said to have been unaware that a military operation was also planned for this area. A U.S. official remarked that "suddenly our entire attack was being broadcast days before it was set to start." The 2 plans were then merged and the fleet set sail May 9 from the

South Vietnamese towns of Chaudoc and Tanchau on the Cambodian border.

Some U.S. Troops Pulled Out

Part of the American force that had participated in the move into Cambodia was reported May 12-16 to have been withdrawn and returned to South Vietnam.

The areas vacated by the U.S. troops were the Ba Thu sector of the Parrot's Beak and the Se San region to the north, 40 miles west of Pleiku. More than 1,000 soldiers were withdrawn May 12-13, and the U.S. high command announced May 16 that a total of 5,500 men had been removed from the Se San front. The withdrawals reduced the strength of the American force in Cambodia to about 18,000 men, most of them in the area north of Tayninh Province, South Vietnam. But up to 1,500 South Vietnamese rangers who had joined the U.S. drive in the Se San area May 5 remained there, assisted by American air cover and logistical support. According to preliminary statistics, the Se San operation had resulted in the capture of 803 Communist weapons and 599 tons of rice. 30 Americans and 184 Communist troops were killed.

(Newsweek magazine reported May 17 that Defense Secy. Melvin R. Laird had said in a top-secret message sent to Gen. Creighton W. Abrams, commander of U.S. forces in Vietnam: "In light of the controversy over the U.S. move into Cambodia, the American public would be impressed" by evidence of the capture of: "1, high-ranking enemy prisoners; 2, major enemy headquarters; 3, large enemy caches." Laird May 18 denied the report and said Newsweek had apologized to him for its publication. Lester Bernstein, Newsweek managing editor, denied that the magazine had apologized to Laird. Newsweek also reported that few Communists had been captured in the allied drive into Cambodia because they had started a major withdrawal from their border sanctuaries along with 20%-50% of their supplies Apr. 20, 10 days before the allied attacks began.)

Allies Open 2 New Fronts

2 new allied thrusts across the Cambodian border were reported May 14 and 17. The burden of the fighting was carried by South Vietnamese forces assisted by American advisers and U.S. supportive fire.

In the first operation, announced May 14, an undetermined number of South Vietnamese troops struck from South Vietnam's Central Highlands, 22 miles south of the Sesan region. The U.S. command reported May 15 that the drive was supported by American advisers, artillery, helicopter gunships and medical evacuation facilities. The South Vietnamese army newspaper reported May 15 that the purpose of the offensive was to relieve Cambodian troops defending the town of Bo Keo, 22 miles inside Cambodia.

The 2d new thrust into Cambodia, reported May 17, was centered in the Mekong Delta region between South Vietnam's Chaudoc Province and the Cambodian province of Takeo. The strike force, including 10,000 South Vietnamese troops supported by 200 American advisers, aircraft and logistical elements, reached Takeo May 17, killing 211 enemy soldiers in the 20-mile thrust.

Sharp fighting erupted May 16 between Cambodian and Communist troops for the major stronghold of Kompong Som. North Vietnamese and Viet Cong forces penetrated the city in force, but Cambodian troops regained Kompong Som the following day. Earlier in the week, the Communists had overrun Tonle Bet, the town directly opposite Kompong Cham on the eastern bank of the Mekong River. Kompong Cham, a provincial capital 74 miles north of Pnompenh, was the Cambodian military headquarters for 3 surrounding provinces. U.S.-made T-28 bombers flown by Cambodian pilots had pounded Communist positions surrounding the city, and Cambodian reinforcements were brought in. The Cambodian counterattacks had forced the Communist forces to withdraw, and Cambodian soldiers were in complete control of Kompong Cham May 17.

The capture of part of COSVN, the Communists' Central Office for South Vietnam, was reported May 17 by Lt. Gen. Michael S. Davison, commander of American forces in Cambodia. He said sections of the North Vietnamese/Viet

Cong base headquarters had been uncovered between May 11 and 13. They were located 4 to 5 miles north of Mimot, about 10 miles inside Cambodia. Davison said the find included parts of the COSVN "post office" and of the base's finance, economy, education and training sections. Casualty figures for the entire Cambodian operation by May 18, according to the allied command, were 7,843 Viet Cong and North Vietnamese killed; 150 Americans killed and 598 wounded; and 700 South Vietnamese soldiers slain and 1,878 wounded. In the first 17 days of the campaign, allied forces had captured 8,611 Communist weapons, 1,095 crew-served weapons, 1,551 tons of ammunition, and 3,223 tons of rice, the U.S. command reported.

South Vietnam Bars Troop Withdrawal

As the fighting raged, a controversy arose over whether South Vietnam would withdraw its troops from Cambodia June 30, the time limit Pres. Nixon had set for the departure of U.S. troops operating in Cambodia.

South Vietnamese Pres. Nguyen Van Thieu said May 8 that his country's forces would not be bound by the June 30 time limit. Thieu said: "We have no deadline, no limits.... When there is a target, we will strike it."

Thieu's statement was coupled with a disclosure that he and Cambodian Premier Lon Nol had reached "agreements in principle" for the continuing operation of Saigon's forces against the Communist sanctuaries in eastern Cambodia. Thieu said the understanding had been agreed to 2 or 3 days before Nixon had announced his decision Apr. 30 to send U.S. forces into Cambodia. Thieu said he already had provided the Pnompenh forces with 4,000 ethnic Cambodian mercenaries who had been fighting with Saigon's soldiers in South Vietnam.

The State Department said May 14 that there had been "no understanding or agreement" between Washington and Saigon on how long South Vietnamese forces would remain in Cambodia. The department did not explain why there had been no such agreement, but it was reported that the U.S. and South Vietnam feared Communist forces might launch a major attack in Cambodia when American troops were pulled out.

The U.S. was reported May 21 to be seeking to reconcile its reported differences with South Vietnam on the mutual withdrawal of their forces from Cambodia June 30. U.S. Amb. Ellsworth Bunker and Gen. Creighton Abrams, head of American forces in South Vietnam, were reported May 21 to have received instructions from Washington earlier in the week to discuss the problem with South Vietnamese Pres. Nguyen Van Thieu.

Vice Pres. Nguyen Cao Ky May 21 reaffirmed previous Saigon government statements that South Vietnamese forces were determined to stay in Cambodia after June 30. "I wish to make clear that we will not let our hands be bound by anyone any more," Ky said. He called the "hypothesis" of a Saigon troop withdrawal along with an American pullout "a silly argument of silly people." Ky said South Vietnamese forces were capable of operating independently in Cambodia and would stay there "not only to destroy the Communists but also to provide protection for the lives and property of 600,000 resident Vietnamese."

South Vietnamese Foreign Min. Tran Van Lam said May 21 that "we have no timetable for the withdrawal of our troops from Cambodia."

The U.S. May 20 had publicly acknowledged for the first time the possibility that South Vietnamese troops might remain in Cambodia beyond June 30. "Determinations have not finally been made" as to whether Saigon's forces would follow the American departure, a State Department spokesman said. Heretofore, Nixon Administration officials had insisted they did not know about South Vietnam's intentions in Cambodia.

Defense Secy. Melvin R. Laird said May 22 that it would "be a mistake . . . to make a firm timetable and establish it here for South Vietnamese forces to withdraw." This remark was in contrast to Nixon's May 8 press conference statement that "I would expect that the South Vietnamese would come out approximately at the same time we do." Speaking on the NBC-TV program "Today," Laird said that announcing the withdrawal of Saigon's forces in advance would "destroy the military or tactical advantage that might be established by keeping . . . the North Vietnamese off guard." Laird stressed, however, that there would be "no American advisers in Cambodia after June 30."

White House Press Secy. Ronald L. Ziegler said May 21 "it would not be appropriate to put a timetable on South Vietnamese forces." The question of whether the U.S. would continue to provide South Vietnamese troops with air support if the Saigon forces remained in Cambodia after June 30 remained unclear. When questioned on this issue, Ziegler said May 22 that he would reserve comment.

State Department press officer Carl Bartch told reporters May 25 that American tactical air support for the South Vietnamese after June 30 was a possibility that was then being left open. He said: "I think it's fair to say that when the United States withdraws its forces from Cambodia June 30, that air and logistic support might also be withdrawn. I am distinguishing between that and what might arise in the future after June 30." While U.S. logistic and air support would be withdrawn June 30, both could be restored July 1, he said.

State Secy. Rogers had said May 24 that the U.S. was "not concerned at all" at reports that South Vietnamese forces would not be removed from Cambodia June 30. The continued presence of those troops in Cambodia, he said, fitted in with Pres. Nixon's doctrine that "Asians work together to solve Asian problems." Rogers affirmed that American troops would be out of Cambodia by July 1. "But insofar as other aspects of the war are concerned, there is no point in signaling the enemy in advance," he said.

Cambodian Foreign Min. Yem Sambaur said May 25 that his government would ask the U.S. to keep its forces in Cambodia until the end of the war. He said the Pnompenh government might ask Thailand for soldiers. Thailand, the Philippines and South Korea had announced May 22 they would provide Cambodia with supplies but not weapons. Manila and Seoul said they would confine their assistance to humanitarian aid. Thailand said it would provide Cambodia with military equipment.

Defense Secy. Laird June 23 defined what he considered the future role of South Vietnamese troops in Cambodia. Speaking at a news conference in London, Laird said that the South Vietnamese would be free to operate in the sanctuary areas in a combat role and that the sanctuary areas could be anywhere in Cambodia. "I can't state what areas will be used as havens by the North Vietnamese or the Viet Cong," he said.

"But I would not want to draw up any limit on South Vietnamese ground forces so far as attacking any sanctuaries that now exist or may come into being."

State Secy. Rogers said June 25 that after the U.S. troops left Cambodia, "the main thrust of our policy is to use our air force for the purpose of interdicting supply lines and communication lines to protect Americans in South Vietnam." He added that the policy "may have a dual benefit—it may serve our purposes and at the same time serve the Cambodian government." Asked whether he could say that U.S. planes "will not fly close air support" in Cambodia, Rogers replied "no."

In San Francisco June 29, Rogers said the North Vietnamese were "attempting to use Cambodian territory to re-establish their disrupted lines of supplies and communication to carry on the war in South Vietnam." "American air power is being used to frustrate these efforts," he said, and the Saigon government "has said that South Vietnamese forces may continue to engage the enemy in Cambodia." "Thus the enemy ... can no longer count on the safe haven in Cambodia," Rogers continued, and would "have to face Thai and South Vietnamese troops and possible interdiction of the American air power."

Saigon Presses Fresh Attacks

A force of 2,500 South Vietnamese troops opened a new front in Cambodia May 20. Supported by U.S. air power and advisers, the South Vietnamese soldiers pushed across the border west of the U.S. Special Forces Camp at Duclap, South Vietnam, 125 miles north of Saigon. The first Communist resistance was encountered May 23. Reports said 20 North Vietnamese and 7 South Vietnamese were killed in the clash, about 6 miles inside Cambodia.

The new thrust brought to 40,000 the number of South Vietnamese troops operating in Cambodia, about twice the total of the previous week. Official sources May 22 estimated U.S. troop strength in the country at about 12,000, up 2,000 over the previous weekend. The additional troops were said to have been sent in to reinforce other ground troops operating to secure and evacuate captured Communist supplies.

About 10,000 South Vietnamese troops May 24 captured Cambodia's largest rubber plantation, a plantation at Chup, about 50 miles northeast of Pnompenh. A regiment of North Vietnamese and Viet Cong troops retreated within the 70-square mile plantation and were said to be surrounded by South Vietnamese troops. The attack was led by the Khmer Krom, ethnic Cambodian mercenaries assigned to the Cambodian army. They had previously fought with U.S. Special Forces in South Vietnam. South Vietnamese air assaults on the plantation May 23 had left it a flaming ruin. The attacks killed 15 civilian workers and injured 80.

In the ground fighting at Chup, 12 members of Khmer Rouge, a Cambodian Communist guerrilla group, were killed and 15 were reported captured. 25 more of the enemy were said to have been slain east of the plantation. 2 South Vietnamese soldiers were killed.

The South Vietnamese force that occupied the plantation was said to have confiscated all its movable assets and to have ordered the French managers to leave in 3 days. Lt. Gen. Do Cao Tri, South Vietnamese commander of the operation, was said to have told the managers that his troops could not occupy the region and, therefore, had to remove all the material to prevent its capture by the Communists, who might return. The plantation at Chup accounted for 50% of Cambodia's rubber production.

In another action May 24, Khmer Krom troops recaptured Tonle Bet, held by the North Vietnamese since May 11. The town, on the east bank of the Mekong River opposite Kompong Cham and less than 10 miles from Chup, had been abandoned by North Vietnamese troops a few hours earlier. Tonle Bet had been pounded by Cambodian artillery and mortars for a week.

In fighting to the south, Saigon troops had linked up with Cambodian soldiers May 20 in a town 25 miles north of Takeo, following a drive launched May 17 from South Vietnam's Chaudoc Province. Saigon forces reported killing more than 400 Viet Cong during the operation. The link-up secured Route 2, a key road running between Pnompenh and Takeo, 54 miles south.

The U.S. Defense Department disclosed May 21 that preliminary intelligence reports indicated that COSVN, the Communists' Central Office for South Vietnam, had been shifted beyond the 21-mile limit set by Pres. Nixon for U.S. ground operations in Cambodia. Deputy Assistant Defense Secy. Jerry Friedheim said it appeared that COSVN, a mobile base headquarters, had been reestablished north of Mimot, a town in the Fishhook area where allied troops struck Apr. 30.

The Cambodian government May 21 reported sabotage in 2 regions previously believed to be secure. An explosion May 19 damaged a bridge on the road to Pnompenh and Angkor Wat, about 75 miles north of the capital near the town of Kompong Thmar. The rail line, linking Pnompenh and Thailand, had been put out of operation May 18 when a rail was removed near Muong, about 140 miles north of Pnompenh. Train traffic was resumed May 21.

Official sources in Saigon reported May 25 that the capture of large caches of Communist weapons and ammunition in Cambodia had resulted in a reduction of enemy firepower in South Vietnam. (As of May 25, more than 14,000 enemy weapons were said to have been seized.) The average enemy shelling attacks dropped to 5 or 6 mortar or artillery shells from the previous rate of 10-12.

North Vietnamese forces May 28 pushed into the provincial capital of Preyveng, 30 miles east of Pnompenh, and engaged the Cambodian garrison in street fighting. A relief force of South Vietnamese government soldiers and more than 1,000 South Vietnamese marines fought their way toward the city May 29 to relieve the beleaguered defenders. (South Vietnamese marines were reported to have killed 19 North Vietnamese in an encounter near Banam, 10 miles southwest of Preyveng. South Vietnamese marines were reported June 15 to have killed 110 more North Vietnamese in 3 battles around Preyveng, 30 miles east of Pnompenh; 12 South Vietnamese were killed and 37 wounded.) The attack on Preyveng was described by official sources as part of the Communists' plan to strengthen their positions east of the Mekong River to obtain a new supply route beyond their invaded sanctuaries along the South Vietnamese border.

The district capital of Tang Krasang, 45 miles northwest of Kompong Cham, was captured by Communist forces May 28. Its fall cut the road from Kompong Thom to Pnompenh. South Vietnamese troops were reported to have killed 72 Communist soldiers in a clash 10 miles east of Kompong Cham. South Vietnamese losses were put at 19 wounded.

About 1,000 Viet Cong troops June 3 captured Set Bo, 11 miles south of Pnompenh. Cambodian troops, assisted by air strikes, recaptured the Bassac River village June 5.

May 26 Saigon had announced the withdrawal of 16,000 South Vietnamese troops, reducing the South Vietnamese strength in Cambodia to 30,000 men. It was reported June 8 that 18,400 U.S. troops had been withdrawn from Cambodia, leaving 12,600 still to be pulled out by the June 30 deadline.

Allied and Communist forces fought a savage battle June 12-16 for the provincial capital of Kompong Speu, 30 miles southwest of Pnompenh. The strategic city was captured by Viet Cong/North Vietnamese forces June 13 and retaken by Cambodian and South Vietnamese soldiers June 16. Kompong Speu was located on Route 4, which linked Pnompenh with the port of Kompong Som (formerly Sihanoukville). Cambodia received all its petroleum through Kompong Som where its only oil refinery was located.

The allied forces that broke into Kompong Speu June 16 found that an enemy force of about 1,400 men had escaped. A total of 4,000 South Vietnamese and 2,000 Cambodians were committed to the battle. In joining the attack, Saigon's forces made their deepest penetration into Cambodia; Kompong Speu was 50 miles from the South Vietnamese border. South Vietnamese authorities reported that their forces had killed 183 Communists and captured 3, while losing 4 men killed and 22 wounded. Casualties among the civilians who remained in Kompong Speu were high; 40 to 50 were reported killed. The South Vietnamese troops in Kompong Speu looted abandoned stores and robbed returning civilians. The South Vietnamese commander forced the soldiers to surrender the loot from the stores but no attempt was made to have them give up the valuables stolen from the civilians.

A Cambodian army officer charged June 22 that as a result of the fighting in Kompong Speu, "the population now has more fear of the South Vietnamese than of the Viet Cong." Maj. Soeung Kimsea, commander of Cambodia's 22d Infantry Battalion, asserted that South Vietnamese troops had gone on a looting rampage, taking "everything—furniture, radios, money. They even broke open safes" and "looted homes of Cambodian officers. Monks were robbed, too."

The war in Cambodia was extended further as North Vietnamese and Viet Cong forces launched attacks across the northern part of the country June 3. Cambodian troops engaged in heavy fighting with the Communists at Kompong Thom, 87 miles northeast of Pnompenh, and at Siemreap, 80 miles to the northwest. Siemreap, situated near the historic ruins of Angkor Wat, was only 65 miles from the Thai border. As a result of the fighting there, Thai forces were reported June 5 to have been put on the alert along the border with Cambodia. The action was taken after North Vietnamese and Viet Cong units were sighted near the Thai provinces of Sisaket and Surin, 250 miles northeast of Bangkok.

The airport serving both Siemreap and Angkor Wat was shut down and all tourists were flown out of the area because of the fighting nearby, government sources reported June 5. Communist forces attacked the airfield June 6, captured it June 7, but lost it to Cambodian troops later that day. A barracks had come under Communist attack during the fighting, in Siemreap, but the main enemy thrust was directed at the airfield. The 1,000 government troops defending Siemreap were reinforced by hundreds of other Cambodian soldiers.

Communist troops were reported June 11 to have seized the ancient temple ruins of Angkor Wat and to have opened a new attack June 12 on Siemreap, four miles from the edge of the huge temple complex. Cambodian troops had fought heavy clashes with the Communists at Siemreap June 3-7. In their latest attacks, the Communists captured the Siemreap airport June 13 and moved into parts of the town the following day. Pnompenh reported June 14 that its troops had regained control of both the airport and the town. Cambodia charged June 15 that the North Vietnamese had established a command post outside Angkor Wat, laid mines and built emplacements at the entrance of the shrine. A Hanoi broadcast June 12 had denied that North Vietnamese and Viet Cong troops had occupied Angkor Wat. Prince Norodom Sihanouk's government-in-exile June 15 denied that its forces had occupied the temple.

In the fighting for Kompong Thom, Communist troops had captured the city and the nearby town of Am Leang June 7. They were driven out of the center of Kompong Thom by Cambodian troops June 8, but sporadic fighting continued near the city. Pnompenh communiques reported that 128 Communists had been killed in and around both centers June 3-7. Government losses were listed at 9 killed and 23 wounded.

U.S. troops engaged in heavy clashes with Communist soldiers June 8-13 within an 11-mile radius of Mimot in the Fishhook region. American casualties totaled 13 killed and 60 wounded. Enemy losses were estimated at 9 killed.

(Thai Interior Minister Praphas Charusathien disclosed June 11 that Thai air force planes were flying reconnaissance missions over Cambodia.)

Communist Attacks Menace Pnompenh

North Vietnamese/Viet Cong attacks north of Pnompenh June 17-21 were said to have almost isolated the Cambodian capital. Communist troops operating in the areas were said to be striking almost at will, and all the roads leading to the city were considered unsafe. Cambodian troops ringed the airport and other key installations in preparation for a possible Communist attack on Pnompenh itself. The principal fighting raged in and around Kompong Thom, 80 miles north of the capital, while similar Communist pressure was being applied along the Mekong River. This phase of the fighting was regarded as a Communist effort to seize the upper reaches of the Mekong River and increase the flow of soldiers and materiel into Cambodia.

Communist troops June 17 severed Cambodia's last working railway line when they seized a section of railway and a freight train carrying more than 200 tons of rice and other food supplies at a station at Krang Lovea, about 40 miles northwest of Pnompenh. The line ran northwest from the capital to the border with Thailand. The capture of the railway section reduced Cambodia's surface transport to only a few passable roads.

2 of those remaining roads, both of them major arteries, were cut, at least temporarily, by Communist forces June 18. They severed Highway 1, linking Pnompenh with Saigon, 30 miles southeast of the capital, and Highway 4, leading southwestward to the port of Kompong Som. The Highway 1 attack consisted of a mine and mortar assault on the village of Koki Thom. The road was a key route for bringing South Vietnamese troops and supplies into Cambodia. The cutting of Highway 4 virtually stopped work on Cambodia's biggest dam development project 40 miles west of Pnompenh.

Kompong Thom came under heavy Communist assault June 17 and 18. By June 19, the Communists had approached to within 200 yards of the city and were reported June 21 to have entered the provincial capital, gaining control of at least half the city. But Cambodian military spokesmen reported June 22 that the enemy forces had withdrawn from Kompong Thom.

Heavy fighting also raged east and south of the city, at Kompong Cham, Tonle Bet, Skoun and Preyveng. South Vietnamese troops June 21 reported killing 32 enemy soldiers in an ambush of a North Vietnamese convoy just south of Preyveng.

A new South Vietnamese thrust into Cambodia, carried out June 20, encountered little enemy resistance. The operation, involving 4,000 troops, took place in the Se Bang Valley, which had not been swept in previous allied offensives.

All Cambodian troops were reported June 27 to have withdrawn from the province of Ratanakiri, virtually leaving the northeastern part of the country under Communist military control. The adjacent provinces of Mondolkiri, Kratie and Stung Treng had been abandoned previously by Cambodian troops. Some South Vietnamese troops were said to be in Kratie. In a 5th northern province, Preah Vihear, a small government garrison remained in the provincial capital of Thbeng Menachey. Maj. Am Rong, a spokesman for the Cambodian military command, indicated that U.S. planes had evacuated 2 government garrisons at Lebansiek and Bo Kheo in Ratanakiri. The withdrawal from the 4 provinces allowed the Cambodian government to concentrate most of its 50,000 soldiers in the area around Pnompenh and east to the South Vietnamese border, where most of the fighting was centered. North Vietnamese and Viet Cong troops launched heavy attacks June 25-29 at Longvek, site of an arms depot, 35 miles north of Pnompenh. Communist forces June 23 had captured Prek Tameak, on the Mekong River, 15 miles north of the capital. Cambodian counterattacks forced the Communists to withdraw and the strongpoint was occupied by South Vietnamese marines, who landed there June 28.

Communist troops renewed assaults against Kompong Speu June 24-26 but failed to retake the provincial capital. The Communists penetrated to within the city's main pagoda June 24 but were thrown back by a Cambodian counterattack. Fighting in the area June 26 blocked Route 4 to the port of Kompong Som.

5,000 South Vietnamese troops launched a new assault in northeastern Cambodia June 24 in an effort to clear Highway 19 and evacuate Vietnamese refugees. 4,250 Vietnamese refugees from the towns of Lebansiek and Bo Kheo along the highway were reported removed to Pleiku, South Vietnam.

U.S. Jets Raid Deep in Cambodia

The U.S. Defense Department acknowledged June 22 that American planes had been bombing Communist infiltration routes deep inside Cambodia. The *Washington Post* quoted other sources as saying that the attacks ranged as far as 100 miles inside the country, well beyond the 21.7-mile limit established by Pres. Nixon for U.S. ground forces. A *N.Y. Times* dispatch from Saigon June 21 said the deep raids had been in progress since the start of allied operations in Cambodia Apr. 30. Nixon Administration officials had repeatedly said that the U.S. would not provide air combat support for South Vietnamese forces beyond the 21.7-mile limit.

Pentagon press spokesman Jerry Friedheim told reporters June 22 that the air strikes had been launched the previous week and were aimed at new enemy supply lines posing a threat to U.S. forces in South Vietnam. He identified the targets as principally Se Kong and Mekong River supply routes west of the Communist border sanctuaries that had been overrun by allied forces. He said these raids might continue after American troops withdrew from Cambodia June 30. Friedheim refused to comment on a UPI dispatch from Saigon that American planes had flown support missions for Cambodian troops as far west as Kompong Thom, 80 miles north of Pnompenh. He would say only that "our organized [air] campaign is not a campaign to save Cambodia."

The *Times* June 23 quoted military witnesses as saying that American planes had bombed Communist positions at Kompong Thom that day and June 22. The raids were followed by South Vietnamese jet attacks and apparently were designed to mark enemy targets for Saigon's pilots.

U.S. ground forces in Cambodia, however, continued to be reduced as the June 30 withdrawal deadline approached. 2 battalions were pulled out of the Cambodian border region June 22, decreasing the American force to 9,700 combat troops.

Cambodians Criticize South Vietnamese Troops

Maj. Am Rong, a spokesman for the Cambodian military command, said in Pnompenh May 21 that Cambodians would rather die than "live under Vietnamese domination." Asked whether this applied to South Vietnamese as well as Viet Cong and North Vietnamese, Am Rong replied that he meant all Vietnamese. A Cambodian government broadcast May 24 denied that Am Rong meant to be critical of Saigon. The statement said: "South Vietnamese forces are in Cambodia to help us liquidate the Viet Cong and North Vietnamese aggressors. The Saigon troops were consequently not aimed at in the spokesman's declaration, which had been exploited out of all proportion."

Posters demanding the withdrawal of South Vietnamese troops from Cambodia were pasted on the walls of the briefing room in which Am Rong made his statement to foreign newsmen. The placards accused Saigon's soldiers of "looting, raping our women, burning and massacring women and children."

The chief of the Cambodian information service asserted May 22 that " we now have 2 invasions being conducted in Cambodia, the North Vietnamese and the South Vietnamese.... The Vietnamese are expansionists, and we fear that if this continues Cambodia will disappear, though we would die before this happens."

A statement criticizing the behavior of South Vietnamese troops had been made available at the Cambodian army information center in Pnompenh May 21 but was quickly withdrawn without explanation. It said: "Americans, withdraw quickly the South Vietnamese army from Cambodian territory. These Vietnamese soldiers have committed inhuman acts against the Cambodian population.... Americans, bring our Cambodian compatriots in South Vietnam to help us kick out the Viet Cong and South Vietnamese who have always wanted to extinguish the Cambodian race from the world." The statement held the U.S. "responsible for these barbarous acts of the South Vietnamese army." The Cambodian government May 22 disclaimed any knowledge of the origin of the statement.

Further Cambodian charges of South Vietnamese troop misbehavior were reported in September-December 1970:

● The Cambodian Foreign Ministry was reported Dec. 5 to have filed another protest with Saigon, charging that South Vietnamese troops had burned the houses of Cambodians and had permitted Vietnamese civilians to take up residence in Cambodia.

● A Cambodian official charged Dec. 9 that more than 400 South Vietnamese peasant families had moved at least 7 miles inside Cambodia and had taken over farms and ricelands abandoned by Cambodian war refugees. Lt. Col. Koh Chhuon, the commander of Svayrieng Province, said the affected area was along a 60-mile stretch from Kompong Trach in the north of Svayrieng to Samraong at the tip of the Parrot's Beak in the south. Chhuon said the squatter movement had started in September. He charged that the Saigon government had ignored repeated Cambodian protests. Chhuon said that in one note handed to the South Vietnamese ambassador in Pnompenh Nov. 25, South Vietnamese soldiers were accused of assisting the infiltrators into the abandoned homes.

● A Cambodian intelligence officer reported Dec. 9 that Viet Cong and North Vietnamese were "in effect" cooperating with the Saigon troops in settling the Cambodian areas in South Vietnam. He said that former Cambodian Communists who had defected to the government side had reported that Viet

Cong and North Vietnamese commanders in the area had ordered their troops not to fire on South Vietnamese soldiers in the Parrot's Beak, but to concentrate instead on killing Cambodian government troops.

U.S. WITHDRAWAL FROM CAMBODIA:
JUNE 29, 1970

All U.S. ground troops were withdrawn from Cambodia June 29, 1970, one day before the scheduled deadline set by Pres. Nixon for ending the American phase of the allied operation that had started Apr. 29-May 1. The completion of the offensive was announced officially by Nixon in a report June 30. He described the operations against Communist border sanctuaries in Cambodia as a success and ruled out further use of American ground forces in Cambodia. The report contained a chronology of events prior to the President's decision to send U.S. troops into Cambodia plus an inventory of enemy arms and supplies captured or destroyed.

South Vietnamese troops remained in Cambodia as the Americans pulled out. The Saigon forces continued their operations against the Communists through the remainder of 1970.

U.S. Troops End Operations

U.S. combat troops completed their withdrawal from Cambodia June 29, ending 2 months of operations against the Communist border sanctuaries there. The last of American advisers assigned to South Vietnamese units withdrew June 30.

The final U.S. troops to return to South Vietnam's Central Highlands through Cambodia's Fishhook region were 1,800 men of the First Cavalry Division (Airmobile). American forces in Cambodia had totaled 18,000 at peak strength. The number had dropped to less than 10,000 in the concluding 2 weeks as the withdrawal rate accelerated. A total of 34,000 South Vietnamese troops remained in Cambodia on what appeared to be an indefinite mission to assist Cambodian soldiers in their fight against the Communist invaders. Most of Saigon's troops were posted near Pnompenh.

U.S. casualties during the entire Cambodian operation totaled 338 killed and 1,529 wounded. South Vietnamese losses as of June 29 were put at 866 killed and 3,724 wounded. Allied military sources claimed Communist losses were 14,488 slain and 1,427 captured.

As the American troops left, Cambodian Premier Lon Nol June 29 expressed hope that the U.S. soldiers would return if his country's military situation deteriorated further. Lon Nol confirmed that the U.S. had been providing Cambodian ground troops with direct tactical air support. He said he had been assured by the U.S. Defense Department that this assistance would continue after the American withdrawal deadline.

The premier's statement appeared to corroborate a report from Pnompenh June 27 that U.S. jets would provide close air support for Cambodian troops engaged in combat anywhere in the country. Military sources were quoted as specifically mentioning "the area all around Pnompenh" and the provincial capital of Siemreap in the northwest. It was pointed out, however, that the nearby temples at Angkor Wat (north of Siemreap), which were occupied by Communist forces, would not be bombed.

Nixon's Report on U.S. Withdrawal

Pres. Nixon's announcement of the withdrawal of U.S. ground forces from Cambodia was made in a written report June 30. The text of this report:

> Together with the South Vietnamese, the armed forces of the United States have just completed successfully the destruction of enemy base areas along the Cambodian-South Vietnam frontier. All American troops have withdrawn from Cambodia on the schedule announced at the start of the operation.
>
> The allied sweeps into the North Vietnamese and Viet Cong base areas along the Cambodian-South Vietnamese border: will save American and allied lives in the future; will assure that the withdrawal of American troops from South Vietnam can proceed on schedule; will enable our program of Vietnamization to continue on its current timetable; should enhance the prospects for a just peace.
>
> At this time, it is important to review the background for the decision, the results of the operation, their larger meaning in terms of the conflict in Indochina—and to look down the road to the future.

It is vital to understand at the outset that Hanoi left the United States no reasonable option but to move militarily against the Cambodian base areas. The purpose and significance of our operations against the Cambodian sanctuaries can only be understood against the backdrop of what we are seeking to accomplish in Vietnam—and the threat that the Communist bases in Cambodia posed to our objectives. Nor can that military action of the last 2 months be divorced from its cause—the threat posed by the constant expansion of North Vietnamese aggression throughout Indochina.

A RECORD OF RESTRAINT

America's purpose in Vietnam and Indochina remains what it has been—a peace in which the peoples of the region can devote themselves to development of their own societies, a peace in which all the peoples of Southeast Asia can determine their own political future without outside interference.

When this Administration took office, the authorized strength of American troops in South Vietnam was 549,500—the high-water mark of American military presence in Southeast Asia. The United States had been negotiating at Paris for 10 months but nothing had been agreed upon other than the shape of the bargaining table. No comprehensive allied peace proposal existed. There was no approved plan to reduce America's involvement in the war—in the absence of a negotiated settlement.

Since January of 1969, we have taken steps on all fronts to move toward peace. Along with the government of South Vietnam, we have put forward a number of concrete and reasonable proposals to promote genuine negotiations. These proposals were first outlined by me 13 months ago, on May 14, 1969, and by Pres. Thieu on July 11, 1969. Through both public and private channels, our proposals have been repeated and amplified many times since.

These proposals are designed to secure the removal of all foreign military forces from South Vietnam and to establish conditions in which all political forces can compete freely and fairly in the future of the country. Our principal goal has been to enable the people of South Vietnam to determine their future free of outside interference.

To indicate our good faith, to improve the climate for negotiations, we changed the orders to our commanders in South Vietnam. This has helped to reduce casualties. We have cut tactical air operations in South Vietnam by more than 20%. We initiated a troop withdrawal program which, during the course of next spring, will bring American troop strength 265,000 men below the level authorized when this Administration took office.

These are not the actions of a government pursuing a military solution. They are the decisions of a government seeking a just peace at the conference table.

But Hanoi has ignored our unilateral gestures and rejected every offer of serious negotiations. Instead it has insisted that—as a precondition to talks—we pledge unconditionally to withdraw all American forces from South Vietnam and to overthrow the elected government.

These proposals are not a basis for negotiation; they are a demand for surrender. For the United States to accept these conditions would make the negotiations meaningless. Acceptance of such conditions would assure in advance Communist domination of South Vietnam.

With Hanoi's intransigence on the negotiating front, this Administration was faced with essentially 3 options.

We could have continued the maximum existing level of American involvement in Vietnam. But this was incompatible with the "Nixon Doctrine" of increasing responsibilities for the Asian countries; and it was unacceptable to the American people.

We could have begun the immediate withdrawal of all our forces. We rejected this course of capitulation which would have only won temporary respite at the price of graver crises later. We also rejected that course as both incompatible with America's commitments and tradition, and disastrous in terms of its long-range consequences for peaee in the Pacific and peace in the world.

We selected instead a third option—that of gradually shifting the total combat burden to the South Vietnamese.

Since the beginning of this Administration 17 months ago, it has been our policy to train and equip the South Vietnamese to take over the burden of their own defense from American troops. Even in the absence of progress at the peace table in Paris, and despite continued enemy pressures in South Vietnam, this policy of "Vietnamization" has permitted us to carry out repeated withdrawals of American troops.

As our policy has been tested, more and more Americans have been brought home. By June of 1969, we could announce the pullout of 25,000 American troops. They came home. In September of 1969, we announced the withdrawal of an additional 35,000 American troops. They came home.

In December of 1969, we announced the withdrawal of 50,000 more American troops. They were home by spring of this year. On Apr. 20, I announced the forthcoming withdrawal of an additional 150,000 Americans to be completed during next spring—50,000 of them will be home or on their way home by the 15th of October.

A POLICY IN TRANSITION

This transfer of primary responsibility for self-defense from American forces to Asian forces reflects our approach to foreign policy. Increasingly, the United States will look to the countries of the region to assume the primary responsibility for their own security—while America moves gradually from a leading to a supporting role.

To be successful this policy requires the striking of a careful balance—whether in South Vietnam or elsewhere in Asia. While the growing strength of our allies, and the growing measure of their regional cooperation allows for a reduction in American presence—they could not survive a sudden and precipitous American withdrawal from our responsibilities. This would lead to a collapse of local strength in the transition period between the old era of principal U.S. involvement to the new era of partnership and emphasis on local and regional cooperation.

Doing too much for an allied people can delay their political maturity, promote a sense of dependency and diminish that nation's incentive to stand on its own feet. But doing too little for an ally can induce a sense of despair, endanger their right of self-determination and invite their defeat when confronted by an aggressor.

As we have proceeded with Vietnamization it has been with these principles in mind.

Looking at American policy in Vietnam these 17 months, this Administration—in the generosity of its negotiating offers, in the limitations on its military actions, and in the consistency of its troop withdrawals—has written a record of restraint. The response from the enemy over those same 17 months has been intransigence in Paris, belligerence from Hanoi and escalation of the war throughout Indochina.

Enemy attacks in Vietnam increased during April.

This past winter Hanoi launched a major offensive against the legitimate government of Laos which they themselves had helped to establish under the 1962 Geneva accords. For years, in violation of those accords, North Vietnamese troops have occupied Laotian territory and used its eastern regions as a highway for the export of aggression into South Vietnam.

In March and April of this year, Communist troops used their long held bases in Cambodia to move against the government of Cambodia in a way which increased the long-term threat to allied forces in South Vietnam as well as to the future of our Vietnamization and withdrawal programs. These new violations, too, took place against a backdrop of years of Communist disregard of the neutrality and territorial integrity of Cambodia— guaranteed in the 1954 Geneva agreements to which Hanoi was a signatory.

BACKGROUND OF THE APRIL 30 DECISION

In assessing the Apr. 30 decision to move against the North Vietnamese and Viet Cong sanctuaries in Cambodia, 4 basic facts must be remembered.

It was North Vietnam—not we—which brought the Vietnam war into Cambodia.

For 5 years North Vietnam has used Cambodian territory as a sanctuary from which to attack allied forces in South Vietnam. For 5 years American and allied forces—to preserve the concept of Cambodian neutrality and to confine the conflict in Southeast Asia—refrained from moving against those sanctuaries.

It was the presence of North Vietnamese troops on Cambodian soil that contributed to the downfall of Prince Sihanouk. It was the indignation of the Cambodian people against the presence of Vietnamese Communists in their country that led to riots in Pnompenh which contributed to Prince Sihanouk's ouster—an ouster that surprised no nation more than the United States. At the end of Sihanouk's rule, the United States was making efforts to improve relations with his government and the prince was taking steps against the Communist invaders on his national soil.

It was the government appointed by Prince Sihanouk and ratified by the Cambodian National Assembly—not a group of usurpers—which overthrew him with the approval of the National Assembly. The United States had neither connection with, nor knowledge of, these events.

It was the major expansion of enemy activity in Cambodia that ultimately caused allied troops to end 5 years of restraint and attack the Communist base areas.

The historical record is plain.

Viet Cong and North Vietnamese troops have operated in eastern Cambodia for years. The primary objective of these Communist forces has been the support of Hanoi's aggression against South Vietnam. Just as it has violated the 1962 Geneva accords on Laos, North Vietnam has consistently ignored its pledge, in signing the 1954 Geneva accords, to respect Cambodian neutrality and territorial integrity.

In a May 1967 Pnompenh radio broadcast, Prince Sihanouk's following remarks were reported to the Cambodian people:

"I must tell you that the Vietnamese Communists and the Viet Cong negotiated with us 3 or 4 times but that absolutely nothing comes out of the negotiations.... After I expelled the French and after the French troops left Cambodia, Viet Minh remained in our country in order to conquer it. How can we have confidence in the Viet Minh?... If we side with the Viet Minh we will lose our independence."

Late in 1969 Prince Sihanouk ordered Cambodia's underequipped and weak armed forces to exercise some measure of control over North Vietnamese and Viet Cong Communist forces occupying Cambodian territory.

At the same time, the Communist forces were actively preparing in their base areas for new combat in South Vietnam. These areas—on the Cambodian side of the Vietnam-Cambodian border—have for years served as supply depots and base camps for enemy troops infiltrated through Laos into South Vietnam. They have also served as sanctuaries for North Vietnamese and Viet Cong headquarters elements and for combat troops to rest, refit and re-supply on their return from South Vietnam.

Our screening of more than 6 tons of documents captured in the Cambodian operations has provided conclusive proof of Communist reliance on Cambodia as a logistic and infiltration corridor and as a secure area from which Communist designs on Vietnam as well as in Cambodia itself could be carried out.

On Jan. 6, 1970 Prince Sihanouk departed on vacation in France. His prime minister, Lon Nol, and deputy prime minister, Sirik Matak, were left in charge. In early March, with Sihanouk still in power, there were public demonstrations, first in the eastern provinces of Cambodia and later in Pnompenh, against flagrant North Vietnamese violation of Cambodia's territorial integrity.

On Mar. 13 Prince Sihanouk left Paris for Moscow and Peking, avowedly to seek Soviet and Chinese assistance in persuading the Vietnamese Communists to reduce the presence of North Vietnamese and Viet Cong forces in Cambodia.

Then, on Mar. 18, the Cambodian National Assembly by unanimous vote declared that Prince Sihanouk was no longer chief of state. Cheng Heng was retained as acting chief of state. Lon Nol and Sirik Matak kept their positions. Reasons for Sihanouk's ouster included growing objections to his mishandling of the economy and to his by-passing of the cabinet and National Assembly; but resentment over North Vietnam's flagrant misuse of Cambodian territory certainly contributed. Sihanouk arrived in Peking the same day and met with the Peking leadership as well as with the North Vietnamese prime minister, who had hastened to Peking to greet him. Thereafter Sihanouk has increasingly identified himself with the Communist cause in Indochina.

This government had no advance warning of the ouster of Sihanouk, with whom we had been attempting to improve relations. Our initial response was to seek to preserve the *status quo* with regard to Cambodia and to try to prevent an expansion of Communist influence. The immunity of the Cambodian sanctuaries had been a serious military handicap for us for many years. But we had refrained from moving against them in order to contain the conflict. We recognized both the problems facing Sihanouk and the fact that he had exercised some measure of control over Communist activities, through regulation of the flow of rice and military supplies into the sanctuaries from coastal ports. We considered that a neutral Cambodia outweighed the military benefits of a move against the base areas.

This is why diplomatically our first reaction to Sihanouk's overthrow was to encourage some form of accommodation in Cambodia. We spoke in this sense to interested governments. And we made clear through many channels that we had no intention of exploiting the Cambodian upheaval for our own ends.

These attempts ran afoul of Hanoi's designs. North Vietnam and the Viet Cong withdrew their representation from Pnompenh. North Vietnamese and Viet Cong forces began to expand their base areas along the border.

By Apr. 3 they were beginning to launch attacks against Cambodian forces in Svayrieng Province. Later these attacks were extended to other outposts in eastern Cambodia, forcing Cambodian troops to evacuate border positions in the Parrot's Beak area by Apr. 10. Communist attacks were also directed against Mekong River traffic.

By Apr. 16 the North Vietnamese and Viet Cong troops began to launch isolated attacks deep into Cambodia, including an attack on the capital of Takeo Province, south of Pnompenh.

Despite escalating Communist activity in Cambodia, we continued to exercise restraint. Though the implications of the Communist actions for our efforts in Vietnam were becoming increasingly ominous, Communist intentions in Cambodia were still not absolutely clear. The military moves by the North Vietnamese and Viet Cong in Cambodia could still be interpreted as temporary actions to secure their base camps in light of the uncertainties following Sihanouk's removal.

When I made my Apr. 20 speech announcing the withdrawal of 150,000 troops over the next year, I knew that we might be at a crossroads in Cambodia. I nevertheless made the announcement because it would leave no doubt about our intention to de-escalate the conflict.

I also used the occasion to restate very forthcoming political principles for a negotiated peace. At the same time I described the pattern of North Vietnamese aggression in Indochina and acknowledged that my withdrawal decision involved some risks when viewed against this enemy escalation. I therefore reiterated my determination to take strong and effective measures if increased enemy action in Laos, Cambodia or South Vietnam jeopardized the security of our remaining forces in Vietnam.

Within days of my Apr. 20 speech, Communist intentions became painfully and unambiguously clear. In the face of our restraint and our warnings, the North Vietnamese continued to expand their territorial control, threatening to link up their base areas. From a series of isolated enclaves, the base areas were rapidly becoming a solid band of self-sustaining territory stretching from Laos to the sea from which any pretense of Cambodian sovereignty was rapidly being excluded.

- On Apr. 20, North Vietnamese forces temporarily captured Saang, only 18 miles south of Pnompenh.
- On Apr. 22, Communist forces assaulted the town of Snoul east of Pnompenh.
- On Apr. 23, they attacked the town of Mimot and an important bridge linking the town of Snoul and the capital of Kratie Province on Route 13.
- On Apr. 24, they moved on the resort city of Kep.
- On Apr. 26, they attacked some ships on the Mekong and occupied the town of Angtassom, a few miles west of Takeo.
- They then attacked the city of Chhlong, on the Mekong River, north of Pnompenh, and the port city of Kampot.
- During this same period, they cut almost every major road leading south and east out of Pnompenh.

The prospect suddenly loomed of Cambodia's becoming virtually one large base area for attack anywhere into South Vietnam along the 600 miles of the Cambodian frontier. The enemy in Cambodia would have enjoyed complete freedom of action to move forces and supplies rapidly across the entire length of South Vietnam's flank to attack our forces in South Vietnam with impunity from well-stocked sanctuaries along the border.

We thus faced a rapidly changing military situation from that which existed on Apr. 20.

The possibility of a grave new threat to our troops in South Vietnam was rapidly becoming an actuality.

This pattern of Communist action prior to our decision of Apr. 30 makes it clear the enemy was intent both on expanding and strengthening its military position along the Cambodian border and overthrowing the Cambodian government. The plans were laid, the orders issued and already being implemented by Communist forces.

Not only the clear evidence of Communist actions—but supporting data screened from more than 6 tons of subsequently captured Communist documents—leaves no doubt that the Communists' move against the Cambodian government preceded the U.S. action against the base areas.

3 OPTIONS

On Apr. 30, before announcing our response, I outlined the 3 basic choices we had in the face of the expanding Communist threat.

First, we could do nothing. This would have eroded an important restraint on the loss of American lives. It would have run the risk of Cambodia's becoming one vast enemy staging area, a springboard for attacks on South Vietnam without fear of retaliation. The dangers of having done nothing would not have fully materialized for several months and this government might have been commended for exercising restraint. But, as withdrawals proceeded, our paralysis would have seriously jeopardized our forces in Vietnam and would have led to longer lists of American casualties. The United States could not accept the consequences of inaction in the face of this enemy escalation. The American men remaining in South Vietnam after our withdrawal of 150,000 would have been in severe jeopardy.

Our 2d choice was to provide massive assistance to Cambodia. This was an unrealistic alternative. The small Cambodian army of 30,000 could not effectively utilize any massive transfusion of military assistance against the immediate enemy threat. We also did not wish to get drawn into the permanent direct defense of Cambodia. This would have been inconsistent with the basic premises of our foreign policy.

After intensive consultations with my top advisers, I chose the 3d course. With the South Vietnamese we launched joint attacks against the base areas so long occupied by Communist forces.

Our military objectives were to capture or destroy the arms, ammunition and supplies that had been built up in those sanctuaries over a period of years and to disrupt the enemy's communication network. At the least, this would frustrate the impact of any Communist success in linking up their base areas if it did not prevent this development altogether.

I concluded that, regardless of the success of Communist assaults on the Cambodian government, the destruction of the enemy's sanctuaries would: remove a grave potential threat to our remaining men in South Vietnam, and so reduce future American casualties; give added assurance of the continuance of our troop withdrawal program; insure the timetable for our Vietnamization program; increase the chances of shortening the war in South Vietnam; enhance the prospects of a negotiated peace; emphasize to the enemy, whether in Southeast Asia or elsewhere, that the word of the United States—whether given in a promise or a warning—was still good.

THE MILITARY OPERATIONS

10 major operations were launched against a dozen of the most significant base areas with 32,000 American troops and 48,000 South Vietnamese participating at various times. As of today, all Americans, including logistics personnel and advisers, have withdrawn, as have a majority of the South Vietnamese forces.

Our military response to the enemy's escalation was measured in every respect. It was a limited operation for a limited period of time with limited objectives.

We have scrupulously observed the 21-mile limit on penetration of our ground combat forces into Cambodian territory. These self-imposed time and geographic restrictions may have cost us some military advantages, but we knew that we could achieve our primary objectives within these restraints. And these restraints underscored the limited nature of our purpose to the American people.

My June 3 interim report pointed up the success of these operations and the massive amounts of supplies we were seizing and destroying. We have since added substantially to these totals. A full inventory is attached as an appendix to the report. Here are some highlights.

According to latest estimates from the field, we have captured: 22,892 individual weapons—enough to equip about 74 full-strength North Vietnamese infantry battalions and 2,509 big crew-served weapons—enough to equip about 25 full-strength North Vietnamese infantry battalions; more than 15 million rounds of ammunition or about what the enemy has fired in South Vietnam during the past year; 14 million pounds of rice, enough to feed all the enemy combat battalions estimated to be in South Vietnam for about 4 months; 143,000 rockets, mortars and recoilless rifle rounds, used against cities and bases (based on recent experience, the number of mortars, large rockets, and recoilless rifle rounds is equivalent to what the enemy shoots in about 14 months in South Vietnam); over 199,552 anti-aircraft rounds, 5,482 mines, 62,022 grenades and 83,000 pounds of explosives, including 1,002 satchel charges; over 435 vehicles and destroyed over 11,688 bunkers and other military structures.

And while our objective has been supplies rather than personnel, the enemy has also taken a heavy manpower loss—11,349 men killed and about 2,328 captured and detainees.

These are impressive statistics. But what is the deeper meaning of the piles of enemy supplies and the rubble of enemy installations?

We have eliminated an immediate threat to our forces and to the security of South Vietnam—and produced the prospect of fewer American casualties in the future.

We have inflicted extensive casualties and very heavy losses in material on the enemy—losses which can now be replaced only from the North during a monsoon season and in the face of counteraction by South Vietnamese ground and U.S. air forces.

We have ended the concept of Cambodian sanctuaries, immune from attack, upon which the enemy military had relied for 5 years.

We have dislocated supply lines and disrupted Hanoi's strategy in the Saigon area and the Mekong Delta. The enemy capacity to mount a major offensive in this vital populated region of the South has been greatly diminished.

We have effectively cut off the enemy from resupply by the sea. In 1969, well over half of the munitions being delivered to the North Vietnamese and Viet Cong in Cambodia came by sea.

We have, for the time being, separated the Communist main force units—regular troops organized in formal units similar to conventional armies—from the guerrillas in the southern part of Vietnam. This should provide a boost to pacification efforts.

We have guaranteed the continuance of our troop withdrawal program. On June 3 I reaffirmed that 150,000 more Americans would return home within a year and announced that 50,000 would leave Vietnam by Oct 15.

We have bought time for the South Vietnamese to strengthen themselves against the enemy.

We have witnessed visible proof of the success of Vietnamization as the South Vietnamese performed with skill and valor and competence far beyond the expectation of our commanders or American advisers. The morale and self-confidence of the army of South Vietnam is higher than ever before.

These then are the major accomplishments of the operations against the Cambodian base areas. Americans can take pride in the leadership of Gen. [Creighton W.] Abrams and in the competence and dedication of our forces.

There is another way to view the success of these operations. What if we had chosen the first option—and done nothing?

The enemy sanctuaries by now would have been expanded and strengthened. The thousands of troops he lost, in killed or captured, would be available to attack American positions and with the enormous resources that we captured or destroyed still in his hands.

Our Vietnamization program would be in serious jeopardy; our withdrawals of troops could only have been carried out in the face of serious threat to our remaining troops in Vietnam.

We would have confronted an adversary emboldened by our timidity, an adversary who had ignored repeated warnings.

The war would be a good deal further from over than it is today.

Had we stood by and let the enemy act with impunity in Cambodia—we would be facing a truly bleak situation.

The allied operations have greatly reduced these risks and enhanced the prospects for the future. However, many difficulties remain and some setbacks are inevitable. We still face substantial problems, but the Cambodian operations will enable us to pursue our goals with greater confidence.

When the decision to go into Cambodia was announced on Apr. 30, we anticipated broad disagreement and dissent within the society. Given the divisions on this issue among the American people, it could not have been otherwise.

But the majority of the Americans supported that decision—and now that the Cambodian operation is over, I believe there is a wide measure of understanding of the necessity for it.

Although there remains disagreement about its long-term significance, about the cost to our society of having taken this action——there can be little disagreement now over the immediate military success that has been achieved. With American ground operations in Cambodia ended, we shall move forward with our plan to end the war in Vietnam and to secure the just peace on which all Americans are united.

THE FUTURE

Now that our ground forces and our logistic and advisory personnel have all been withdrawn, what will be our future policy for Cambodia?

The following will be the guidelines of our policy in Cambodia:

1. There will be no U.S. ground personnel in Cambodia except for the regular staff of our embassy in Pnompenh.

2. There will be no U.S. advisers with Cambodian units.

3. We will conduct—with the approval of the Cambodian government—air interdiction missions against the enemy efforts to move supplies and personnel through Cambodia toward South Vietnam and to re-establish base areas relevant to the war in Vietnam. We do this to protect our forces in South Vietnam.

4. We will turn over material captured in the base areas in Cambodia to the Cambodian government to help it defend its neutrality and independence.

5. We will provide military assistance to the Cambodian government in the form of small arms and relatively unsophisticated equipment in types and quantities suitable for their army. To date we have supplied about $5 million of these items principally in the form of small arms, mortars, trucks, aircraft parts, communications equipment and medical supplies.

6. We will encourage other countries of the region to give diplomatic support to the independence and neutrality of Cambodia. We welcome the efforts of the Djakarta group of countries* to mobilize world opinion and encourage Asian cooperation to this end.

---

*Australia, Indonesia, Japan, Korea, Laos, Malaysia, New Zealand, Philippines, Singapore, South Vietnam, Thailand.

7. We will encourage and support the efforts of 3d countries who wish to furnish Cambodia with troops or material. We applaud the efforts of Asian nations to help Cambodia preserve its neutrality and independence.

I will let the Asian governments speak for themselves concerning their future policies. I am confident that 2 basic principles will govern the actions · of those nations helping Cambodia:

● They will be at the request of, and in close concert with the Cambodian government.

● They will not be at the expense of those nations' own defense—indeed they will contribute to their security which they see bound up with events in Cambodia.

The South Vietnamese plan to help. Of all the countries of Southeast Asia, South Vietnam has most at stake in Cambodia. A North Vietnamese takeover would, of course, have profound consequences for its security. At the same time, the leaders of South Vietnam recognize that the primary focus of their attention must be on the security of their own country. Pres. Thieu has reflected these convictions in his major radio and TV address of June 27. Our understanding of Saigon's intentions is as follows:

1. South Vietnamese forces remain ready to prevent re-establishment of base areas along South Vietnam's frontier.

2. South Vietnamese forces will remain ready to assist in the evacuation of Vietnamese civilians and to respond selectively to appeals from the Cambodian government should North Vietnamese aggression make this necessary.

3. Most of these operations will be launched from within South Vietnam. There will be no U.S. air or logistics support. There will not be U.S. advisers on these operations.

4. The great majority of South Vietnamese forces are to leave Cambodia.

5. The primary objective of the South Vietnamese remains Vietnamization within their country. Whatever actions are taken in Cambodia will be consistent with this objective.

In this June 27 speech [South Vietnamese] Pres. [Nguyen Van] Thieu emphasized that his government will concentrate on efforts within South Vietnam. He pledged that his country will always respect the territory, borders, independence and neutrality of Cambodia and will not interfere in its internal politics. His government does not advocate stationing troops permanently in Cambodia or sending the South Vietnamese army to fight the war for the Cambodian army.

Under the foreign policy guidelines first outlined at Guam a year ago, I stressed that a threatened country should first make maximum efforts in its own self-defense. The Cambodian people and soldiers are doing that against the superior force of the North Vietnamese and Viet Cong invaders. The majority of the Cambodian people support the present government against the foreign intruders. Cambodian troops have remained loyal and have stood up well in the face of great pressures from a better-armed and experienced foe.

Secondly, our policy stresses there should be regional cooperation where a country is not strong enough to defend herself. Cambodia's neighbors are providing that cooperation by joining with her in a collective effort. Each of them is a target of Communist aggression; each has a stake in Cambodia's neutrality and independence.

3d, the U.S. will assist such self-help and regional actions where our participation can make a difference. Over the long term, we expect the countries of Asia to provide increasingly for their own defense. However, we are now in a transitional phase when nations are shouldering greater responsibilities but when U.S. involvement, while declining, still plays an important role.

In this interim period, we must offset our lower direct involvement with increased military and economic assistance. To meet our foreign policy obligations while reducing our presence will require a redirection—both quantitatively and qualitatively—in our assistance programs.

Prince Sihanouk wrote in Dec. 1969 about the Communist threat to his country and the balance presented by American forces in Southeast Asia. In a generally anti-American article in the official Cambodian government party newspaper he stated:

"On the diplomatic and political plane, the fact that the U.S. remains in our region and does not yet leave it allows us maneuverings. . . . to assure on the one hand our more than honorable presence in the concert of nations. . . . this presence (and this is an irony of fate for the anti-imperialists that we are) is an essential condition for the 'respect,' the 'friendship' and even for the aid of our Socialist 'friends.' When the U.S. has left these regions, it is certain that the Cambodia of the Sangkum will be the objective of the shellings of the heavy Communist guns: unfriendliness, subversion, aggressions, infiltrations and even occupations."

THE SEARCH FOR PEACE

In our search for a lasting peace in Southeast-Asia, we are applying the 3 basic principles of our foreign policy which are set forth in the [Presidential] foreign policy report to Congress last February: partnership, strength and willingness to negotiate.

● The partnership of our Vietnamization program and of our support for regional defense efforts.

● The strength of our action against the Communist bases in Cambodia and the steadfastness of the American people to see the war through to an honorable conclusion.

● The willingness to negotiate expressed in our generous proposals for a settlement and in our flexibility once Hanoi agrees to serious negotiations.

All 3 elements are needed to bring peace in Southeast Asia. The willingness to negotiate will prove empty unless buttressed by the willingness to stand by just demands. Otherwise negotiations will be a subterfuge for capitulation. This would only bring a false and transitory peace abroad and recrimination at home.

While we search for genuine negotiation we must continue to demonstrate resolution both abroad and at home, and we must support the common defense efforts of threatened Asian nations.

To the leaders in Hanoi, I say the time has come to negotiate. There is nothing to be gained in waiting. There is never an ideal moment when both sides are in perfect equilibrium.

The lesson of the last 2 months has reinforced the lessons of the last 2 years—the time has come to negotiate a just peace.

In Cambodia, the futility of expanded aggression has been demonstrated. By its actions in Cambodia, North Vietnam and the Viet Cong provoked the destruction of their sanctuaries and helped to weld together the independent states of Southeast Asia in a collective defense effort, which will receive American support.

The other side cannot impose its will through military means. We have no intention of imposing ours. We have not raised the terms for a settlement as a result of our recent military successes. We will not lower our minimum terms in response to enemy pressure. Our objective remains a negotiated peace with justice for both sides and which gives the people of South Vietnam the opportunity to shape their own future.

With major efforts the North Vietnamese can perhaps rebuild or readjust Cambodia supply areas over a period of months. They can pursue their war against South Vietnam and her neighbors. But what end would a new round of conflict serve? There is no military solution to this conflict. Sooner or later, peace must come. It can come now, through a negotiated settlement that is fair to both sides and humiliates neither. Or it can come months or years from now, with both sides having paid the further price of protracted struggle.

We would hope that Hanoi would ponder seriously its choice, considering both the promise of an honorable peace and the costs of continued war.

We repeat: all our previous proposals, public and private, remain on the conference table to be explored, including the principles of a just political settlement that I outlined on Apr. 20.

We search for a political solution that reflects the will of the South Vietnamese people and allows them to determine their future without outside interference.

We recognize that a fair political solution should reflect the existing relationship of political forces.

We pledge to abide by the outcome of the political process agreed upon by the South Vietnamese.

For our part, we shall renew our efforts to bring about genuine negotiations both in Paris and for all of Indochina. As I said in my address last September to the United Nations General Assembly:

"The people of Vietnam, North and South alike, have demonstrated heroism enough to last a century.... The people of Vietnam, North and South, have endured an unspeakable weight of suffering for a generation. And they deserve a better future."

We call on Hanoi to join us at long last in bringing about that better future.

Communist Losses

The White House June 30 also made public this summary of "significant" Viet Cong/North Vietnamese losses in Cambodia as of June 29:

```
Ammunition: *
  Machinegun rounds .............................  4,067,177
  Rifle rounds ..................................  10,694,990
    Total small arms (machinegun and rifle rounds)........ 14,762,167
  Anti-aircraft rounds ..........................    199,552
  Mortar rounds .................................     68,539
  Large rocket rounds ...........................      2,123
  Small rocket rounds ...........................     43,160
  Recoilless rifle rounds .......................     29,185
  Grenades ......................................     62,022
  Mines .........................................      5,482
Weapons:
  Individual ....................................     22,892
  Crew-served ...................................      2,509
Food:
  Rice (pounds) .................................  14,046,000
  Man months of rice............................     309,012
  Total food (pounds) ...........................  14,518,000
Facilities:  Bunkers/structures destroyed .........     11,688
Transportation:
  Vehicles ......................................        435
  Boats .........................................        167
Examples of other equipment:
  Radios ........................................        248
  Generators ....................................         49
  Total communications equipment (pounds).......     58,600
  Miscellaneous explosives (pounds) (including 1,002 satchel
    charges) ....................................     83,000
  Medical supplies (pounds) .....................    110,800
  Documents (pounds) ............................     12,400
Personnel:
  Enemy killed in action ........................     11,349
  Prisoners of war (includes detainees)..........      2,328
```

Communists Distrust U.S. Departure

North Vietnam charged July 1 that, despite the complete withdrawal of American troops from Cambodia, the U.S. was "prolonging and expanding the war in Cambodia through the

*Not including 70 tons of assorted ammunition.

service of the mercenary clique supplied by the reactionary authorities in Southeast Asia." Hanoi radio said American aid to Cambodia and other countries sending their forces to fight there represented "an implementation of Nixon's doctrine of making Asians fight Asians for the realization of United States neocolonialism in Asia." The broadcast called the U.S. operation in Cambodia "a disastrous failure" that belied Nixon's June 30 report "about military wins which have never existed."

The Soviet Union July 1 also characterized the American operation as a failure. The Soviet news agency Tass said the U.S. failure was evidenced by the fact that Communist forces still controlled large areas of the country. "Washington's miscalculations in Cambodia are evident, and no bragging in the President's [June 30] report can conceal them," Tass said.

Communist China charged in an article published July 2 that the U.S. had announced the expansion of bombing raids on Cambodia "while playing with the trick of troop withdrawal." The Communist Party newspaper *Jenmin Jih Pao* said the purpose of this action was to enable the U.S. to continue its "criminal scheme of making Asians fight Asians."

ARMS AID TO CAMBODIA

Cambodia had appealed to the U.S. and to Asian countries Apr. 14, 1970 for arms assistance against the invading Communist forces. The plea brought a positive response, and weapons began arriving even before the allied incursion into Cambodia. Under a pact signed Aug. 19, the U.S. agreed to provide Cambodia with $40 million worth of military equipment. Thailand and South Vietnam signed separate pacts May 27-28 to provide Cambodia with direct military aid. The Saigon agreement broadened South Vietnam's authority to continue operations in Cambodia.

A shipment of several thousand rifles and ammunition captured from Communist forces in South Vietnam was flown to Cambodia Apr. 23, 1970. The weapons were AK-47 automatic rifles of Soviet design and Chinese manufacture. The U.S. and the Pnompenh regime confirmed the arms shipment Apr. 23 and 24. A White House statement said the weapons were being supplied to Cambodia by South Vietnam "with our knowledge and approval." The American decision to send the guns had been transmitted by Washington Apr. 17 to Lloyd M. Rives, the U.S. charge d'affaires in Pnompenh. But Rives had been instructed to warn Pnompenh officials against "inflated expectation" of further military assistance. Washington's message was said to have expressed American readiness to ship 1,500 AK-47 rifles immediately and 4,000 to 5,000 more within 2 or 3 weeks.

Cambodian Premier Lon Nol Apr. 20 had sent to Pres. Nixon a personal appeal for extensive military equipment. The premier also had urged that Cambodian mercenaries assisting U.S. Army Special Forces in South Vietnam be sent back to Cambodia to help fight the Communist invaders. (Most were sent to Cambodia.)

Lon Nol's general appeal for international arms assistance, broadcast Apr. 14, had been formally transmitted to diplomatic missions in Pnompenh the following day. Foreign Min. Yem

Sambaur handed the envoys a covering letter and a copy of
Lon Nol's broadcast statement.

Pnompenh government sources reported Apr. 22 that
Indonesia had agreed in principle to provide military aid to
Cambodia and that the assistance would be arriving soon. Lon
Nol was said to be negotiating the matter with Indonesian
representatives.

U.S. Widens Assistance

The U.S. embassy in Pnompenh disclosed June 24 that the
U.S. had stepped up the shipment of arms to Cambodia and
that all of the $7.9 million in arms aid promised for the current
fiscal year either had arrived or would arrive shortly.

Jonathan F. Ladd, political-military counselor at the
embassy, said the equipment already received included 20,000
M-1 rifles and M-2 carbines, some pistols, some 30-caliber light
machine guns, and ammunition. Ladd disclosed that the
Pnompenh government was also charged with the cost of repair
and maintenance of Cambodia's 10 T-28 trainer planes
converted into fighter-bombers and with the outfitting of 2,000
Khmer Krom, the ethnic Cambodian Special Forces who had
been fighting in South Vietnam and who were brought into
Cambodia May 1.

The U.S. was reported June 27 to be recruiting more ethnic
Cambodians in South Vietnam for fighting in Cambodia. Col.
Richard W. Ellison, senior American adviser in the Mekong
Delta's Vinhbinh Province, said 230 Cambodian militiamen had
been shipped out the previous week. About 200 of them were
described as either members of or sympathizers with Khmer
Serei, a Cambodian rightist movement. Ellison said the
recruiting drive came to a halt when the province chief
complained to Pres. Nguyen Van Thieu that the men were
being enrolled without his knowledge. Other American officials
said that the recruitment of Cambodians was continuing in
other delta provinces.

Under a pact concluded in Pnompenh Aug. 19, the U.S.
agreed to provide $40 million worth of more military
equipment to Cambodia. The military assistance agreement,
confirmed by the U.S. State Department Aug. 24, provided for
small arms, ammunition, communications equipment, spare

parts and training funds to be furnished to Cambodia. The funds were to cover the fiscal year ending June 30, 1971. Cambodia had received $8.9 million in emergency military aid from the U.S. in May-June 1970. Additional military funds to be given to Cambodia during the current fiscal year depended on the progress of the fighting, State Department officials said.

In a previous action aimed at helping Pnompenh fight the Communist invaders, the U.S. State Department Aug. 14 had confirmed a "tentative" agreement to provide American aid to the 5,000 troops being recruited or trained in Thailand for operations in Cambodia. "The nature and extent of whatever support we may provide will depend in part on arrangements, including the training and disposition of the troops involved," the department said. According to the department, "no final overall agreement on U.S. support for troops recruited or trained in Thailand" had yet been reached. The agreement covered 3,000 Thai troops described as "ethnic Cambodians" and about 2,000 Cambodians being trained in Thailand.

Sen. Frank Church (D., Ida.) charged Aug. 14 that if Washington implemented the Cambodian-Thai troop aid arrangement it "would represent the 2d violation of the Senate-approved Cooper-Church amendment within a week's time." The "first violation," Church said, "was the disclosure that direct air support is now being extended to Cambodian troops."

South Vietnam & Thailand Sign Aid Pacts

South Vietnam and Thailand also agreed to provide direct military assistance to Cambodia in its struggle against the Vietnamese Communists. The separate agreements were reached in Saigon May 27 and in Pnompenh May 27-28. The Saigon agreement gave South Vietnam a broad mandate to pursue its military operations in Cambodia. Thailand said it would send a volunteer force to Cambodia that was to be armed and equipped by the U.S., but the Thais later canceled this plan.

The tripartite military efforts followed appeals by the U.S. for South Vietnam, Thailand and Cambodia to undertake joint defense plans.

The South Vietnamese-Cambodian agreement was announced in a 17-point communique signed May 27 following 3 days of talks in Saigon. The statement, signed by Cambodian and South Vietnamese Foreign Mins. Yem Sambaur and Tran Van Lam, said Saigon's military forces had entered Cambodia to "help Cambodian troops to drive out the Viet Cong and North Vietnamese forces [and] will withdraw when their task is completed." The 2 ministers also signed 3 other documents reestablishing diplomatic relations (broken since 1963), providing for economic cooperation and dealing with the treatment of Vietnamese residents in Cambodia.

The agreement on sending the Thai volunteer force to Cambodia was announced by the Bangkok government June 1. A follow-up announcement June 2 said the troops would take up defense duties in Pnompenh and other Cambodian cities, releasing regular Cambodian troops for combat. The force would be composed of Thais of Cambodian descent and would be drawn mainly from an estimated half million ethnic Cambodians residing in the 8 Thai provinces along the Cambodian border. In addition, Thailand agreed to provide Cambodia with clothing, medical supplies and 20 gunboats to patrol the Mekong River. The 2 countries also announced their resumption of full diplomatic relations.

The U.S. government June 1 expressed support for the agreement on the Thai expeditionary force, and it announced June 2 that it would provide the arms and equipment. State Department officials had said May 27 that the South Vietnamese and Thai governments were authorized to provide the Cambodian army with military equipment that had been supplied to them under terms of the U.S. defense treaties with the Saigon and Bangkok regimes.

The refusal of Thailand to send ground troops to Cambodia was the subject of talks between Cambodian Premier Lon Nol and Thai Premier Thanom Kittikachorn in Bangkok July 22-23. Lon Nol failed to win assurances of Thai troop aid but was given promises of other military assistance.

Lon Nol confirmed at a news conference that Thai air force planes were conducting bombing and strafing missions in northern Cambodia at the request of the Pnompenh government. Other Thai assistance included military training for ethnic Cambodians and regular Cambodian troops, military equipment and medical supplies and services.

Thanom, following his July 22 talks with Lon Nol, said that the Bangkok government "has under serious consideration other measures that may become necessary to meet the mounting Communist onslaughts and to stem the tide of aggression."

Thailand's reluctance to provide Cambodia with troops had been criticized July 17 by Lt. Gen. Do Cao Tri, commander of South Vietnamese forces in Cambodia. Tri said the Thais were shirking their responsibilities because the U.S. would not meet their request to finance a Cambodian operation.

Assistance to the hard-pressed Pnompenh government had been the topic of a high-level meeting of South Vietnamese and Cambodian officials in Neak Leung, Cambodia July 17. After meeting for 2 hours with Lon Nol, Deputy Premier Sisowath Sirik Matek and Chief of State Cheng Heng, South Vietnamese Pres. Nguyen Van Thieu said: "The most important thing that we agreed together was that the other nations of the free world should come as rapidly as possible to help Cambodia and not permit the Communists to take the initiative." Thieu dismissed a recent suggestion by Vice Pres. Nguyen Cao Ky that Cambodia, Thailand and South Vietnam form a joint anti-Communist front in Southeast Asia. Thieu said the idea was "not feasible" because "we don't need a classical or rigid alliance."

U.S. DISSENT: APRIL-DECEMBER 1970

The American military drive into Cambodia triggered explosive dissent in the U.S. Violent protests took place on college campuses. The most tragic incident, a confrontation between National Guardsmen and students at Kent State University in Ohio May 4, 1970, resulted in the deaths of 4 students. Nearly 500 colleges and universities throughout the country were closed or went on strike in expressions of student and, in many cases, faculty opposition to the expanded conflict. (Classes generally returned to normal for summer and fall sessions.)

Pres. Nixon acted quickly to try to mitigate the animosity between his Administration and the campus community. Holding his first TV news conference in 3 months, the President May 8 engaged student protesters in discussions and conferred with leading educators, governors and labor leaders as he sought to explain his decision to commit American troops in Cambodia. Opposition to the new military move reached into the President's own cabinet. Interior Secy. Walter J. Hickel sent a letter of protest to Nixon. He warned against alienating the youth and complained of lack of consultation with cabinet members. There were reports of other disagreements within the cabinet on the Cambodian venture, although the members allegedly involved publicly avowed their support of Nixon's policy. Several government officials outside the cabinet resigned their posts with statements assailing the Cambodian incursion.

The U.S. drive into Cambodia evoked surprise and considerable criticism in the Senate. Opposition was also voiced—but to a lesser extent—in the House of Representatives. Congressional anger was particularly aroused over the Administration's alleged failure to consult with legislative leaders in advance. This led to increasingly vocal concern about a possible Constitutional conflict between the President and Congress over the chief executive's right to engage in military ventures without the consent of Congress. In a move aimed at restricting further Administration moves in Indochina, the House and Senate Dec. 29 approved a measure that barred the introduction of American ground forces into Thailand and Laos and prohibited the use of funds for military support of Laos or Cambodia. A measure calling for the withdrawal of all American troops from Vietnam by the end of 1971 was defeated in the Senate Sept. 1.

4 Students Slain at Kent State University

The 4 students killed at Kent State University in Ohio were gunned down May 4 when 100 National Guardsmen fired into a group of antiwar demonstrators. 11 other students were wounded.

Ohio Adjutant Gen. Sylvester T. Del Corso said in a statement May 4 that the troops had run out of tear gas and had fired in reaction to sniper fire "from a nearby rooftop." Corso retracted this assertion May 5 and said that "there is no evidence" of sniper fire. Reporters and students at the scene said that demonstrators had thrown rocks and paving stones at the troops but that there were no shots before the National Guardsmen suddenly fired their M-1 rifles at the students. One Guardsman hit by a stone was treated at the hospital and released.

The 4 victims were Allison Krause, 19, of Pittsburgh; Sandra Lee Scheuer, 20, of Youngstown, Ohio; Jeffrey Glenn Miller, 20, of Plainfield, N.Y.; and William K. Schroeder, 19, of Lorain, Ohio. None were described as radicals.

The shooting occurred 20 minutes after the troops had used tear gas to disperse a student protest against the use of U.S. forces in Cambodia. 600 National Guardsmen had been ordered onto the campus the previous day after the university's ROTC building had been burned to the ground during a 2d night of disruptions by antiwar students.

Just before the shooting started May 4, a few students had thrown rocks at the Guardsmen as they retreated up a campus hill. A couple of students threw back a tear gas canister. In all, about 20 rocks were allegedly thrown at the troops, who were about 40 yards from the 500 to 600 advancing students when they turned around, formed a skirmish line and began to fire. Witnesses said many students dropped to the ground but others remained standing, apparently believing the troops were firing into the air.

Maj. Gen. D. E. Manly, commander of an Ohio Highway Patrol unit that was working with the National Guardsmen, May 5 denied earlier National Guard reports that his men, circling above the campus in a helicopter, had spotted snipers on a rooftop. Brig. Gen. Robert Canterbury, officer in command of the Guards, said May 5: "In my opinion, the fact that there is or is not a sniper is not important.... I think the reason the people fired was because they were being assaulted with rocks and concrete." He said that there were no orders to open fire, but the men had made "individual decisions" to shoot when they feared their lives were threatened.

Gov. James A. Rhodes called on FBI Director J. Edgar Hoover to investigate the shooting, and FBI men were on the campus May 5 making a preliminary study. The Kent State Student Senate had accused Rhodes May 3 of political motivation when he ordered troops onto the campus. (Rhodes was engaged in a primary battle with Rep. Robert Taft for the Republican nomination for the U.S. Senate.) The Defense Department said May 5 that it would not investigate the shooting because the troops were on non-federal status under the command of the state.

Robert I. White, president of the university, ordered the school closed May 4 after the shooting, and students were sent home. Students on other campuses around the nation, however, continuing to demonstrate against the use of U.S. troops in Cambodia, protested against the events at Kent State and held memorial services for the dead students.

Pres. Nixon, in a statement released by White House Press Secy. Ronald L. Ziegler May 4, said the deaths at Kent State "should remind us all once again that when dissent turns to violence it invites tragedy." Nixon said: "It is my hope that this tragic and unfortunate incident will strengthen the determination of all the nation's campuses ... to stand firmly for the right which exists in this country of peaceful dissent and just as strongly against the resort to violence as a means of such expression."

Vice Pres. Spiro T. Agnew said the incident was "predictable and avoidable." He said that he had called attention to the "grave dangers which accompany the new politics of violence and confrontation" and that events at Kent State "make the truth of these remarks self-evident."

Student Strikes & Demonstrations

Students at colleges and universities throughout the U.S. went on strike starting in early May in protest against the American involvement in Cambodia. The editors of campus newspapers at 11 major Eastern colleges May 4 published a common editorial saying a strike was necessary "to free the academic community from activities of secondary importance and open them up to the primary task of building renewed opposition to the war." Much of the protest activity that followed appeared to be almost inextricably entangled with opposition to the Indochina fighting in general and with other complaints involving the draft, racial antagonism and student problems.

The presidents of 37 colleges and universities May 4 joined in a letter warning Pres. Nixon of "the incalculable dangers of an unprecedented alienation of America's youth" as a result of the U.S. invasion of Cambodia and renewed bombing of North Vietnam. The letter had been drafted by Dr. James M. Hester, president of New York University. It carried, *inter alia,* the signatures of the presidents of Princeton, Columbia, Radcliffe, Cornell, Stanford, Dartmouth and the Universities of Notre Dame and Pennsylvania. The presidents said they shared the "severe and widespread apprehensions on our campuses" and called on Nixon to "take immediate action to demonstrate unequivocally your determination to end the war quickly."

Firebombings were reported on a number of campuses May 6-7.

In Washington May 4, leaders of the National Student Association (NSA) and the former Vietnam Moratorium Committee officially called for a nationwide strike of indefinite duration. The NSA and student body presidents from 10 campuses had called on the House of Representatives May 1 to begin impeachment proceedings against Pres. Nixon. 68

members of the Cornell University faculty, in a May 1 resolution, had also called for Nixon's impeachment.

According to a May 5 statement from Brandeis University (Waltham, Mass.), where a National Strike Information Center was set up, more than 115 schools across the nation were already on strike. The College Press Service estimated May 5 that 208 schools were closed or were planning to close, including Yale University, whose president and campus newspaper had opposed the strike May 3. Yale Pres. Kingman Brewster Jr., while attacking the spread of the war as a "dreadful policy," said May 5 that he hoped students could find an alternative to the strike call "to demonstrate our distress."

A student and faculty strike began at Stanford University in Palo Alto, Calif. May 4 when whole departments, including the School of Law, voted to discontinue classes in protest against Nixon's actions in Cambodia. The walkout had been preceded Apr. 30 by violent antiwar demonstrations in which 42 rock-throwing students were arrested by police. The incident followed a day-long peaceful sit-in at the university's Student Union by anti-ROTC protesters. (ROTC had been the subject of sharp controversy at the school earlier in April. The students had voted by a slim majority to permit the ROTC program to stay on campus without academic credit. Anti-ROTC protests continued, however, and fires caused $50,000 to $100,000 damage to the Stanford Center for Advanced Studies in the Behavioral Sciences Apr. 24. The university said the work of 10 visiting scholars was destroyed in the blaze.)

Maryland Gov. Marvin Mandel declared a state of emergency on the University of Maryland campus in College Park May 4 and called in National Guardsmen after student demonstrators blocked traffic along a major highway for the 2d time in 4 days. The demonstrations had begun May 1 when students ransacked the university's ROTC office, causing $10,000 damage. The police used tear gas to disperse the protesters blocking the highway. Some students had thrown rocks at the officers. The confrontation May 1 resulted in 25 arrests and 50 injuries. The demonstrations, in reaction to the decision to send troops into Cambodia, followed unrest over the arrest of more than 80 students Mar. 24 after a building occupation protest against the school's refusal to grant tenure to 2 assistant professors. National Guard troops carrying unloaded rifles were brought back to the campus May 14 as antiwar students continued to demonstrate and to block a nearby highway. Martial law was declared May 15, but a midnight-to-6 a.m. curfew was lifted May 19 on condition that no further trouble developed.

The faculty at Princeton University, where immediate plans for a strike had been adopted by 2,300 students May 1, voted May 5 to approve a 2-week recess immediately before the Nov. 3 national elections to permit students and faculty to work to elect antiwar candidates to Congress. This Princeton plan was adopted quickly on other campuses.

At the University of Wisconsin in Madison, Mayor William Dyke declared a state of emergency, and Gov. Warren Knowles ordered National Guardsmen to stand by May 5 after about 3,000 students tried to raid a Selective Service office. Local police drove back the rock-throwing demonstrators with tear gas. Guardsmen stood by with bayonet-tipped rifles May 6 to keep campus buildings open to students who wished to attend class. The troops used tear gas to disperse protesters; 20 persons were injured, including 3 policemen and 2 Guardsmen, and 25 protesters were arrested.

2 National Guardsmen suffered injuries as they tried to break up student demonstrations at the Ohio State University campus in Columbus May 5. Students, seeking to seal off the entrances to the university, had thrown bricks at the troops. The university was ordered closed May 6.

Gov. Ronald Reagan ordered the 9 campuses of the University of California and the 18 state colleges closed May 6 through May 10 to provide "time for rational reflection away from the emotional turmoil and [to] encourage all to disavow violence and mob action." In San Diego, a University of California student, George M. Winne Jr., 23, died May 11. He had set himself afire May 10 in protest against the war.

Pennsylvania State University, with 18 campuses, was closed May 6 but was reopened May 7.

The 27 colleges of the University of Georgia system were also shut temporarily.

Gov. Louie B. Nunn sent 250 National Guardsmen "with mounted bayonets and live ammunition" May 5 to the University of Kentucky, where 6 students were arrested and 1,000 other protesters dispersed.

Illinois Gov. Richard Ogilvie ordered 5,000 National Guard troops on duty at various troubled campuses throughout the state May 6. A state of emergency was declared at Southern Illinois University (Carbondale) May 8 as Guardsmen hurled tear gas and advanced with fixed bayonets to rout demonstrators. Officials at the university decided May 18 to close the school for the rest of the term. 3 students from the university had been injured May 15 when an explosion damaged a house in a predominantly Negro section of Carbondale. Assistant Dean George Turner of Illinois State University (Normal) was hospitalized with a head injury received during a battle between about 50 students and an equal number of police May 14. 33 people were arrested in an antiwar disruption at Northern Illinois University in De Kalb May 19.

Texas Rangers and highway patrolmen were stationed at the state capitol in Austin May 6 in preparation for an expected protest by University of Texas students.

At Harvard University, truck drivers belonging to the Teamsters union honored student picket lines around campus buildings May 6.

Gov. Robert E. McNair dispatched 150 troops May 7 to the University of South Carolina in Columbia, where 36 students were arrested after a sitdown strike in a campus building. McNair declared a state of emergency on the campus May 11 after police and National Guardsmen confronted brick-throwing students. A curfew was maintained at the university May 14, but Gov. McNair praised faculty and student leaders for helping to reduce tension.

At least 4 students were reported wounded by birdshot pellets at the University of Buffalo (N.Y.) May 7, but police denied firing on students and said they did not carry shotguns.

Troops moved onto the University of New Mexico campus May 8, and a university information officer said there were reports that at least 7 students had been wounded by bayonets. 3 students had been reported stabbed May 6 in a flag-raising dispute at the university.

Helmeted construction workers broke up student antiwar demonstrations in New York City's Wall Street May 8. 70 people were injured in the fighting, including 3 policemen. The workers, yelling "All the way U.S.A." and "Love it or leave it," then stormed City Hall and forced officials to raise to full staff the U.S. flag that had been placed at half staff in mourning for the students killed at Kent State University. At a news conference May 9, Mayor John Lindsay said that New Yorkers had "witnessed a breakdown of the police as the barrier between them and wanton violence." He said that violence by "marauding bands of construction workers" had been appalling, and he charged that police had failed to contain it.

2,000 construction workers and their supporters again marched through Wall Street May 11. Enough police were on hand to control the demonstration, but several bystanders were punched and kicked. The workers carried signs saying "Lindsay is a bum" and "Impeach the Red Mayor." Lindsay praised the police May 11 for acting "alertly, skillfully and professionally" to control the crowds.

Construction workers again gathered on Wall Street May 12 across police barricades from about 1,000 antiwar students from a dozen graduate business schools of Eastern universities. The students had short hair, wore coats and ties and claimed that they voiced opposition to the war from the "Establishment."

Troops were ordered on standby at the University of Iowa May 9. State police arrested 68 protesters at the University of Virginia May 9 after an apparently spontaneous demonstration in Charlottesville.

A Miami, Fla. circuit court judge ordered the resumption of classes at the University of Miami in Coral Gables May 9 in a ruling on a suit brought by 2 law students.

The State Court of Appeals in Albany, N.Y. held May 12 that law students must complete a specified number of classroom hours and take final exams to be eligible for state Bar examinations. Law students at New York University (NYU) and at other campuses had voted to boycott classes, and an NYU spokesman had said students who elected to stay out of class could receive course credits.

Michigan Gov. William Miliken declared a state of emergency and a dusk-to-dawn curfew at Eastern Michigan University in Ypsilanti May 13 as police used tear gas to disperse antiwar demonstrators.

At the University of Denver, National Guardsmen moved onto the campus May 13 after antiwar protesters evacuated a shantytown commune that had been built on the campus. The troops had been alerted May 12 following campus demonstrations.

2,000 college students gathered on the Kansas state capitol grounds in Topeka May 13 to petition Gov. Robert Docking to call a special session of the legislature to consider antiwar legislation.

Northwestern University (Evanston, Ill.) resumed classes May 13 after students voted to end a strike, but 5 buildings were closed May 14 because of bomb threats.

Ohio University (Athens) was closed early May 15, and about 1,500 National Guardsmen with loaded rifles patrolled the campus after the 2d night of disturbances involving rock-throwing students and police armed with tear gas.

Protests at a number of schools May 15 centered on the death of 2 students shot by highway patrolmen at Jackson State College in Mississippi.

About 500 University of Pennsylvania students walked out of commencement exercises for 3,784 graduates May 18. The walkout was urged by an antiwar speaker. Protests and disruptions at a number of campuses May 19 led to arrests by state and local police: University of Alabama (Tuscaloosa), 37 arrests; Florida Memorial College (Opa-Locka), 46 arrests; and Michigan State University (Lansing), 132 arrests.

The strike movement waned by mid- and late May. The strike center at Brandeis University had reported as of May 10 that 448 universities and colleges were on strike or closed. The Brandeis center said May 12 that 286 colleges continued on strike "indefinitely" and that class boycotts continued at some of the 129 schools in 49 states that had officially reopened May 11. It reported strike activity at 281 colleges and universities May 19, while news agency reports indicated that 15 institutions throughout the nation remained officially closed as of May 15.

Senate Aroused by Move into Cambodia

The first announcement of U.S. involvement in the Cambodia incursions, supporting the South Vietnamese thrust into the Parrot's Beak sector Apr. 29, had drawn angry Senate responses, some from those who generally supported the Administration's Vietnam policy. Sen. George D. Aiken (R., Vt.) said Apr. 29 that he "did not think the President would do what he reportedly has done." Sen. John Sherman Cooper (R., Ky.) called the action a "U-turn" in the Administration's Southeast Asia policy. Sen. Norris Cotton (R., N.H.) expressed shock and dismay and said he anticipated early Senate action "to register its disapproval." Senate Democratic Leader Mike Mansfield (Mont.) announced his backing of a move to bar Congressionally appropriated funds for military operations in Cambodia.

Other criticism came from New York Republican Sens. Jacob K. Javits (who said it meant "the President's decision to expand the war") and Charles E. Goodell (who said it "demonstrates how the strategy of Vietnamization has failed and how it pulls us inexorably into a wider war").

The Parrot's Beak action was backed Apr. 29 by Chairman John Stennis (D., Miss.) of the Senate Armed Services Committee, assistant Senate Republican Leader Robert P. Griffin (Mich.) and Sens. John G. Tower (R., Tex.) and Peter H. Dominick (R., Colo.). Stennis said it "could be a turning point in the war for us for the good." It was not, in itself, "an escalation—not yet, not yet," Stennis said. Griffin said the President's national security adviser, Henry A. Kissinger, had advised him that the operation was "a limited action" undertaken to protect U.S. troops in Vietnam and was in no way related to the Cambodian request for U.S. military assistance. Chairman J. William Fulbright (D., Ark.) of the Senate Foreign Relations Committee, whose committee had met 2 days earlier with State Secy. William P. Rogers, said the Cambodia action was "directly contrary to what we had been led to believe." He warned that it might lead to a North Vietnamese "move on Pnompenh, and then one thing leads to another." His committee approved a statement expressing "deep concern" over the possibility of further U.S. involvement in Cambodia.

As U.S. forces became directly involved in the fighting, driving into the Fishhook area of Cambodia Apr. 30, Senate critics of the Administration voiced increasing concern.

Cooper said he thought that "the risks of escalation and prolongation of our presence in South Vietnam are much greater than the possible benefits." Aiken warned that "the President is taking a long chance." Sen. Lee Metcalf (D., Mont.) said Nixon "has definitely made it his war. The risks are considerable." Sen. Edmund S. Muskie (D., Me.) said the President was either "wrong 10 days ago" when he announced plans to withdraw 150,000 troops "or he is wrong now." Sen. Fred R. Harris (D., Okla.) said Nixon had indicated that he "might hold off the troop withdrawals and might in some way escalate the war, depending on Hanoi's reactions." Sen. Edward W. Brooke (R., Mass.) said the President had "undertaken an extremely hazardous policy."

In contrast, Sen. Marlow W. Cook (R., Ky.) said he thought Nixon had "shown more honesty than anyone involved in this thing." Stennis said "it was time to do it if we are going to continue Vietnamization." Sen. John G. Tower (R., Tex.) said the logic of the action was "unassailable" in that it was not a new war nor another Vietnam but "it is Vietnam."

Fulbright, while stressing the Senate Foreign Relations Committee's attempt to exercise its responsibility in a "restrained" way to persuade the President to adopt its way of thinking, made clear May 1 that his committee nearly unanimously opposed the dispatch of U.S. troops into Cambodia, which he said could result in "a major enlargement" of the war. He also brought up, as did Sen. Albert Gore (D., Tenn.), the issue of Constitutional authority.

Mansfield said on the Senate floor May 1 that the "vital" concern of the nation "must be to end our involvement in the war in Vietnam. It is not to become bogged down in another war in all of Indochina." But Senate Republican Leader Hugh Scott (Pa.) defended the President's action as a "courageous" decision that could shorten the war.

Informed May 2 of the new U.S. bombing of North Vietnam, Mansfield said "events are piling upon events in a way which indicates that there is without question a stepup in the fighting, which means, in plain English, an escalation of the war." "It is a difficult situation to reconcile one's mind to," he said, "because the outlook seems to be getting grimmer by the day." Fulbright said "it looks as if the President is following what he has been urged to do by many members of Congress—

to seek a military decision and knock North Vietnam out of the war."

The Senate Foreign Relations (Fulbright) Committee charged May 4 that the executive branch over the years had been "conducting a Constitutionally unauthorized, Presidential war in Indochina." It said the Nixon Administration, by sending U.S. troops into Cambodia "without the consent or knowledge of Congress," was usurping Congress' war-making powers. The White House, in a statement by Press Secy. Ronald L. Ziegler, rejected the charge and said the President's action had been taken as commander-in-chief to protect the security of U.S. forces in Vietnam. The committee's charges were made in a report urging the repeal of the 1964 Tonkin Gulf Resolution, often cited by the Johnson Administration as the legal basis for the U.S. military buildup in Vietnam. (The report was withdrawn May 5 and returned to committee for deletion of the Cambodia references after 2 members, Cooper and Sen. John J. Williams [R., Del.] objected and pointed out that the report had not been approved by the full committee.)

The Senate Foreign Relations Committee May 1 had requested a meeting with Nixon to discuss the Cambodian developments. The White House assented but broadened the proposed session to a joint meeting with the House Foreign Affairs Committee. In addition, it invited the Senate and House Armed Services Committees to a separate joint session. While accepting the offer May 4, the Fulbright committee indicated that it would still seek a separate Presidential consultation. The chairman of the House counterpart committee, Rep. Thomas E. Morgan (D., Pa.) commented May 4 that "the House and Senate share an equal responsibility in this vital matter." The meetings, attended by 28 Senators and 72 Representatives, were held May 5.

Afterwards, several participants reported that Nixon had expressed "a firm commitment" that U.S. troops would be withdrawn from Cambodia in 3 to 7 weeks and would not penetrate deeper than 30-35 kilometers (18.6-21.7 miles) into Cambodia without Congressional approval being sought. Sen. Stuart Symington (D., Mo.), a member of both the Armed Services and Foreign Relations Committees, reported on the Senate floor that the White House session did "little to lessen my apprehension." Aiken said that "not a wealth of new information was presented ... nor would I say that many minds were changed." Fulbright also said he had heard "nothing new" and objected to the format of the meeting, which Nixon conducted like a news conference with, Fulbright said, no chance for informative discussion.

(In broadcast interviews May 17, Mansfield and Fulbright again denounced the thrust into Cambodia. Mansfield, on the CBS "Face the Nation" program, viewed the Senate proposal to cut off funds for future Cambodia-like operations as "a protective device which will give ... [the President] support and strength when he needs it because there will be other voices, undoubtedly, at that time trying to bring about a change in the situation." Fulbright, on the ABC "Issues and Answers" broadcast, called the Cambodian thrust "a serious international disaster" that would prolong the war and had already "clearly weakened our power to influence the situation in the Middle East or nearly anywhere else." He accused Nixon of having "subverted the Constitution in invading another country without authorization of Congress.")

Student Protesters Shift Focus to Washington

Increasing numbers of students and faculty members turned from street and campus demonstrations to an intensive lobbying effort in Washington in an attempt to persuade members of Congress to oppose the war in Vietnam and the use of U.S. troops in Cambodia.

Almost the entire student body at Haverford College (Pa.)—accompanied by professors, administration members, employes and Bryn Mawr students—converged on Washington May 7 for a day of discussions with Congress members.

A law school lobbying effort against the war was started at a meeting of student leaders from 12 Northeastern law schools at New York University the night of May 5-6. Students and professors taking part in this effort began converging on Washington, where they went to headquarters set up at George Washington University and sought meetings with virtually every member of Congress.

Columbia University professors began a phone campaign May 6 to mobilize colleagues at campuses across the nation on behalf of a newly organized Academic & Professional Lobby for a Responsible Congress. By the following day, the group's spokesmen reported, faculty delegations for antiwar lobbying had been set up at 13 schools, most of them in the Northeast.

With student lobbyists milling through Capitol halls May 7, the House rejected, 220-134, a proposal by Rep. Edward P. Boland (D., Mass.) to set a July 1 cutoff for funds used to maintain ground combat troops in Cambodia. The House was considering a $20.2 billion defense authorization bill. Rep. Ogden R. Reid (R., N.Y.) Apr. 30 had introduced an amendment to bar funds for the support of U.S. ground troops in Cambodia, Laos or Thailand. But a vote, taken May 6, came on an amendment offered by Rep. Paul Findley (R., Ill.) as a substitute for the Reid proposal. The Findley amendment, indorsed May 5 by Nixon as "splendid," would have barred funds in the bill for the introduction of ground troops into those areas without the consent of Congress unless the President deemed the action necessary to protect the lives of U.S. forces in Vietnam. The Findley amendment was tentatively approved May 6 by 171-144 vote but rejected by a 221-32 final vote. (The seeming reversal was interpreted as a way of both approving the President's action and skirting the Constitutional issue involved in the President's acting without specific sanction from Congress.)

Among college lobbying groups in Washington May 11 were 600 Brandeis University students, a delegation from the small Church of the Brethren school in Indiana, representatives from 9 eastern Pennsylvania colleges and groups from the University of California, the University of Minnesota, Colgate University and the University of Virginia.

In an outgrowth of Princeton's decision to declare a 2-week recess before the November elections for political activity, student and faculty representatives from 29 universities had met in New York May 9 to create a Movement for a New Congress. The group formed a steering committee with headquarters at Princeton and started plans for campaigning efforts on behalf of peace candidates facing primary battles in a number of states.

12 Harvard professors, each of whom had served as a Presidential adviser, met May 8 with Pres. Nixon's national security affairs adviser, Henry A. Kissinger, to announce their public break with Nixon Administration domestic policies and policies in Southeast Asia. Among the group were Edwin Reischauer, former ambassador to Japan; George Kistiakowsky, chief science adviser to the late Pres. Dwight D. Eisenhower; Richard Neustadt, who had been a member of ex-Pres. Harry S. Truman's White House staff; Ernest May, a former Army historian; Thomas Schelling, consultant to the Defense Department; Francis Bator, former special assistant to ex-Pres. Lyndon B. Johnson; Adam Yarmolinsky, former special assistant to the Defense Secretary; and William Capron, former assistant director of the budget.

Antiwar Rally in Washington

A crowd estimated at 60,000 to 100,000 held an antiwar demonstration in Washington May 9. The rally had been hastily organized by the New Mobilization Committee to End the War in Vietnam (New Mobe) after Pres. Nixon's announcement Apr. 30 of the U.S. thrust into Cambodia, but a more massive assembly was quickly arranged after the deaths at Kent State University.

More than 5,000 troops had been placed on alert, but the mass demonstration proved to be peaceful. After the rally ended, however, police used tear gas to disperse small bands of demonstrators who roamed through the streets causing disruptions and throwing rocks.

The White House approached the demonstration in a more conciliatory manner than the previous mass protest in the capital in Nov. 1969. Troops remained out of sight. Nixon voiced his belief that the demonstrators had peaceful intentions; he made a surprise dawn appearance at the Lincoln Memorial, and Administration aides mingled with the crowd. A requirement of 15 days' advance notice for demonstrations in the capital was waived at the government's request, and protesters were allowed to rally at the Ellipse, south of the White House.

The crowd was overwhelmingly young and white; it consisted mainly of college students. Speakers at the rally denounced the President and his policy in Vietnam and Cambodia. Stewart Meacham of the American Friends Service Committee urged the group to "shut down the production of weapons ... not just the universities." David Livingston of the Wholesale, Retail & Office Workers Union called for the impeachment of Nixon and a nationwide general strike against the war. Although Congress members were not among the speakers, 9 members of the House appeared on the speaker's stand, and Republican Sens. Jacob K. Javits (N.Y.), Charles E. Goodell (N.Y.) and Edward W. Brooke (Mass.) mingled with the crowd.

As the rally began to break up, some 700 persons bearing coffins draped in black marched to Arlington Cemetery. More militant protesters, some carrying rocks and sticks, moved toward the Justice and Labor Department buildings. 30 persons tried to turn over one of a line of buses blocking off the White House area. Police began to use tear gas to disperse the demonstrators. At the end of the day police said 14 persons had been arrested; 5 of them were counter-protesters, including 3 identified as members of the American Nazi Party.

More serious disturbances occurred the next morning. Protesters set fire to a car and truck early May 10 and stoned police and firemen on the George Washington University campus. After leaving the campus, students caused disruptions at the Washington Monument, and a bomb exploded at the headquarters of the U.S. National Guard Association. Police arrested about 375 persons, mostly at the university. Damage was estimated at $1,000,

The Administration at first had refused to permit the demonstrators to rally near the White House. It had said that the protest would have to be confined to the Washington Monument grounds. The New Mobe had originally sought use of Lafayette Square, directly across the street from the White House. Ron Young, organizer of the New Mobe protest, had said May 6 that the protesters would demonstrate as close to the White House as police barricades allowed. He added that if police and troops "gas us and beat us ..., then it is their demonstration, their violence." Later that night the committee asked that the Ellipse be approved as a compromise site.

After pleas from city officials and Congress members, the Administration said May 8 that the rally could be held at the Ellipse. White House Press Secy. Ronald L. Ziegler said the Ellipse "will provide appropriate space and an environment in which people can peacefully express themselves, and the President is convinced that the vast majority have that in mind."

New Mobe had announced plans for the rally May 1. At a news conference called by the committee May 5, Dr. Benjamin Spock, a leading antiwar activist, had said: "The government is committing titanic violence in Vietnam and Cambodia.... We must stand up in opposition to the government's illegal, immoral and brutal war." Rabbi Balfour Brickner, a member of the steering committee of Clergy & Laymen Concerned About Vietnam, said in reference to the Kent State shootings: "The shots that were fired were the first shots fired in a new and terrifying civil war in America."

Spock had been one of 75 persons arrested May 3 during a peaceful rally across from the White House called by the clergy and laymen group and the Fellowship of Reconciliation in protest against Nixon's decision to send troops into Cambodia. The protesters, charged with disorderly conduct, had been arrested because they failed to give police the required 15 days' notice of their demonstration. Others arrested included Sam Brown, David Hawk and David Mixner of the disbanded Vietnam Moratorium Committee; the Rev. Dr. John C. Bennett, retiring president of the Union Theological Seminary; the Rev. David R. Hunter, deputy general secretary of the National Council of Churches; and the Rev. Richard Fernandez, executive secretary of Clergy & Laymen Concerned About the War in Vietnam.

Nixon & Agnew Score Campus Rioters

Pres. Nixon had provoked controversy May 1 when he contrasted the "bums ... blowing up the campuses" with the "kids" fighting the war in Vietnam, who, he said, were "the greatest."

Speaking informally with civilian employes at the Pentagon, where he attended a briefing on the Cambodia developments, Nixon said: "You see these bums, you know, blowing up the campuses. Listen, the boys that are on the college campuses today are the luckiest people in the world, going to the greatest universities, and here they are burning up the books, storming around about this issue. You name it. Get rid of the war there will be another one. Then out there [in Vietnam] we have kids who are just doing their duty. They stand tall and they are proud.... They are going to do fine and we have to stand in back of them."

Earlier remarks by Vice Pres. Spiro T. Agnew on college turmoil had also stirred bitter dispute. Speaking at a GOP fund-raising dinner in Hollywood, Fla. Apr. 28, Agnew, denouncing student violence, had referred to students at Cornell University "who, wielding pipes and tire chains, beat a dormitory president into unconsciousness." Cornell Pres. Dale R. Corson, in a telegram April 29, said "no such incident has ever occurred at Cornell." Agnew's office acknowledged that the incident had occurred not at Cornell but at the University of Connecticut, but it listed a number of violent student activities at Cornell. Corson rebutted these charges as containing "inaccuracies and disrespect for the judicial process."

A dispute had also flared between Agnew and New York Mayor John V. Lindsay, who had referred Apr. 29 to "the intemperate language of the Vice President" heightening tension "at a university [Yale] already on the edge of turmoil." Speaking at the University of Pennsylvania in Philadelphia, Lindsay expressed "unending admiration" for those "heroic" enough to refuse to serve in Vietnam and willing to take the consequences. He stressed, however, that the course of justice would not be served "if we embrace revolutionary violence." Agnew, in a Washington speech May 4, referred to Lindsay and criticized "men, now in power in this country, who do not represent authority, who cannot cope with tradition and who believe that the people of America are ready to support revolution as long as it is done with a cultured voice and a handsome profile."

Nixon Seeks to Assure Nation

Pres. Nixon held a televised news conference May 8 to defend the use of U.S. troops in Cambodia as a necessary step to speed the end of American involvement in the war in Indochina. The President said preliminary briefings from U.S. field officers indicated that the joint operations of South Vietnamese regulars and U.S. troops were so successful that some American units could be shifted out of Cambodia by May 16. He said all U.S. ground forces would be redeployed outside Cambodia by the end of June.

Nixon, noting that his decision had triggered a wave of protests on college campuses across the country, said he shared the goals and objectives of his critics, but he added that time and history would prove that his decision "served the cause of a just peace in Vietnam."

Among remarks made by Nixon at his May 8 press conference:

Progress of the war —U.S. operations in Cambodia would win 6 to 8 months of time for the further training of South Vietnamese regulars and thus shorten the time of U.S. involvement. Most American troops would be out of Cambodia by the middle of June, and some combat units would be withdrawn during the week ending May 16. The move into Cambodia would not necessarily jeopardize Nixon's avowed plans to withdraw 150,000 men from Vietnam by the spring of 1971.

Nixon's decision to move troops into Cambodia was precipitated by reports of increased enemy action in Cambodia. Those Communist moves could "leave the 240,000 Americans who would be there [in South Vietnam] a year from now without many combat troops to help defend them ... in an untenable position"

Despite the new moves into Cambodia, the U.S. would continue to seek an accord at the peace talks in Paris.

The units of the South Vietnamese army that had been participating in the Cambodian operations with U.S. troops would not necessarily be bound by the June deadline that Nixon had set for the withdrawal of American forces. Nixon, however, expected the pullback of South Vietnamese forces to come "approximately at the same time that we do, because when we come out our logistical support and air support will also come out with them."

Nixon was planning a televised speech to the American people in June to explain the outcome of the U.S. operation in Cambodia. Nixon intended to respond in full at that time to questions about the success of the mission. However, all preliminary reports indicated that the operation was a success. "We have also saved, I think, hundreds if not thousands of Americans. Rockets by the thousands and small arms by the millions have already been captured, and those rockets and small arms will not be killing Americans in these next few months."

As for new U.S. bombing strikes against North Vietnam, "if the North Vietnamese did what some have suggested they might do—move a massive force of 250,000-300,000 across the DMZ [demilitarized zone] against our Marine Corps people who are there—I would certainly not allow those men to be massacred without using force and more effective force against North Vietnam."

The U.S. would continue to explore all diplomatic channels in an attempt to secure Cambodia's neutrality once U.S. troops were withdrawn. The U.S. would seek continued sessions with the Soviet Union, Britain and Asian nations "to see that neutrality is guaranteed without having the intervention of foreign forces." In line with the Nixon Doctrine, the U.S. did not intend to send American troops to protect Cambodia itself.

Nixon was not responsible for the war in Vietnam, and the move into Cambodia did not represent an expansion of the war. When he had become President, "I found 525,000 Americans [in Vietnam], and my responsibility is to do everything that I could to protect their lives and to get them home as quickly as I can." Considering that the U.S. was involved in the war, "if we do what many of our sincere critics think we should do—withdraw from Vietnam and allow the enemy to come into Vietnam and massacre the civilians there by the millions, as they would—if we do that, let me say that America is finished insofar as a peacekeeper in the Asian world is concerned."

Domestic reaction —The intensity of the protests against his decision on Cambodia had not taken Nixon by surprise. He shared the goals and concerns of student protesters, and "I know that what I have done will accomplish the goals they want." He was concerned about the protesters "because I know how deeply they feel." Nixon would like to open meaningful communications with the nation's youths. To achieve that end, Alexander Heard, chancellor of Vanderbilt University, had agreed to take a 2-month leave from his post to seek to establish more open dialogue between the youths and their government. Heard's task would be to keep the President "fully and currently informed on the thinking of the academic community." (Nixon had announced Heard's appointment as his personal adviser on campus problems earlier May 8.)

The President said he would not "censor" Vice Pres. Agnew. He thus contradicted reports from a spokesman for 8 university presidents who had conferred with him May 7. Nixon also said he would make no effort to restrain Interior Secy. Walter J. Hickel, who had called the Administration insensitive to the concerns of students. The President said he would "of course, be interested in his [Hickel's] advice."

The President also clarified his May 1 comment on the use of the word "bums" to describe some student rioters. He said he regretted that his use of the word was "interpreted to apply to those who dissent." He said "when students on university campuses burn buildings, when they engage in violence, when they break up furniture, when they terrorize their fellow students and terrorize the faculty, I think bums is perhaps too kind a word to apply to that kind of person. Those are the kind I was referring to."

The President declined to elaborate on the Kent State shootings "in advance of getting" all the facts. Nixon said that he had seen the pictures of the slain students in a newspaper and that he had vowed "that we are going to find methods that would be more effective to deal with the problems of violence ... methods that would not take the lives of innocent people."

Nixon's May 8 news conference had been preceded and followed by personal meetings with students, college presidents, state governors and labor leaders. In these discussions, Nixon reiterated his defense of his decision to move into Cambodia and continued to express optimism about the ultimate success of the operations.

The President met with student protesters May 6 and 9.
The first meeting was at the White House with 6 Kent State
University students who had come to Washington to see their
Congressman, Rep. J. William Stanton (R., Ohio). The 2d
meeting was a pre-dawn visit to the Lincoln Memorial.
The Kent State students had met May 5 with Presidential
Assistant John D. Ehrlichman. They had already met with
Stanton, who had called the White House. The Presidential
invitation followed. The students later reported telling Nixon
that the campus unrest was caused by opposition to the
Vietnam war, the extension of it to Cambodia and a lack of
communication between youth and college administrations and
the federal government. They said the President promised a full
report on the killing of the Kent State students "to find out
where the errors were made." He also suggested, they related,
basic goals that might "minimize" the student dissent—ending
the war in Vietnam, avoiding similar overseas entanglements in
the future, slowing the arms race and creating a volunteer
army. (Another student confrontation with high-level
Administration personnel took place May 6—10 students and 5
faculty members from Stanford University met with
Ehrlichman and Henry A. Kissinger, the President's adviser on
national security affairs.)

The President's pre-dawn tour May 9, the day of the
student antiwar protest in Washington, lasted 3½ hours and
involved an hour's chat with youths on the steps of the Lincoln
Memorial. Nixon was accompanied only by a valet and several
Secret Service men. On his return to the White House, Nixon
told a *Washington Star* reporter that he had tried "to relate" to
the students "in a way they could feel that I understood their
problems." He asked them, he said, "to try to understand what
we are doing," that "I know you think we are a bunch of so and
sos—I used a stronger word to them. I know how you feel—you
want to get the war over.... Sure, you came here to
demonstrate and shout your slogans on the Ellipse. That is all
right. Just keep it peaceful. Remember, I feel just as deeply as
you do about this."

2 Syracuse University students present commented later.
Ronnie Kemper said: "It was unreal. He was trying so hard to
relate on a personal basis, but he wasn't really concerned with
why we were here." Joan Pelletier said: She hoped "it was

because he was tired, but most of what he was saying was absurd. Here we had come from a university that's completely uptight, on strike, and when we told him where we were from, he talked about the football team. And when someone said he was from California, he talked about surfing."

Nixon met with the presidents of the 8 universities May 7 and reportedly assured them that hostile attacks on students by members of his Administration would cease. The educators later said that they had found the President "an attentive listener" while they had spoken of "the deep and widening apprehensions on campuses everywhere and the reasons for them." In a statement, they said they had given the President their "assessment of the distress, frustration and anger among students and faculty across the nation—reactions that result from the developments in Southeast Asia, hostile comments by members of the Administration about campus events and persons and the tragic incidents that have occurred on several campuses."

Harvard Pres. Nathan Pusey, who read the statement, was asked if the President had assured the group that the hostile statements would cease. He replied "yes." In addition to Pusey, the university heads meeting with Nixon were Malcolm C. Moos (University of Minnesota), William C. Friday (University of North Carolina), Fred H. Harrington (University of Wisconsin), Alexander Heard (Vanderbilt), Charles J. Hitch (University of California), Edward H. Levi (University of Chicago), and W. Allen Wallis (University of Rochester).

At his news conference May 8, Nixon said that the educators had "raised questions" about Agnew and "other people in the Administration, about the rhetoric," but that he "did not indicate to them that I was going to muzzle" Agnew or "censor" him. Nixon said that he would not try "to tone" Agnew down and that he hoped everyone in his Administration would keep in mind "a rule that I have always had, . . . when the action is hot, keep the rhetoric cool."

The Cambodian decision and campus turmoil were the subjects of a 4-hour White House meeting May 11 with 46 state and territorial governors. In addition to Nixon, the group also heard from Agnew, State Secy. Rogers and Labor Secy. George P. Shultz. The need for more and better communication between the government and the public, especially the campus community, and between the various levels of government, reportedly was stressed. According to Gov. Raymond P. Shafer (R., Pa.), "the problem of communication was discussed in great depth and it was suggested that channels of communication should be established by the governors. It is very clear most of the problems are based on a lack of understanding."

There were conflicting accounts of Agnew's role and language during the meeting. Some said he had an exchange with Gov. Frank Licht (D., R.I.). Others, including Licht, denied any "confrontation." Some said Agnew spoke of the "anti-intellectuals" dominating many campuses and the need to restore "authority" and clear out the "radicals and rascals." White House Press Secy. Ronald L. Ziegler said he heard no such words. Agnew, he said, "referred to the fact that he would like to go on campuses and speak" and "to the fact that it is difficult to do so because of the problem of being heard."

Nixon told labor leaders May 12 that the operations in Cambodia were an "enormous success"—that 5,000 of the enemy had been killed in action and more ammunition captured than the enemy had expended in South Vietnam in the last 5 or 6 months. AFL-CIO Pres. George Meany reported that the President had said "they're knocking out the sanctuaries ahead of schedule." (Nixon made the remarks during a surprise visit to AFL-CIO headquarters, where its executive council was beginning a 2-day quarterly meeting. The 35-man council May 13, with only 3 dissents and one absention, indorsed a May 1 statement by Meany in support of Nixon's Cambodia operation.)

At a Medal of Honor ceremony May 14 Nixon said the war in Southeast Asia was often "not understood and not supported in this country," but "as time goes on, millions more of your countrymen will look back and they will reach the conclusion that you served the cause of the land of the free by being brave—brave beyond the call of duty."

The President conferred May 14 with Raymond Gallagher, national commander of the Veterans of Foreign Wars, who expressed support for the Nixon policies in Southeast Asia. (Gallagher and American Legion National Commander J. Milton Patrick were taken by Senate Republican Leader Hugh

Scott May 13 to the Senate press gallery, where they released a joint statement condemning the actions of Senators "who would tie the President's hands" with proposals that amounted to "a declaration of surrender to Communist forces" and constituted "a stab in the back for our boys in combat." Scott May 15 sent a letter of apology to Fulbright and others sponsoring such proposals. Dissociating himself from the statement, he said the veterans' leaders had been taken to the gallery at the request of the White House, and he had not known beforehand what they were going to say.)

Dissent Within the Administration

A letter urging Nixon to establish communication with the nation's youth in view of their violent opposition to the war had been sent to the President by Interior Secy. Walter J. Hickel May 6. Hickel suggested that Agnew stop attacking youth and urged the President to consult with members of Congress. The letter, purportedly a private communication, was leaked to the press shortly after its transmittal to the White House. Hickel stressed in his letter that "youth in its protest must be heard." He warned that the Administration was "embracing a philosophy which appears to lack appropriate concern" for youth and that a deliberate attempt to alienate youth was wrong "politically or philosophically." "A vast segment" of the young people, he said, felt there was "no opportunity to communicate with government ... other than through violent confrontation."

Nixon sent an aide, John C. Whitaker, to confer with Hickel May 7. Asked at his news conference May 8 about the incident, Nixon said that Hickel was "outspoken" and "courageous" and held "very strong views." That was why he was in the cabinet and why the President had defended him when Hickel had come under earlier attack, Nixon said. As for Hickel's advice, Nixon said he would, of course, "be interested" in it. Hickel May 8 lauded the President's remarks at his news conference on the nation's youth, saying young people "should be reassured by the President's determination to work together with all those millions of Americans who share his loyalty to the nation, if not always the same views."

Other dissent within the Administration over the Cambodian military involvement was reported although cabinet members reportedly involved later affirmed their support of the President in his action.

According to press reports May 6, Defense Secy. Melvin R. Laird and State Secy. William P. Rogers had serious reservations about the use of U.S. troops in Cambodia, largely because of concern about domestic political repercussions. Laird was said to have held out for no more involvement than the assignment of advisers and air support to South Vietnamese troops. Rogers was quoted (in excerpts released May 5 from secret Congressional testimony given Apr. 23, 4 days before the final decision on Cambodian troop use) as saying the Administration had "no incentive to escalate" since "we recognize that if we escalate and we get involved in Cambodia with our ground troops that our whole program [presumably Vietnamization] is defeated." "Our whole incentive is to de-escalate," he told a House Appropriations subcommittee. The "one lesson" that the Vietnam war "has taught us," he said, "is that if you are going to fight a war of this kind satisfactorily you need public support and congressional support."

Laird announced May 6 that he had "supported fully" the President's decision. He stressed May 11 that the U.S. operation in Cambodia "was to last from 3 to 6 weeks, and the timetable will be met." The U.S. troops had to be withdrawn from Cambodia before the monsoons began, he said. He specifically noted that the timetable would be met despite reports from field commanders in Cambodia that the deadline would not allow enough time to search all the occupied territory and remove or destroy all the enemy supplies found.

Nixon, asked at his news conference if Rogers had opposed the Cambodian decision, said May 8 that "every one of my advisers" had "raised questions about the decision and, believe me, I raised the most questions because I knew the stakes that were involved," "the division that would be caused in this country," "the problems internationally" and "the military risks." "I made this decision," the President said. "I take the responsibility for it. I believe it was the right decision. I believe it will work out. If it doesn't, then I am to blame."

2 other cabinet members made public statements about the U.S. involvement in Cambodia:

● Health, Education & Welfare Secy. Robert H. Finch said, after a series of meetings with young war protesters May 9, that the President would have a "very serious case of credibility" if the U.S. troops were not withdrawn from Cambodia by the July 1 target date. Finch had told reporters May 7 that the campus turmoil had reached the proportions of a "national crisis" and that the Cambodian venture was "the straw that broke the camel's back."

● Housing & Urban Development Secy. George Romney, in a New York speech May 11, called the Vietnam war "the most tragic foreign policy mistake in the nation's history." He said he did not believe a democracy could "successfully engage in foreign military operations, except when responding to attack, without following constitutional processes." He defended the U.S. move into Cambodia, however, as a "tactical" operation. Romney commented on the Hickel letter at a news conference May 11. He said that Hickel had "rendered a real service" and that he was pleased the President "recognized that he had made a sound suggestion and acted promptly."

Anthony J. (Toby) Moffett Jr., 25, head of the new Office of Students & Youth in the Office of Education, announced his resignation May 7. He had said May 6 that recent events had "convinced me that the advocacy function is impossible within the Nixon Administration." He objected to recent Presidential statements—Moffett called them "irresponsible"—on the killing of 4 Kent State University students and on certain student rioters as being "bums."

Morton H. Halperin said May 11 that he had indicated his protest against the Cambodia operation by submitting his resignation May 6 as a consultant to the National Security Council.

Non-Administration Leaders Protest

Vigorous criticism of the Cambodia operation came also from many public figures outside the Nixon Administration.

Ex-Defense Secy. Clark M. Clifford charged in the May 22 issue of *Life* magazine, published May 16, that the Cambodia incursion was "reckless" and "foolhardy" and that Vietnamization was "a formula for perpetual war." The U.S. should "get out of Vietnam on a scheduled and orderly basis no later than the end of 1971," Clifford said, and it should inform the North Vietnamese that a more rapid withdrawal could come if the safety of U.S. troops were assured by a cease-fire and cessation of military pressures in Laos and Cambodia. Clifford, who had served in the Johnson Administration, said the combat role of GIs in Southeast Asia should be ended no later than Dec. 31, 1970.

4 Protestant church leaders had assailed Nixon at a Washington news conference May 6 for sending U.S. troops into Cambodia. In a joint statement, the churchmen said "We have heard a pledge to bring us together, and see action which is at this moment further tearing our already weakened social fabric." They estimated that more than 500 church leaders and representatives were in Washington that day lobbying against the expansion of the war. The statement was issued by Bishop John Wesley Lord of Washington, president of the Council of Bishops of the United Methodist Church; Cynthia Wedel of Alexandria, Va., president of the National Council of Churches; William P. Thompson, chief executive of the United Presbyterian Church; and the Rev. Robert V. Moss of New York, president of the United Church of Christ.

W. Averell Harriman, chief negotiator at the Paris peace talks under the Johnson Administration, and Paul C. Warnke, Johnson's Assistant Defense Secretary for international affairs, said May 7 that the Cambodian action was an unwarranted expansion of the war. Both men were speaking at a Washington news conference on behalf of the Democratic Policy Council's International Affairs Committee. Harriman, chairman of the Committee, said: The intervention in Cambodia and renewed bombing of North Vietnam were "serious mistakes of judgment.... There is no conceivable military success in Cambodia worth the awful price we are paying at home and abroad." The Cambodian action was "demonstrable proof that the President does not have and never has had an effective plan for peace in Vietnam.... The simple truth is that there is no way of achieving a political victory in Vietnam through military actions."

John T. Connor, chairman of the board of the Allied Chemical Corp. and ex-Commerce Secretary under Lyndon B. Johnson, said May 8 that Nixon's decision to send U.S. troops into Cambodia "shakes the confidence of many Americans in his judgment and intentions." Addressing the Business Council, meeting in Hot Springs, Va., Connor said the President's action "will result in more widespread dissension in this country involving many other loyal citizens besides most of the young, the intellectuals and the blacks."

Lawrence F. O'Brien, Democratic National Committee chairman, charged May 9 that the Nixon Administration had attempted to "divide us as a nation, to polarize us, and to create anarchy." In a speech prepared for delivery at a Jefferson-Jackson Day dinner in Milwaukee, O'Brien said in reference to the Kent State tragedy: "I can only wonder with all of you whether those triggers would have been pulled if the elected leaders in this country had acted differently." He said that the President, in his news conference May 8, had been unable to supply any good reasons why U.S. troops had moved into Cambodia and instead had chosen "to fall back on lame military arguments and political rationalizations." He said Nixon's policy was "an open-ended U.S. commitment to sustain the existing South Vietnamese government by military force." (Democrats in Washington, where a copy of O'Brien's speech was released, saw the address as a major element in a Democratic offensive against the Nixon Administration's Indochina policy.)

6 prominent urbanists, in Washington to meet with Presidential aide Daniel P. Moynihan, said May 11 that they would try to dramatize "the connection between the war and domestic spending requirements." Charles M. Haar, Harvard University law professor and ex-Assistant Housing & Urban Development Secretary, said that "unless federal priorities are realigned ..., the crisis of the cities remains dangerously unmet." Others in the group were ex-HUD Undersecy. Robert C. Wood, who had served briefly as interim HUD secretary; William A. Doebele, Harvard professor of design; Bernard J. Frieden, Massachusetts Institute of Technology professor of urban planning; Lee Rainwater, Harvard professor of sociology; and Alonzo S. Yerby, associate dean of Harvard's school of public health.

Urban Coalition Chairman John W. Gardner, ex-HUD secretary, said May 13: "The nation disintegrates" and there was a "growing crisis of confidence in our leadership." "Nothing we are doing to help or harm our friends or foes in

Southeast Asia can compare to what we are doing to ourselves as a nation. The erosion of spirit that we have experienced is beyond calculation." Gardner's remarks were from a speech he was to have given at the Illinois Constitutional Convention in Springfield, Ill. The speech was canceled when convention leaders learned through an advance text that Gardner planned to assail Nixon's leadership. Gardner refused to change his speech, returned to Washington and released the address at a news conference.

Ford Foundation President McGeorge Bundy, an adviser to Presidents Kennedy and Johnson, said May 15: Another action like the Cambodian intervention "would tear the country and the Administration to pieces." It was imperative to "call in the Congress as a required partner in any such decision" and "a track that would have Congressional support" would be the withdrawal of U.S. troops from South Vietnam "at a rate which will be increased—and never decreased—until only volunteer supporting forces remain." "The maintenance of our own society is now more important by far than the precise rate of our disengagement in Vietnam."

At least one major voice was raised, however, to suggest a diminution of the criticism buffeting the President. At a dinner attended by Democratic Party members in Chicago May 1, ex-Pres. Johnson had said that Nixon should have the support of all "who want freedom" while he deliberated policy in Southeast Asia. "I hope," continued Johnson, "our President's voice is not drowned out by those other voices which are without knowledge and the responsibility to make this agonizing decision."

Administration Officials Explain Move

Nixon's pledge to limit the operations of American troops in Cambodia was further explained by Defense Secy. Melvin R. Laird and State Secy. William P. Rogers.

Laird, appearing May 12 before the Senate Armed Services Committee, said that several thousand U.S. troops had already been withdrawn from Cambodia, that by June 15 "the major portion of our forces" would be withdrawn and that all would leave Cambodia by the end of June.

Laird also said that: (a) the Cambodian government "was informed and it had no objections" to the operation prior to its initiation; (b) he would "not permit South Vietnamese forces to be tied down [in Cambodia] to such an extent that it in any way slows down the withdrawal of American forces"; (c) he would not rule out the possibility that South Vietnamese forces might return to Cambodia on their own in the future if Communist forces moved back into the sanctuary areas; (d) "the important thing that had an effect" on the President's decision to strike into Cambodia was information that the North Vietnamese "would in the coming months be using sanctuaries at an increasing rate to increase American casualties, and this would have a decided effect on public opinion in the United States."

Laird told reporters May 14 that in mid-April the Communists had begun moving out of their Cambodian sanctuaries westward toward Pnompenh, and "this was the time to hit" the sanctuaries because of the reduced risk to U.S. forces. The reduction in risk, he said, "changes my mind" concerning sending U.S. troops into Cambodia since, "at the start" of the planning for incursion, the Fishhook area "looked like a very tough area."

Laird was one of 3 top Administration officials—along with State Undersecy. Elliot L. Richardson and Henry A. Kissinger, the President's national security adviser—sent by Nixon May 14 to meet with Republican Senators to discuss strategy against proposed legislation to cut off funds for future military involvement in Cambodia without Congressional approval. Their argument was that passage of such a measure would imply a lack of confidence in the President and, in light of Nixon's pledge to withdraw U.S. troops from Cambodia by the end of June, could impair the President's "credibility" abroad.

In a Presidential statement released from Key Biscayne, Fla. May 15, White House Press Secy. Ronald L. Ziegler said: "It is our feeling there should be no restraint on the powers of the President as Commander in Chief" as "stated under the Constitution."

Rogers made a surprise appearance at a routine State Department briefing May 13 to affirm that the U.S. would not become "militarily involved" with troop or air support to defend the Cambodian government. He said that South

Vietnam and Thailand would be encouraged to cooperate with Cambodia in repulsing the Communist threat and that this policy was in line with the Nixon Doctrine idea of fostering cooperation among the Asians to handle their own problems. Rogers stressed that the Cambodian incursion was "not an escalation" nor "an attempt to win a military victory." He said Nixon had "committed himself to limitations of time and distance, and events will answer these anxieties." These limits, Rogers said, would also mellow the foreign reaction to the move, which initially had been "reserved or negative."

Nixon Gives Optimistic Progress Report

Pres. Nixon June 3 called the U.S. and South Vietnamese military thrust into Cambodia "the most successful operation of this long and very difficult war" in Indochina. Reporting to the nation in a televised address from the White House, Nixon said the successful operation "insured the continuance and success of our troop withdrawal program." He said 50,000 of the 150,000 U.S. troops whose withdrawal from Vietnam he had announced Apr. 20 "will now be out on Oct. 15."

Nixon said that the Cambodia operations also "guaranteed that the June 30 deadline I set for withdrawal of all American forces from Cambodia will be met" and that "this includes all American air support, logistics and military adviser personnel." "The only remaining American activity in Cambodia after July 1," he added, "will be air missions to interdict the movement of enemy troops and material where I find that is necessary to protect the lives and security of our men in South Vietnam." As for the South Vietnamese activity in Cambodia, Nixon said, "our discussions with the South Vietnamese government indicate that their primary objective remains the security of South Vietnam" and that their activity in Cambodia "after their withdrawal from the sanctuaries will be determined by the actions of the enemy in Cambodia."

If the enemy increased its attacks "in a way that jeopardizes the safety of the remaining [U.S.] forces in Vietnam," Nixon warned, "I shall, as my action 5 weeks ago clearly demonstrated, take strong and effective measures to deal with that situation."

The President said that "the door to a negotiated peace remains wide open. Every offer we have made at the conference table, publicly or privately, I herewith reaffirm. We are ready to negotiate whenever they are ready to negotiate." He reiterated his commitment to attain "a just peace in Vietnam." He called it "essential if there is to be a lasting peace in other parts of the world." "I pledged to end this war," Nixon said. "And I shall keep that promise. But I am determined to end the war in a way that will promote peace rather than conflict throughout the world. I am determined to end it in a way that will bring an era of reconciliation to our people—and not an era of furious recrimination.... We have a program for peace—and the greater the support the Administration receives in its efforts, the greater the opportunity to win that just peace we all desire."

The President took note of the "unprecedented barrage of criticism in this country" directed against his Cambodia decision. He expressed his "deep appreciation to the millions of Americans who supported me" and his understanding of "the deep divisions in this country over the war." He realized, he indicated, that many Americans were "deeply troubled" and wanted peace and "to bring the boys home." But, he said, "no group has a monopoly on those concerns. Every American shares those desires. I share them very deeply. Our differences are over the best means to achieve a just peace." Nixon's responsibility as President was to listen to those "who disagree with my policies" but also to make the "hard decisions" necessary to protect the lives of the U.S. troops in Vietnam, he asserted. If he had failed to meet the "clear threat" to these troops that "was emerging" in Cambodia a month before, he asked, "would those nations and peoples who rely on America's power and treaty commitments for their security—in Latin America, Europe, the Mideast, other parts in Asia—retain any confidence in the United States?"

Between Apr. 20 and 30, Nixon said, the Communists had attacked "a number of key cities" in Cambodia in an operation designed to link their bases together. "This posed an unacceptable threat" since the entire 600-mile Cambodia-South Vietnam border would then "become one continuous hostile territory from which to launch assaults upon American and allied forces." Furthermore, Nixon said, the enemy acted despite "an explicit warning from this government." Therefore, he concluded, "failure to deal with the enemy action would have eroded the credibility of the United States before the entire world." The Cambodia thrust had been ordered, he said, to destroy the major enemy bases along the Cambodian frontier, and he reported "that all of our major military objectives have been achieved."

The 43,000 South Vietnamese and 31,000 U.S. troops that took part in the operations, he said, "moved with greater speed and success than we had planned" and "captured and destroyed far more in war materiel than we anticipated." In addition, casualties were "far lower than we expected," he continued. "In the month of May, in Cambodia alone, we captured a total amount of enemy arms, equipment, ammunition and food nearly equal to what we captured in all of Vietnam in all of last year." The rice captured amounted to "more than enough ... to feed all the enemy's combat battalions in Vietnam for over 3 months," Nixon reported. It would take the enemy months "to rebuild his shattered installations" and replace the captured and destroyed equipment. (The President utilized film clips to show some of the captured war materiel and rice.)

In assessing the long-range effects, Nixon said, in addition to insuring the success of the U.S. withdrawal, the Cambodia thrust had eliminated an immediate security threat to the troops in Vietnam and had gained "precious time" for the South Vietnamese to prepare themselves to carry the burden of the war and release the U.S. troops. He said the splendid performance of the South Vietnamese army was "one of the most dramatic and heartening developments of the operation." Their "effectiveness, the skill, the valor with which they fought far exceeded our expectations," Nixon declared, and the operation "clearly demonstrated that our Vietnamization program is succeeding."

Nixon said he was encouraged "by the resolve of 11 Asian countries at the Jakarta conference to seek a solution to the problem of Cambodia." Here was an opportunity, he said, for Asian cooperation to support Cambodia's effort to maintain its neutrality, independence and territorial integrity. "We shall do what we can to make it possible for these Asian initiatives to succeed," he declared.

Congress Curbs Moves in Indochina

A measure to curb Nixon's war-making powers in Cambodia and elsewhere in Indochina was approved by Congress Dec. 29 following a series of parliamentary actions that had started in May.

The measure, an amendment to a foreign military appropriations bill, was proposed by Sens. Frank Church (D., Ida.) and John Sherman Cooper (R., Ky.). It was adopted by the House by 234-185 vote and by the Senate by 70-2 vote. The curbs, incorporated in a $66.6 billion defense appropriation for fiscal 1971, barred the introduction of U.S. ground troops into Thailand or Laos (a Senate attempt to extend the ban to Cambodia was deleted), and it stipulated that a $2½ billion fund for "free world forces" in Southeast Asia could not be used for military support of the government of Cambodia or Laos. The stipulation made clear that nothing in the restriction would prevent the support of any action required to insure a safe withdrawal of U.S. forces.

Under the original Cooper-Church amendment, approved by the Senate June 30 by 58-37 vote, the President would have been barred from spending any funds without Congressional consent after July 1 to: (a) retain U.S. forces in Cambodia; (b) send military advisers to instruct Cambodian forces; (c) provide air combat support to Cambodian forces; (d) provide financial assistance to advisers or troops of other countries aiding Cambodia. During protracted debate prior to the June 30 vote, the preamble to the amendment was revised to specify that the proposal was being made "in concert" with Nixon's declared objective of avoiding involvement in Cambodia after July 1 and expediting the U.S. withdrawal from Cambodia. Another phrase acknowledged the Constitutional power of the President to protect the lives of U.S. troops "wherever deployed." A phrase affirming the Constitutional power of Congress to declare war and to "make rules for the government and regulation" of the U.S. armed forces was also added. Proposed by Sen. Jacob K. Javits (R., N.Y.), it was adopted by 73-0 vote June 26.

In a move by Administration supporters to blunt the effect of the Cooper-Church amendment, Sen. Gordon P. Allott (Colo.), chairman of the Senate Republican Policy Committee, had introduced June 25 a "stop-the-war amendment" drafted by Senate doves. Sponsored by Sens. George McGovern (D., S.D.) and Mark O. Hatfield (R., Ore.), it would have cut off funds for combat activities in Vietnam after Dec. 31 and would have required the withdrawal of all U.S. forces from Vietnam by mid-1971. The dove faction planned to bring up the amendment for debate later in the summer after an advertising campaign to gain public support. Allott's commandeering of their proposal, with the express intent of engineering its defeat, was rebuffed. The Senate voted 62-29 June 29 to reject Allott's maneuver. The Hatfield-McGovern amendment, however, was defeated when it came up for Senate vote Sept. 1.

The Cooper-Church amendment had been approved by the Senate Foreign Relations Committee May 11 by 9-4 vote. The approval came after the receipt of a State Department letter opposing it on the Constitutional ground that the Presidential power to protect U.S. armed forces should not be restricted.

Prior to the beginning of Senate debate on the amendment May 13, Chairman John Stennis (D., Miss.) of the Armed Services Committee, a foe of the proposal, said that he viewed the enemy sanctuaries in Cambodia as "part of the South Vietnamese battlefield" and that a curb on Presidential powers while the battle "is still going on" would be a "grave mistake." Warning that it might be necessary to send U.S. forces back in 4 or 5 months if the sanctuaries were rebuilt, he asked what would the President "have to do" then? "Get a law passed?"

In the Senate May 13, Church said the use of U.S. troops in Cambodia, "though presently limited in scope, could easily become the first step toward committing the United States to the defense of still another government in Southeast Asia." The Vietnam war, he said, "has already stretched the generation gap so wide that it threatens to pull the country apart." The Foreign Relations Committee report on the amendment said it was time for Congress "to assert its Constitutional powers in order to prevent a widening of the war."

Stennis and Chairman J. W. Fulbright (D., Ark.) of the Foreign Relations Committee clashed sharply May 15. Fulbright said since the President had pledged the pullout by June 30, there was nothing wrong with legislation to hold him to it. Stennis asked him if he believed the pledge. "No, I don't believe him," Fulbright answered. "I don't think he knows what's going to happen. No government is run just on people's words. It's run on laws." "If he wants to go into another sanctuary," Fulbright said, "let him come to the Senate. One of those sanctuaries may be in China, another in Laos, why shouldn't he come ask the sanction of the Senate?"

Senate GOP whip Robert P. Griffin (Mich.) told the Senate May 20 that he knew it was not the intention of the amendment's sponsors "to aid the enemy," but "it does aid the enemy when we tie the hands of the commander-in-chief." Democratic leader Mansfield insisted May 20 that the amendment was not "an affront to the President as commander-in-chief" but "consistent with the President's pledge on Cambodia." When Griffin objected May 26 to the amendment as still "a slap in the face of the President," even with the preamble, which he described as "cosmetics," Cooper replied if the implication was that he was trying to "undermine" the President, "I challenge you from the very bottom of my soul." "All we are saying," Cooper said, "is that before the operation is extended and leads us into a war in Cambodia, under the Constitution, the President must come to Congress and get its approval." Mansfield added that there was "a general air of malaise in this chamber that carries with it innuendoes and aspersions that are not a healthy sign."

The final day of debate on the Cooper-Church amendment prior to the June 30 vote was the day of the announcement of the completed withdrawal of U.S. forces from Cambodia. A Republican effort to delay a vote on the amendment until the completion of the withdrawal was climaxed by Griffin's declaration June 30 that the amendment had become legally meaningless because all U.S. troops had left Cambodia. But the amendment's supporters, who had maintained that the proposal was intended to prevent future Cambodia incursions, persisted and, prior to the final vote, rebuffed a last Administration attempt to dilute the original amendment. With White House instigation, Griffin proposed a revision to authorize additional pay for foreign troops going to the military assistance of Cambodia. It was offered on the ground that the amendment as worded would interfere with the Nixon Doctrine pledge of the U.S. to help Asians defend themselves. The Cooper-Church forces contended that their amendment was designed only to bar the "hiring" of troops, or mercenaries, to fight in Cambodia and that it would not bar supplying military assistance to other countries helping Cambodia. On the 4th vote, the Griffin revision was rejected 50-45.

The Cooper-Church amendment was attached to a bill authorizing $300 million in credit sales of arms to foreign countries and imposing restrictions on the disposal of surplus weapons to other countries. The bill, carrying the Cooper-Church amendment, was passed by 75-20 Senate vote later June 30.

(The bill carried an amendment repealing the 1964 Gulf of Tonkin resolution, which Pres. Lyndon B. Johnson had cited as authorization to escalate the war in Vietnam. The 1964 resolution expressed Congressional approval of any "necessary measures" by the President to prevent further aggression in Southeast Asia. The repeal motion, approved June 24 by 81-10 vote, had been brought before the Senate in a controversial manner. The motion was offered by Sen. Robert J. Dole [R., Kan.] despite the fact that another repeal motion, originating in the Senate Foreign Relations Committee, was on the Senate calendar for later debate. Committee Chairman Fulbright, a leading war critic, voted against the Dole proposal "to preserve the integrity of the procedures of the Senate." The Nixon Administration had denied that the Tonkin Gulf resolution was the basis for its war-making authority in Southeast Asia. It asserted that it drew on the Constitutional authority of the President as commander-in-chief to protect the lives of U.S. military forces.)

The House rejected the Cooper-Church amendment July 9 without debate. Chairman Thomas E. Morgan (D., Pa.) of the House Foreign Affairs Committee had moved to send the military sales bill and amendment to conference with the Senate. Following some parliamentary confusion, Rep. Wayne Hays (D., O.) offered a motion to kill the proposal by tabling it. His motion was accepted, 237-153.

Vice Pres. Agnew May 17 had denounced Congressional proposals to cut off funds for future operations in Indochina. He said the Congressional move "to jerk the rug out from under the commander-in-chief and the troops" was tainted with political motivation and a "reprehensible attitude on the part of the Congress and those that support those resolutions." Agnew also said: Some speakers at the antiwar rallies May 9 were "the same old tired radicals that everybody in the country's sick of listening to"; "I certainly don't agree that the demonstrations are really indicative of deep-seated student hostility to the Cambodian decision"; "the best place and the first place" to begin cooling the rhetoric "is on the editorial pages of some of the Eastern newspapers."

In the midst of the debate on the Cooper-Church amendment, Sen. Dole, a supporter of Nixon's Asia policy, had introduced a proposal to bar legislative curbs on the President's war-making authority in Cambodia as long as Americans were held prisoner in Cambodia. The proposal was defeated June 3 by 54-36 vote.

Another move to head off or nullify the adoption of the Cooper-Church amendment had been made June 3 by Sen. Robert C. Byrd (D., W. Va.), who offered to add the words that the prohibition would not "preclude the President from taking such action as may be necessary to protect the lives" of U.S. forces in South Vietnam "or to hasten the withdrawal" of U.S. forces from South Vietnam. Griffin joined in co-sponsoring the Byrd proposal, and Nixon informed Senate GOP leader Hugh Scott (Pa.) by letter June 4 of his indorsement of the Byrd effort. Until then, the Administration had officially opposed any amendment on Cambodia.

Hatfield-McGovern Amendment Rejected

The "amendment to end the war" in Vietnam was rejected by the Senate Sept. 1 by 55-39 vote (34 R & 21 D vs. 32 D & 7 R). The amendment, proposed by Sens. Mark O. Hatfield (R., Ore.) and George S. McGovern (D., S.D.), provided that no more than 280,000 U.S. troops could be retained in South Vietnam after Apr. 30, 1971 and that all U.S. troops would have to be withdrawn by the end of 1971. In the event of an "unanticipated clear and present danger," the amendment provided that the President could keep the troops in Vietnam for 60 more days and submit to Congress a request for authorization of a new total withdrawal date.

In arguing against the adoption of the Hatfield-McGovern amendment, Sen. John C. Stennis (D., Miss.) had told the Senate prior to the vote that the move was constitutional and Congress had "the sole power to appropriate money." But, he urged, "Let's not stampede, let's go on down the road with whatever power our chief executive has as a negotiator, as a man of discernment."

McGovern, in his final words before the vote, said that "every Senator in this chamber is partly responsible for sending 50,000 young Americans to an early grave and ... for that human wreckage at Walter Reed [Army Hospital] and all across this land—young boys without legs, without arms, or genitals, or faces, or hopes. If we don't end this damnable war, those young men will some day curse us for our pitiful willingness to let the Executive [Branch] carry the burden that the Constitution places on us."

The vote on the Hatfield-McGovern amendment climaxed the protracted debate on a $19.2 billion military procurement bill, which was approved later Sept. 1 by 84-5 Senate vote and sent to conference with the House.

INTERNATIONAL REACTION: APRIL-JUNE 1970

The U.S.-South Vietnamese drive into Cambodia was sharply condemned by Communist countries—notably the Soviet Union and Communist China. Neither state, however, took overt action. The incursion also precipitated violent anti-American demonstrations in various world capitals. France deplored the move, and Britain questioned the wisdom of Pres. Nixon's action. India, Indonesia and Japan expressed regret. The only outright international support for Washington's decision was expressed by the U.S.' loyal allies in Asia—South Vietnam, Thailand, South Korea and Nationalist China.

The sudden widening of the Indochina war spurred further international efforts and appeals for joint action to end the conflict. A meeting of foreign ministers of 12 Asian nations was held in Jakarta, Indonesia May 17, but its call for a new international conference to stop the fighting produced no positive responses. France had advanced a similar appeal Apr. 1 as the Cambodian crisis was building to a climax. Its proposal for a multinational meeting to create a "zone of neutrality and peace" in Vietnam, Laos and Cambodia was indorsed by the U.S. The Soviet Union, however, rejected the idea, reiterating its opposition to the reconvening of a Geneva-type conference. Supporting the position of North Vietnam and the Viet Cong, Moscow contended that the withdrawal of American and allied troops from Indochina was the only way to achieve peace. UN Secy. Gen. U Thant also proposed an international conference on Cambodia, but North Vietnam rejected the idea.

Invasion Evokes Criticism, Ire & Skepticism

Pres. Nixon's decision to send U.S. troops into Cambodia was sharply assailed by the Soviet Union and Communist China May 4.

Speaking at a rare news conference in Moscow, Soviet Premier Aleksei N. Kosygin charged that, in ordering the drive into Cambodia and the resumption of air raids on North Vietnam, Nixon was, "in effect, also tearing up the decision of his predecessor, Pres. Johnson, to end ... all aerial bombing and other action involving the use of force" against North Vietnam. Kosygin said, "the real meaning" of Nixon's Apr. 30 speech announcing the incursion and U.S. policy in general in Southeast Asia "is to eliminate 'progressive regimes in the countries of the region [and] to stifle the liberation movement" there.

Kosygin warned that the U.S.-South Vietnamese drive would probably result in "the further complication of the general international situation."

The USSR Apr. 30 had condemned the U.S.-supported South Vietnamese thrust into Cambodia Apr. 29 as "a direct aggression against a member of the United Nations." The statement called the action "the grossest violation of Cambodia's neutrality."

In the May 4 Peking statement denouncing the U.S., Communist China pledged support for "the 3 Indochinese people" (Cambodia, Laos and Vietnam) in their "patriotic struggle" against American forces. Peking supported a statement in which Prince Norodom Sihanouk May 2 had urged international condemnation of the U.S. "armed intervention" in Cambodia.

The strongest Communist reaction had come from the North Vietnamese government newspaper *Nhan Dan* May 3. The Communist Party journal said that Nixon had been attempting to justify the "U.S. aggression in Cambodia" but that his Apr. 30 speech was "even more absurd, unwittingly proving his dirty trickery."

The incursion had drawn sharp denunciations May 1 from the North Vietnamese and Viet Cong delegations to the Paris peace talks. They described Nixon's actions as "warlike and perfidious."

Nixon's decision to send U.S. troops into Cambodia drew praise May 1 from Washington's Asian allies—Thailand, South Korea and Nationalist China. Indonesian Foreign Min. Adam Malik expressed regret over the move. Japanese Foreign Min.

Kiichi Aichi called the intervention an "unavoidable step" under present circumstances.

UN Secy. Gen. U Thant said May 3 that, in the extension of the fighting to Cambodia, "we see the tragedy of the war in Vietnam threatening to engulf the Indochinese peninsula."

Thant May 5 issued an appeal for an international conference to seek a peaceful settlement of the Indochinese war. He expressed fear that if the parties to the conflict "do not take urgent ... measures toward peace, it will become increasingly difficult to end a war" that threatened not only Indochina but "the whole of mankind."

Thant's statement followed a U.S. note informing the President of the Security Council earlier May 5 of the American action in Cambodia and the reasons for it. U.S. Amb.-to-UN Charles W. Yost had advised Thant of the contents of the letter May 4. It accused North Vietnam of aggression and described the dispatch of allied troops into Cambodia as "appropriate measures of collective self-defense by the armed forces" of the U.S. and South Vietnam.

In statements issued by State Secy. William P. Rogers May 6 and by British Amb.-to-UN Lord Caradon May 7, the U.S. and Britain supported Thant's call for an international conference.

Cambodian Premier Lon Nol had said May 1 that the U.S. and South Vietnam had not given him prior notice of their plans to invade his country to attack Communist sanctuaries. He was first informed of the attack by U.S. Charge d'Affaires Lloyd M. Rives, who brought him the text of Nixon's speech announcing the incursion. Lon Nol called the operation a violation of Cambodia's territorial integrity. He said he would have preferred that "our friends give us the arms to do the operation ourselves."

But Lon Nol May 2 modified his criticism of the allied attack. He said that the operations represented a positive response to Cambodia's request for military aid. Visiting Philippine Sen. Benigno Aquino Jr., who interviewed Lon Nol, said that although the premier did not approve the American intervention, he did not criticize the action. Lon Nol said the number of Communist forces in Cambodia was 150,000, compared with the 50,000 previously estimated.

British Prime Min. Harold Wilson, refraining from direct criticism of the American action, expressed fear May 5 that U.S. forces might penetrate further into Cambodia than the limits set by Nixon and thus cause a reversal in Washington's policy of withdrawal of troops from Vietnam. Speaking in House of Commons debate, Wilson voiced "apprehension and anxiety" that the new American military moves would "add a new dimension to the area and scale of the fighting."

French Foreign Min. Maurice Schumann warned May 5 that any escalation of the war in Indochina would only solidify the Communists. Schumann said that a speech made by ex-Pres. Charles de Gaulle in 1966 calling for the withdrawal of American troops from Vietnam "contained something of an advance reply" to Nixon's Apr. 30 address announcing the U.S. move into Cambodia. Schumann gave these views at a special session of the National Assembly's Foreign Affairs Committee on the Cambodian crisis. A French government statement issued after a cabinet meeting May 6 said France was "concerned by the worsening of the international situation caused, almost everywhere, but essentially in the Far East, by a number of recent events, which we deplore." The French government had said May 1 that it "can only deplore anything that aggravates, prolongs and extends the conflict."

Indian Prime Min. Indira Gandhi May 6 called the invasion a "dangerous step" and urged Nixon to reconsider his move.

Laotian Premier Souvanna Phouma said in an interview published May 8 that further U.S. and South Vietnamese penetration of Cambodia would imperil his country because it could force the North Vietnamese and Viet Cong to pull back into Laos.

5,000 antiwar demonstrators marched on the U.S. embassy in London May 9 in protest against the campaign in Cambodia and against U.S. actions in Vietnam. Police blocked attempts by the marchers to force their way to the entrance of the building. 60 demonstrators who fought past police lines were arrested. 19 demonstrators and 60 police were injured.

Thousands of antiwar demonstrators, hurling stones and gasoline bombs, fought police in front of the U.S. cultural center in West Berlin May 9. 3 persons were wounded by police bullets. Demonstrations had been held May 6 in Montreal,

Canada, Calcutta, India, where the library of the American University Center was sacked, Caracas, Venezuela, Canberra, Australia and Auckland, New Zealand. 2 high school pupils were shot to death by sniper fire during continued protest rallies in Caracas May 7.

About 200,000 persons took to the streets in Melbourne, Sydney and other Australian cities May 8 to begin 3 days of organized protest against Australian and U.S. involvement in the Vietnam war. (Australian Prime Min. John Gorton had announced May 5 that his government supported American military moves in Cambodia.) Police used tear gas to disperse an anti-American demonstration by 300 Filipino youths in front of the U.S. embassy in Manila. About 3,500 students and workers marched in Tokyo in protest against American action in Cambodia and an Asian conference on Cambodia, scheduled to open in Jakarta May 16.

An anti-American protest in Paris May 10 was attended by French Socialists and Viet Cong and Cambodian supporters of ousted Prince Norodom Sihanouk and by Xuan Thuy, head of the North Vietnamese delegation to the Paris peace talks.

Non-Communist Asians Seek Indochina Peace

The convening of a new international conference to end the conflict in Indochina and the reactivation of the International Control Commission (ICC) in Cambodia were recommended at a 2-day meeting of foreign ministers of 12 Asian nations, held in Jakarta, Indonesia May 16-17.

Participating states in the conference, convened specifically to consider the crisis in Cambodia, were Indonesia, Australia, New Zealand, Japan, South Korea, South Vietnam, Laos, Thailand, Malaysia, Singapore and the Philippines. Cambodia attended as a "special invitee."

A final communique issued May 17 urged "respect for the sovereignty, independence, neutrality and territorial integrity of Cambodia." It called for the immediate end of the fighting there and the withdrawal of all foreign troops. The statement urged the participants in the 1954 Geneva Conference on Indochina to cooperate in achieving those ends. The foreign ministers of Japan, Malaysia and Indonesia were appointed as a "task force" to start immediate talks with Britain and the

Soviet Union, co-chairmen of the Geneva conference, to reactivate the ICC and to promote the new international peace conference. The task force also was authorized to meet with UN Secy. Gen. U Thant to encourage UN intercession to help restore peace.

Indonesian Foreign Min. Adam Malik, chairman and organizer of the meeting, was instructed to continue consultations with the Jakarta conference participants and other interested nations on "further possible steps toward a peaceful solution in Cambodia."

The Jakarta communique made no mention of a reported Pnompenh government message, presumed to have been received at the opening meeting May 16, calling on Asian and Pacific nations to send troops to Cambodia to help fight the Communist invaders. The message reportedly was sent by the ruling National Committee of Salvation over the signature of Premier Lon Nol.

The *Pnompenh Courier,* a pro-government newspaper, criticized the Jakarta conferees May 19 for having "talked about everything except the economic and military aid that our government delegation had gone to ask for." Cambodian Foreign Min. Yem Sambaur had said in Jakarta May 17 that he was not disappointed by the conference's refusal to provide his country with military aid. He said he came to the conference anticipating only "moral support and sympathy and understanding for the current situation in Cambodia."

The Jakarta conference task force led by Foreign Min. Malik met with Soviet officials in Moscow June 16-17 but received a negative response to its peace proposals. Malik said that Soviet Foreign Min. Andrei A. Gromyko had rejected the idea of a Geneva conference at that time and blamed the U.S. for the trouble in Cambodia. The Jakarta conference was assailed June 19 by the Soviet news agency Tass. It charged that the meeting "constituted an attempt to divert attention from the armed invasion of Cambodia by the United States. Naturally, it was met with a negative attitude by the majority of the countries of the world, including the Soviet Union."

The Jakarta conference task force discussed its peace formula with Indian officials in New Delhi June 19 but failed to receive Indian indorsement. Foreign Secy. T. N. Kaul told the delegation that India could not support a "piecemeal solution" relating only to Cambodia.

France Calls for International Conference

The French government Apr. 1 had proposed a general international conference on Vietnam, Laos and Cambodia with the goal of creating "a zone of neutrality and peace." The proposal failed to evoke wide acceptance, and the meeting never materialized.

Asserting that the Vietnam war was spreading to Cambodia and Laos, France's Apr. 1 statement said that "the extension of a war that tends to become indivisible can be avoided only by negotiation between all interested parties with a view to seeking and guaranteeing the bases for peace, itself indivisible." A French government spokesman said one approach could be the reconvening of the 1954 Geneva Conference, which had ended the French-Indochinese war. The Paris statement implied that such a parley could replace the Paris peace talks on Vietnam, which had been deadlocked since their initiation in 1968.

France had proposed Mar. 11 that U.S. and North Vietnamese troops be withdrawn from Laos to help end the fighting in that country. "Any international solution must result in a return to the Geneva accords, their current application, a complete termination of foreign interference and the respect for Laotian neutrality," Foreign Min. Maurice Schumann was quoted as saying.

France Mar. 19 renewed its appeal for the preservation of Laos and Cambodia as neutral states. It urged "all interested parties" to prevent the Vietnam war from spreading to all of Indochina. "The remaining chances of re-establishing peace in Vietnam itself can only be compromised by such a development while international tension would dangerously increase in that part of the world," the statement said.

France's Apr. 1 call for an international conference won support in the U.S. Senate Apr. 2. A resolution advocating such a conference was introduced by Sens. Fred R. Harris (D., Okla.) and James B. Pearson (R., Kan.). The "indivisibility of the conflicts" in Laos, Cambodia and Vietnam, and the need for an overall "political settlement" were cited by Chairman J.

W. Fulbright (D., Ark.) of the Senate Foreign Relations
Committee in a Senate speech Apr. 2. Fulbright indorsed the
French proposal for negotiations to make all Indochina into a
"zone of neutrality and peace."

The French initiative also received favorable comment
Apr. 2 from U.S. State Secy. William P. Rogers, who said the
French "proposals talk about negotiations," and "we are
interested in any kind of negotiations that would lead to
peace." He made the comment to newsmen after testifying
before the Fulbright committee on the Administration's effort
to maintain the neutrality of Cambodia and to avoid
entanglement in an all-Indochina war. Senate Democratic
leader Mike Mansfield (Mont.) said after hearing Rogers'
testimony that "the attitude of the Administration [toward
Cambodia] is a correct one." "All the Administration wants—
and all I want," he said, "is maintenance of neutrality and no
involvement in what could become an Indochina war."

(The State Department Mar. 12 had indorsed France's
Mar. 11 appeal for the withdrawal of all U.S. and North
Vietnamese troops from Laos. The department also called on
the 14 nations which had signed the 1962 Geneva accords
neutralizing Laos to "live up to their responsibilities.")

The USSR suggested Apr. 16 that a new Geneva
conference be convened to deal with the crisis in Southeast
Asia, but Moscow reversed its position the following day. The
original statement and the followup remarks were delivered by
Yakov A. Malik, the Soviet Union's chief delegate to the UN.
Malik said at a news conference Apr. 16 that the situation in
Southeast Asia "is not a matter for the United Nations." He
said that since the 1954 and 1962 Geneva agreements on Laos,
Cambodia and Vietnam had not been carried out, "only a new
Geneva conference could bring a new solution and relax
tensions." "If this was the point of the French proposal [for the
reconvening of an international parley on Indochina], then it is
deserving of attention," Malik said.

But in an apparent retraction of this Apr. 16 statement,
Malik said in an ABC radio interview Apr. 17 that the
reconvening of a Geneva conference "is unrealistic because the
source of conflicts and tensions in Indochina is rooted in the
overt armed intervention of the United States and its allies in
Vietnam and other countries in the area." Malik said that

lasting peace could be achieved only by "the withdrawal of American and allied troops from Indochina." A "clarification" circulated by the Soviet delegation at the UN Apr. 20 reiterated Malik's view that a new conference on Indochina was "unrealistic at this time."

Malik's original remarks had aroused U.S. interest. Statements on the matter were issued by the White House Apr. 17 and by State Secy. William P. Rogers Apr. 18. Rogers said he had instructed U.S. Amb.-to-UN Charles Yost to ask Malik for further clarification. Rogers said the U.S. "welcomes initiatives by countries in or outside the area which might lead to progress toward restoration of peace in Southeast Asia."

Following the apparent reversal of Moscow's position, Rogers criticized the USSR Apr. 25 for failing to take steps to reconvene the Geneva conference. Speaking in New York at a dinner of the American Society of International Law, Rogers said such a meeting was warranted by North Vietnamese military activity in Laos and Cambodia, which he asserted was in violation of the 1954 and 1962 Geneva agreements. The failure of the Soviet Union, as co-chairman of the Geneva conference, to reconvene the international meeting, he said, represented a "flouting" of its "international responsibilities." Rogers noted that Malik had first proposed reconvening the Geneva conference but that Moscow "has been back-pedaling ever since."

The Viet Cong Apr. 20 had rejected France's proposal for talks on Indochina. Mrs. Nguyen Thi Binh, foreign minister of the Viet Cong's Provisional Revolutionary Government, said in Paris that the French plan "could not contribute to solving the problems" of Vietnam, Laos and Cambodia. She noted that an international conference on South Vietnam was already in progress in Paris, that there had been an agreement on Laos and that the deposed Cambodian chief of state, Prince Norodom Sihanouk, had called for the withdrawal of U.S. forces. "Thus to settle these problems only requires that the United States end its policy of aggression and let the people of each of these 3 countries settle their own affairs," Mrs. Binh said.

The French peace proposal had evoked differing reactions Apr. 4 from 2 high-ranking South Vietnamese government officials—Vice Pres. Nguyen Cao Ky and Foreign Min. Tran Van Lam. Ky expressed approval of the proposal, but Lam dismissed it as "unrealistic and inapplicable to the present situation."

Thant Appeals for Peace

UN Secy. Gen. U Thant June 11 proposed an international conference to end the fighting in Cambodia. The proposal was rejected by North Vietnam June 13 and 16.

Thant suggested in his June 11 statement that the participants in the conference include all the parties involved in the fighting, the Cambodian government of Premier Lon Nol and the forces supporting Prince Norodom Sihanouk, the ousted chief of state, the U.S., Britain, France, the Soviet Union, Communist China and the 3 members of the International Control Commission—India, Poland and Canada.

Nguyen Thanh Le, the North Vietnamese press spokesman at the Paris peace talks, denounced Thant's proposal June 13 as "sheer hypocrisy." Le said Thant had "lumped the usurpers of power in Cambodia together with the legitimate leaders of the country and placed them on the same footing. In effect, he has recognized the Lon Nol regime by this proposal, while we do not."

The North Vietnamese Communist Party newspaper *Nhan Dan* said June 16 that Thant's plan was aimed at shielding "atrocious aggressive acts of U.S. aggression."

AFTERMATH OF U.S. WITHDRAWAL:
JUNE-DECEMBER 1970

The withdrawal of U.S. troops from Cambodia June 29, 1970 brought no letup in the fighting that had been raging there since the allied entry ·in late April. With the departure of the U.S. soldiers, Saigon's forces assumed the major role in combatting the Viet Cong and North Vietnamese armies on Cambodian soil. Cambodian forces also expanded their operations. Although Pnompenh's troops fought independently of South Vietnam's soldiers, there were a few instances of joint allied operations.

The Communist and allied troops carried out heavy offensives and counter-offensives during 1970 with apparently neither side gaining an advantage over the other. The intensity of combat was sustained through the end of 1970, and high losses were reported on both sides. The heaviest fighting took place in eastern and central Cambodia. In the central sector, the Communists carried out major assaults within a short distance of Pnompenh in August. Strong Cambodian resistance, however, neutralized the threat to the capital.

Although American ground troops were no longer in Cambodia, the U.S. continued to exert strong military pressure in the form of air power. American planes pounded Viet Cong/North Vietnamese concentrations with the avowed purpose of interdicting Communist supply routes in order to protect U.S. troops in South Vietnam. U.S. newsmen, however, reported in August that the air attacks were being mounted in direct support of Cambodian troops. This action would have violated Pres. Nixon's June 30 pledge to restrict the aerial strikes to neutralizing the Communist supply routes. In denying the allegations, the Administration insisted that the American air role in Cambodia did not exceed the limited directives issued by the President.

Central Cambodia Clashes

Cambodian and South Vietnamese forces engaged Communist troops in scattered battles throughout central Cambodia beginning June 29. Among actions reported:

● About 3,000 South Vietnamese troops June 29 lifted a siege of an arms depot at Longvek, 23 miles north of Pnompenh. Cambodian troops had been trapped in the town by Communist soldiers since June 25.

● More than 5,000 South Vietnamese troops launched a sweep of areas north of Pnompenh July 1 but made no significant contact with the enemy. Meanwhile, more than 800 Khmer Krom, ethnic Cambodians, arrived from South Vietnam to bolster the defense of Pnompenh. The reinforcements, trained by U.S. Special Forces, joined 4,000 other Khmer Krom from Vietnam assigned to the defense of the capital.

● North Vietnamese/Viet Cong forces July 5 entered the town of Saang, 20 miles south of Pnompenh, but began pulling out later in the day after the arrival of Cambodian reinforcements in the area. The Cambodians surged into Saang July 6, cleaned out the remaining Communist troops and retook complete control of the town. The Cambodian command reported that 250 Communists were killed in the fighting. Cambodian losses were listed as 32 killed and 47 wounded. Saang, which had been heavily battered in April, suffered further damage in the latest fighting.

● The Saigon command reported July 5 that its troops had killed 34 Communists in repelling attacks on South Vietnamese positions near Svayrieng and along Route 7 west of the Chup rubber plantation, close to the Vietnamese frontier. South Vietnamese losses were given as 8 killed and 3 wounded.

● The withdrawal of Communist troops from the ancient temple ruins at Angkor Wat was reported July 6. Cambodian patrols that entered Angkor reported no damage to the country's greatest cultural shrine after a Communist occupation of more than a month. There was no explanation as to why the Viet Cong, the North Vietnamese and Khmer Rouge troops had abandoned the area, where they had set up supply dumps and fortified positions. The entire Angkor area had been treated as an "open city" by the Cambodians, who made no effort to attack the Communist positions there. The Communists were said to remain entrenched in other temples in the jungles around Angkor and nearby Siemreap.

● The Saigon command July 8 reported the completion of a 6-week drive in the Parrot's Beak, in southeastern Cambodia. The offensive, the command claimed, resulted in the killing of 1,119 Viet Cong and North Vietnamese and the capture of 8,427 rifles and 158 heavy weapons. South Vietnamese losses were listed as 878 killed and 3,832 wounded.

● Communist forces July 11 captured a Cambodian military base at a mountaintop resort at Kirirom, 50 miles west of Pnompenh, after routing 400 government defenders. Kirirom was astride Highway 4 linking Pnompenh with the port of Kompong Som on the Gulf of Siam. Cambodian counterattacks were assisted by South Vietnamese air strikes. 2 battalions of Khmer Krom were sent from Pnompenh July 12 to capture the road leading to the summit of the mountain, but they were halted about 3 miles from the top by heavy Communist fire and withdrew to Highway 4. The ethnic Cambodians staged new diversionary attacks July 13 and reported killing 50 of the estimated 1,000 North Vietnamese and Viet Cong. Cambodian troops recaptured Kirirom July 16. Retreating Communist soldiers set fire to some of the village buildings. Government losses were described as "fairly heavy." Fighting for Kirirom continued intermittently. Communist troops made a new attempt to recapture it July 27 and forced the Cambodian government garrison to withdraw July 28. Maj. Am Rong, a Cambodian military spokesman, said the 2,000-man Cambodian force withdrew in the face of enemy seizure of the helicopter landing zone and harassing fire from sniper and mortar positions.

● Cambodian intelligence sources reported July 21 a large enemy build-up in the Angkor-Siemreap area. A Pnompenh military spokesman said air strikes north of Siemreap July 24 had killed 600 soldiers and wounded 200 near the Angkor Wat ruins.

● A force of 2,500 South Vietnamese troops entered Cambodia July 26 on a new search and destroy mission, raising Saigon's forces in the country to about 20,000 men. (About 2,000 South Vietnamese irregulars had been reported July 8 to have been withdrawn from Cambodia.) The new troops were flown by U.S. helicopters July 26 to a staging area at Donphuc in South Vietnam's western Mekong Delta, 3 miles from the Cambodian border. From there, the South Vietnamese pushed across the border 6 miles east of Kompong Trabek on the main Saigon-Pnompenh highway. The South Vietnamese reported killing 35 Communist soldiers in their initial contacts with the enemy and finding the bodies of 26 Communists killed earlier by allied air strikes southeast of Kompong Trabek.

● The town of Skoun was seized by North Vietnamese and Viet Cong forces Aug. 1, retaken briefly by Cambodian troops Aug. 2 and recaptured the same day by the Communist forces. Skoun, located at a key intersection 40 miles northeast of Pnompenh, was then recaptured Aug. 7 by Cambodian soldiers. A Pnompenh military spokesman reported that Cambodian soldiers re-entering Skoun were assisted by allied air strikes. (Although the spokesman did not specify whether the planes were American, the announcement called attention to a growing controversy over whether stepped-up U.S. air strikes in Cambodia were in direct support of Cambodian troops or were intended only to interdict Communist supplies.)

● Kompong Thom, 76 miles north of Pnompenh, was encircled Aug. 8 by a Communist force estimated at 8,000 men. The town was considered important to the Communists because it controlled the western edge of the enemy's Mekong River infiltration route from Laos. A force of 2,000 to 3,000 Communists had fought its way into the center of Kompong Thom July 31 behind heavy fire from mortars and automatic weapons. The invaders were driven out by Cambodian troops Aug. 3, but the village remained besieged.

● Communist forces launched heavy attacks Aug. 8 against 3 towns north and south of Pnompenh and another near Angkor, but all were repulsed. The largest assault was centered on Saang, 12 miles south of the capital. The Cambodian government reported that a "number of North Vietnamese" had been killed in an attack on Preytoung, 40 miles northeast of the capital.

Cambodian Rebels Establish Command

The existence of 3 rebel regional military commands in Cambodia headed by ministers in Prince Norodom Sihanouk's government-in-exile was disclosed by the Communist Chinese weekly *Peking Review* (reported July 12).

The commands were: the eastern region, under Defense Min. Khieu Samphan; the southwestern, under Interior Min. Hou Youn; and the northwestern, under Information Min. Hu Nim.

Sihanouk had said that the forces fighting to overthrow the Lon Nol government totaled about 63,000, but he insisted that the North Vietnamese and Viet Cong did not constitute the majority. Other sources, however, estimated the number of Vietnamese Communists fighting in Cambodia to be 30,000-60,000, with Cambodian rebels totaling 1,000-3,000.

The northwestern command, along the Thai border, was said to be a stronghold of the Cambodian Communists, supported by the Thai Communists.

U.S. Air Support Controversy

In announcing the withdrawal of U.S. troops from Cambodia June 30, Pres. Nixon had pledged that the American military role in the continuing campaign there would be limited to air attacks on Communist troops and supplies that endangered U.S. forces in South Vietnam. Subsequent reports by American journalists strongly indicated that this pledge was being violated and that U.S. planes were flying bombing missions in direct support of Cambodian troops.

Defense Secy. Melvin R. Laird denied Aug. 6 that U.S. planes were supporting Cambodian troop operations. Referring to a battlefield incident the previous day, Laird said that bombings by U.S. jets in front of a battalion of Cambodian troops fighting at Skoun were part of a general interdiction campaign to prevent the Communists from reopening sea supply routes through Cambodian coastal towns. Laird emphasized that the Administration's policy of conducting only interdictory attacks against Communist forces in Cambodia to protect American troops applied to virtually all of Cambodia, particularly "along the sanctuary areas, or along the river route." He conceded that such raids would provide the Cambodians with "ancillary benefits," but he did not specify what these benefits would be.

In explaining the distinction between "ancillary benefits" and direct air support, Defense Department spokesman Jerry Friedheim said Aug. 6: "The difference is how it looks to the Cambodians and how it looks to us. How it looks to the Cambodians is that ancillary benefits are direct support for his troops. It looks to us like an interdiction campaign conducted in the context of our interdiction operations aimed at protecting the safety and security of our forces in South Vietnam."

A Cambodian military spokesman, Maj. Am Rong, confirmed Aug. 6 that "American air intervention is being carried out in Cambodia to interdict supply routes and to protect the lives of Americans in South Vietnam."

An AP report on the Aug. 5 fighting at Skoun had said that 7 American planes provided direct air support to Cambodian ground troops. The attacks were directed by a Cambodian ground controller trained by U.S. Special Forces, according to the report.

A U.S. military command directive issued Aug. 6 advised all unit commanders to restrict their comments about American air involvement in Cambodia. The statement, whose contents were made public Aug. 8, said that, when asked about these operations, the commanders were to reiterate only that the purpose of the bombings was "to protect Americans in Vietnam, the Vietnamization program, to enhance continuing American withdrawals and to reduce American casualties."

Senate Majority leader Mike Mansfield (D., Mont.) questioned Aug. 7 whether Nixon had gone back on his pledge to limit American air involvement in Cambodia. "I think we better call things what they are," Mansfield said. "It seems to me their reasoning is a bit tortured." Mansfield had warned Aug. 5 that U.S. air support of Cambodian troops could lead the U.S. into "a full-fledged war."

In a further explanation of American air policy in Cambodia, the Defense Department said Aug. 26 that the U.S. raids were linked to the prevention of an enemy takeover but not directly to the support of the Lon Nol government. But Daniel Z. Henkin, a department spokesman, refused to comment on whether the U.S. was committed to the support of

Lon Nol's regime. "We have a Vietnamization program," Henkin said. "Our interdiction missions in Cambodia are linked to that objective." He added that "without regard to any specific government," a Communist takeover of all of Cambodia would "present [an] increased threat to our U.S. and allied personnel in South Vietnam."

Informed Saigon sources had said Aug. 22 that U.S. pilots were free to go anywhere in Cambodia and attack enemy troops and supply lines. But the informants insisted that this represented no change in policy. The pilots could attack whenever military officials believed enemy troops might pose a threat to forces in South Vietnam, the sources said. Final judgment on a threat rested with Gen. Creighton W. Abrams, commander of the U.S. forces.

(Military spokesmen said that American B-52 bombers had crossed into Cambodia Aug. 23 to bomb North Vietnamese infiltration routes and suspected troop concentrations.)

Communist Forces Menace Pnompenh

Cambodian soldiers fought Communist troops 7½ miles from Pnompenh Aug. 20 in the nearest battle to the capital since the Cambodian war began in April. The threat to Pnompenh was successfully contained.

A force of 1,500 Viet Cong and North Vietnamese had attacked a 700-man government unit at Puk Rusey on the eastern bank of the Mekong River, breaking a 10-day lull in the fighting. The 9-hour clash was followed by a Communist mortar attack on government positions at Arey Ksach on the eastern bank of the Mekong below Puk Rusey, only one mile from the center of Pnompenh. The brief shelling was reported to have caused no damage or casualties. According to government estimates, about 300 Communists were killed in the fighting at Puk Rusey, while Cambodian losses totaled 19 killed and 124 wounded.

Cambodian troops carried out clearing operations in the vicinity of Puk Rusey Aug. 22 in an attempt to uncover enemy soldiers left behind after the Aug. 20 fighting.

In other fighting around the capital, 8 Cambodian infantry battalions were dug in at Prek Tameak Aug. 25 with orders to hold the east bank of the Mekong River. Communist forces mounted a major assault on Prek Tameak that same day. Vietcong and North Vietnamese units Aug. 26 continued shelling the town, located 9 miles northeast of Pnompenh.

Fighting was reported 6 miles from the capital Aug. 29 at Moat Krasas Krao and other outer defenses of Pnompenh, but the enemy reportedly withdrew that day.

A Sept. 2 report said Communist troops had moved to within easy mortar and rocket range of the capital but had not begun any shelling. An AP report said Communist sources had indicated that the USSR had warned Hanoi against any major attack on Pnompenh unless it could be proved that it was carried out by Cambodian guerrilla units.

Fierce fighting was reported Aug. 31 28 miles southwest of the capital at the town of Srang, which had been taken by enemy troops Aug. 30. Cambodian government troops Sept. 1 made a 2d attempt to recapture the town but met stiff enemy resistance as Communist reinforcements were moved up Sept. 2. Enemy troops withdrew from Srang Sept. 3, and the town was reoccupied by government forces.

A force of 1,000 South Vietnamese rangers was reported Sept. 4 to have moved across the border into Cambodia's Fishhook area. The Vietnamese met with little resistance.

In clashes elsewhere in Cambodia:

● Cambodian Communist forces were reported to have captured the offshore island of Koh Kong in the Gulf of Thailand Aug. 18. Thai provincial sources said 135 Cambodian women and children had fled the island to Thailand's Trad Province, about 300 miles northeast of Bangkok.

● A 4,000-man South Vietnamese force Aug. 21 opened a new drive against Communist troops in an area 12 miles southeast of Neak Luong near the main highway linking Pnompenh and Saigon.

● In a report on the completion of a 10-day campaign, Saigon authorities announced Aug. 22 that an 1,800-man South Vietnamese ranger force had killed 47 Communists.

● A Cambodian military spokesman reported Aug. 24 that 500 North Vietnamese and Viet Cong troops had been killed by allied air strikes Aug. 9-11. The Communist troops had been attacked by air while operating in a sanctuary along the South Vietnamese border near Kompong Trach, 67 miles southeast of Pnompenh. The raids also destroyed a Communist command post and a weapons factory. The Cambodian command said it had only learned of the attack Aug. 23 from information received from villagers and Cambodian troops operating near the area. The Cambodian military spokesman declined to identify the allied planes involved in the air strikes.

Cambodian Offensive Stalled

The Cambodian army launched a major offensive Sept. 7 along Route 6, but the drive stalled after less than 2 weeks. The ground attacks were supported by U.S. aircraft.

The provincial capital of Kompong Thom, goal of the offensive, was reportedly reached by a flotilla of patrol boats Sept. 9. The Cambodian command announced that their arrival had broken a 3-month siege by Communist forces. Ground forces were reported to be 36 miles from the city, having moved about 10 miles in the first 3 days of the offensive.

Cambodian military spokesmen acknowledged Sept. 12, however, that the 8-battalion force was stalled at that point, while army engineers attempted to repair a bridge along the route. Sharp fighting was reported Sept. 13 as the Viet Cong attacked the government forces. A Sept. 15 report said Communist troops were maneuvering behind government lines, while other enemy units moved southwest of Skoun in an attempt to cut that city's road link with Pnompenh.

Senior Cambodian commanders directing the government offensive were reported to be in Pnompenh Sept. 16 for urgent talks with the high command. A relief force of about 1,500 government troops was reported moving toward the main concentration of stalled troops Sept. 17 in an attempt to cut off the enemy forces that had closed in behind the lines. The relief troops linked up with the main force Sept. 18. (Meanwhile, Saigon sources reported that U.S. fighter-bombers flew raids along Route 6 Sept. 17. One plane was lost in a raid; it was the first such loss in more than 2 months.)

Both government and Communist forces moved up reinforcements Sept. 19 in what then appeared to be preparations for a showdown battle. The expected government advance did not take place, however, as enemy troops blew up the newly built bridge virtually in the midst of the government force. Brig. Gen. Neak Sam, commander of the Cambodian troops, described the situation as "very, very serious." Neak was removed from command Sept. 21 and replaced by Brig. Gen. Phan Moeung. Premier Lon Nol, who visited the stalled column of troops Sept. 21, said he was "satisfied" with his units.

Government troops Sept. 21 began a flanking move with 3 battalions of paratroops swinging east from Route 6 behind Tangkok. Other battalions moved west in a pincer operation against the estimated 3,500 guerrillas deployed in and around Tangkok. Military spokesmen said Sept. 23 that the government troops had succeeded in occupying several villages in the area. Sharp enemy resistance prevented government forces from penetrating Tangkok itself; unofficial reports Sept. 25 said Viet Cong guerrillas holding the town had forced back an assault by 10,000 government troops.

(New fighting had also been reported Sept. 8 near the ruins of the temples at Angkor Wat. Communist troops were reported Sept. 11 to be about 500 yards from the southern edge of Siemreap, just south of Angkor. Communist forces were also threatening the Siemreap airport.

(A South Vietnamese naval task force Sept. 19 had launched a major operation in Cambodia along the Bassac River 35 miles southeast of Pnompenh. The force, made up of 200 vessels and more than 1,500 Vietnamese marines, was aimed at destroying enemy base areas between the Bassac and Mekong Rivers.)

Communist & South Vietnamese Offensives

After stopping the Cambodian government offensive in September, Communist forces launched a drive of their own at the end of the month. South Vietnamese troops also carried out major operations in October and continued to bring more troops into Cambodia.

The Communist forces launched an attack on vital road links Sept. 29 and forced the closing of several of the highways leading to Pnompenh. Other enemy operations were directed at the area around the central village of Taing Kauk, scene of bitter fighting since early September.

The Communist drive had been preceded by the capture of Taing Kauk by Cambodian government forces Sept. 26. Assisted by massive U.S. air strikes, the government soldiers forced enemy troops to abandon the stronghold and claimed their first major victory of the war.

The drive against the highways followed a report Sept. 29 that large numbers of North Vietnamese and Viet Cong troops had moved out of the Kirirom area, 55 miles northwest of Pnompenh, and were approaching one of the roads, Route 4, linking the capital with the port of Kompong Som, 57 miles to the southeast. By Oct. 1, Route 4 as well as Routes 1 and 5 were reported to be cut or under attack. Route 4 was completely sealed off after the enemy seized control of one section of it. Route 5 was virtually severed when Communist attacks were directed at 4 points of the road, which led from Pnompenh to the west and northwest. The Communists threatened Route 1, leading from Pnompenh to Saigon, when they attacked a government garrison 20 miles south of the capital. That road was reported by the Cambodian command Oct. 2 to have been entirely closed because of a mine detonation near the South Vietnamese border. But a government communique said Oct. 2 that Route 5 had been reopened and that it and Route 7 were the only major roads open to traffic. The latter highway connected Pnompenh with the provincial capital of Kompong Cham, 47 miles to the northeast.

A major clash erupted Oct. 5 when Communist forces attempted to overrun a government garrison at Sre Khlong on Route 4. The defenders repulsed the attackers after 11 hours of fighting.

Communist forces began to apply pressure in the Taing Kauk area Oct. 5. Their attacks forced government troops to retreat from a village about 2 miles to the east. Jet bombers from South Vietnam Oct. 6 bombed suspected enemy bunkers at Kanthum, a village outside Taing Kauk. The planes were called in after Cambodian troops had come under fire for 6 hours from the Communist stronghold.

Sharp clashes occurred Oct. 7 and 10 around Prakham, site of a government brigade headquarters 4 miles south of Taing Kauk. 9 Cambodians and at least 12 enemy soldiers were killed in the first clash. Communist troops attacking a large Cambodian column were driven back in a 9-hour battle in the 2d clash.

The Cambodian military command reported Oct. 11 that Communist forces had eased their pressure in the Taing Kauk area. Local commanders said the pause was due to the enemy's supply and manpower problems.

The South Vietnamese command had reported Oct. 6 the completion of a 3-month operation in southeast Cambodia around Neak Luong and Takeo and the withdrawal of the Saigon force involved. The communique said that 453 North Vietnamese and Viet Cong had been killed in the operation. South Vietnamese losses were said to total 93 killed and 642 wounded.

South Vietnamese forces fought sharp engagements with Communist troops at 3 points along the Cambodian frontier Oct. 13. 2 of the clashes occurred just inside Cambodia and the other in South Vietnam. The largest battle was fought in the 7 Mountains area just inside South Vietnam.

South Vietnamese forces opened 2 separate offensives in Cambodia Oct. 24 and 25.

● The Oct. 24 drive was centered in Cambodia's Fishhook and the Parrot's Beak regions. The operation was aimed at lifting a North Vietnamese threat to Saigon and 11 surrounding provinces, a region from which U.S. forces were being withdrawn rapidly.

● The Oct. 25 offensive involved a force of 6,000 South Vietnamese troops that crossed the border into the Fishhook area and captured the abandoned town of Snoul Oct. 26. The drive, which had encountered little Communist resistance, brought the number of South Vietnamese troops in Cambodia to about 17,500. The attack was aimed at offsetting North Vietnamese pressure against the Saigon area. It was supported by American artillery operating from bases in South Vietnam. The invading troops fanned out along 3 key highways used by the North Vietnamese as supply and infiltration routes into the southern half of South Vietnam.

20,000 Cambodian troops, massed in the Taing Kauk area, 47 miles north of Pnompenh, came under heavy Communist mortar attack Oct. 27. The troops had been stationed there since Sept. 7 in preparation for a drive toward the surrounded provincial capital of Kompong Thom, 25 miles to the north.

Fighting accelerated Nov. 2-11 with South Vietnamese troops taking an increasingly active role.

Hundreds of Saigon militiamen crossed into Cambodia Nov. 2 about 100 miles west of Saigon and launched attacks along the eastern bank of the Mekong River, 50 miles southeast of Pnompenh. Saigon claimed the killing of 43 North Vietnamese and Viet Cong in the attacks.

In an area more than 100 miles to the northeast, other South Vietnamese troops reported finding 65 North Vietnamese bodies near Snoul. Most were reported killed by air and artillery strikes.

A 6,000-man South Vietnamese task force swept into southeastern Cambodia Nov. 6. But the invading units were reported Nov. 11 to have withdrawn after making contact with the enemy but failing to trap part of the 5th Viet Cong Division in the Fishhook area. The drive reportedly was aimed at countering North Victnamese attempts to bring reinforcements and supplies to the Seven Mountains region in southeastern South Vietnam.

Saigon troops came under heavy Communist shelling during fighting Nov. 8. About 500 enemy shells hit bases and posts along the frontier. In ground clashes, the Saigon command reported that 62 Communists and one South Vietnamese had been killed in 6 encounters along Routes 1 and 7. The heaviest fighting was said to have occurred 2 miles north of Snoul, about 5 miles inside Cambodia. 41 North Vietnamese were reported slain in this action.

A force of 7,000 South Vietnamese and Cambodians was reported Nov. 8 to have launched a combined operation between Routes 2 and 3, 24 miles south of Pnompenh. The principal purpose of the drive was to re-establish government control in the area, a Cambodian spokesman said.

Cambodian military positions and towns northeast of the capital were subjected to heavy Communist attacks Nov. 9. A command spokesman said 5 Cambodians had been killed and 6 wounded in an assault on the airport at Kompong Cham, 50 miles northeast of Pnompenh. The government reported 5 Cambodians and 85 Communists killed. 15 North Vietnamese were reported killed in fighting around Skoun, a command center for a large Cambodian force, west of Kompong Cham. A key bridge linking Skoun with Pnompenh was blown up by the Communists Nov. 10. The blast occurred at Batheay on Route 6, 30 miles north of the capital. Another span west of Skoun also was blown up. The destruction of the Batheay bridge also severed an important road link between the capital and Kompong Cham. The cutting of the 2 road links required the government to temporarily supply its forces in the area by air. Communist forces ambushed 2 Cambodian battalions about 5 miles east of Skoun Nov. 11, but there was no word about the fate of the trapped government force. A Pnompenh military spokesman said enemy units had been operating along virtually the entire 32 miles of Highway 7 between Kompong Cham and Skoun.

The fighting Nov. 9-Dec. 1 was marked by the opening of a new Communist drive northeast of Pnompenh and by further South Vietnamese thrusts into the country. In launching their offensive Nov. 9, North Vietnamese/Viet Cong troops attacked and isolated Kompong Cham and assaulted fortified towns nearby. The Cambodian high command reported that it had lost contact with Troeung, 8 miles west of Kompong Cham. The attack on Kompong Cham cut the city's road links with Pnompenh, 50 miles northeast. Skoun, halfway between Pnompenh and Kompong Cham, was hit by the Communists, but the Cambodian defenders repulsed the attack and killed 15 Viet Cong.

Kompong Cham came under constant enemy attacks through Nov. 12. A Cambodian garrison at Chuon Nath, 5 miles west of Kompong Cham, was forced to withdraw Nov. 15 in the face of heavy enemy fire. 11 soldiers who made it to safety were wounded, 3 seriously, according to a command communique.

2 elements of a 20,000-man Cambodian task force were reported Nov. 16 to have been battered by North Vietnamese troops 50 miles north of Pnompenh. A high command account of the action said 13 soldiers had been killed and 49 wounded. 7 North Vietnamese were reported killed.

A force of 4,500 South Vietnamese soldiers crossed into Cambodia's northernmost Ratankiri Province bordering Laos Nov. 17. This was the first time that Saigon's soldiers had crossed the Cambodian frontier in that area in 6 months. The operation centered 36 miles east of Lomphat, the provincial capital. The South Vietnamese drive made little contact with the enemy but uncovered big food and equipment dumps. 4 caches containing 254 tons of ammunition were found Nov. 17. The South Vietnamese command reported Nov. 18 that since then 20 houses, 20 bunkers and 5 acres of crops and a base camp had been destroyed as the task force probed deeper into the province.

Another South Vietnamese task force, comprising 1,000 men, crossed Nov. 19 into Cambodia about 15 miles northeast of the Vietnamese border town of Boduc. This force, too, failed to meet enemy resistance.

Communist forces renewed their attacks Nov. 23, directing their assaults south of Pnompenh. They forced the destruction of Cambodia's only munitions factory and seized a 6-mile stretch of Highway 4, the country's supply lifeline to the Gulf of Siam. The munitions factory, at Stung Chral, 60 miles southwest of the capital, came under heavy enemy rocket, mortar and machine gun fire, forcing a government battalion in the building to withdraw. Before pulling out, the Cambodian defenders blew up the factory and the munitions stocks.

The Communists' southward drive toward Pnompenh was renewed Nov. 27 with a 5-hour attack on government positions 10 miles northeast of the capital. A Cambodian military spokesman said the enemy had taken control of Route 6 on the northern bank of the Mekong River and had captured the vital ferry point at Prek Khdam on the Tonle Sap River, 20 miles north of Pnompenh. The ferry was the only connection to the land route to the northern area of Cambodia. Its loss cut off about 30,000 government troops on the northern front. Other Communist forces were said to have captured some points along a 32-mile stretch of Route 7, about 50 miles north of Pnompenh. The enemy assaults prompted government counterstrikes with air and artillery barrages, and Cambodian forces recaptured the Prek Khdam ferry point Dec. 1. The new government drive reportedly was led by a Cambodian battalion recruited and trained in South Vietnam. Prek Khdam was the southernmost penetration thus far of the Communist offensive.

A South Vietnamese task force operating in southeastern Cambodia came under North Vietnamese attack Nov. 27 near the town of Krek. The Saigon forces repelled the assault on the headquarters of the 52d Task Force, killing 48 North Vietnamese. The South Vietnamese command listed its losses as 10 killed and 20 wounded.

A Cambodian military district headquarters about 40 miles east of Pnompenh was overrun by Communist forces Dec. 6. Pnompenh claimed, however, that Cambodian troops had inflicted heavy casualties on Viet Cong/North Vietnamese soldiers in fighting elsewhere through Dec. 21. The intensified fighting took place after a Cambodian report Dec. 4 of large Communist reinforcements moving into the northern part of the country.

The district headquarters captured by the Communists was at Peam Chikang on the northern bank of the Mekong River. A Cambodian spokesman said a battalion of government defenders and the attackers had both suffered heavy losses. The fighting raged in the area of Route 7, where, according to Pnompenh's Dec. 4 report, 8,000-10,000 Viet Cong had been operating along a 32-mile stretch of Route 7 between Pnompenh and Kompong Cham, isolated by the Communists since September. A government report Dec. 21 said Cambodian troops had ousted the enemy from the road and that it was currently under Pnompenh control.

The Pnompenh military command claimed that 217 North Vietnamese and Viet Cong were killed Dec. 8 in a 5-hour battle north of Svayrieng, an area rarely challenged by the Communists since the allied incursion in the spring had wiped out enemy bases in the sector. The Communists suffered the heavy casualties after opening a strong assault against the government's northern defense line.

A Saigon communique reported Dec. 10 that South Vietnamese forces had suffered 30 killed and 41 wounded in the Fishhook area just inside Cambodia Dec. 9 during a Communist rocket and mortar assault. The shelling also destroyed several trucks. The communique claimed that the defenders had killed 48 members of the 200-man North Vietnamese force in repulsing the attack.

Cambodian forces Dec. 9 recaptured the northwestern district town of Puok, held by the North Vietnamese for more than a month. The North Vietnamese defenders were driven out after fierce street fighting, Premier Lon Nol's office reported.

Heavy fighting raged Dec. 12-15 at Prey Totung, a district town 26 miles north of Pnompenh, between Kompong Cham and Skoun, the last major Cambodian government stronghold on the northern front. A government military spokesman reported Dec. 15 that government defenders, assisted by repeated air strikes, had killed at least 2,000 of the enemy. A convoy moving troop reinforcements up the Mekong River to Kompong Cham came under Communist rocket fire Dec. 12 from both banks of the stream. 4 boats were reportedly sunk within minutes. The U.S. command in Saigon reported that an American plane was shot down Dec. 12 by Communist ground fire in Kompong Cham Province. The pilot was rescued.

A force of 3,000 South Vietnamese troops was reported Dec. 15 to have been airlifted to Kompong Cham in 40 helicopters. The troops were brought in as a result of a personal appeal by Premier Lon Nol to Pres. Nguyen Van Thieu. The Saigon forces were said to have moved into an area believed to contain at least 6,000 North Vietnamese and Viet Cong soldiers.

Cambodian forces were reported Dec. 21 to have launched a major drive to clear enemy forces from Route 4, linking Pnompenh with Kompong Som, Cambodia's only deepwater port on the Gulf of Siam and the site of its only oil refinery. The Cambodian government troops, aided by bombers, were driving southwest along the road, which had been closed by enemy pressure since Nov. 20. The isolation of the port and oil refinery had forced the government Dec. 11 to ration gasoline for consumers for the first time. Military fuel and aviation gasoline were not affected. Civilian reserves were said to have been reduced to 134,500 gallons. Cambodia reported Dec. 22 that its forces had cleared a 50-mile stretch of Route 4. Brig. Gen. Sosthene Fernandez said government soldiers had encountered only Communist harassment as they pushed toward the beleaguered port of Kompong Som. The general estimated that 400 to 500 Communist soldiers had been slain since government forces began their drive down the road. The government said its losses thus far totaled 10 killed and 60 wounded.

Foreign newsmen who visited Prey Totung Dec. 17 had reported that the village, 44 miles north of Pnompenh, had been destroyed by U.S., South Vietnamese and Cambodian air attacks. South Vietnamese forces had linked up with the remaining Cambodian defenders in the village after the allied air strikes.

The Cambodian command Dec. 27 reported fierce fighting with Communist forces at Chambak and Tram Khnar, 2 towns close to the main supply corridor in southern Cambodia. 30 North Vietnamese and Viet Cong were said to have been killed at Chambak, 22 miles south of the capital. No casualties were given for the fighting at Tram Khnar which was 24 miles southwest of Pnompenh.

Government troops Dec. 27 fought hand-to-hand for 7 hours with a 400-man attacking Communist force at Rokakong, a key river village on Pnompenh's outer defense ring. The attackers withdrew from the area, 22 miles north of the capital, after suffering 10 killed and 25 wounded, according to government reports. The defenders lost 4 killed and 12 wounded.

INDEX

Note: This index follows the Western usage in regard to most Vietnamese names but not Cambodian ones. A Vietnamese individual, therefore, would be listed not under his family name but under the last section of his full name. *E.g.,* Huyn Van Cao would be indexed thus: CAO, Huyn Van (not HUYN Van Cao). Exceptions are usually the cases of monks or others (*e.g.,* Ho Chi Minh) who use adopted names; such persons are generally listed under the first sections of their names (HO Chi Minh, not MINH, Ho Chi). A Cambodian, on the other hand, would have his first—or family—name appear first in the index, thus: NORODOM Sihanouk, Prince (not SIHANOUK, Prince Norodom); LON Nol, Lt. Gen. (not NOL, Lt. Gen. Lon), etc.

220 CAMBODIA & THE VIETNAM WAR

SYRACUSE University (Syracuse, N.Y.)—162
SYRIA—70

T

TACHHOR (island)—82
TAEY—22
TAFT Jr., Robert—143
TAING Kauk—201-3
TAKEO Province—50, 67, 75, 78, 81, 84, 102, 104, 109, 125, 202
TANCHAU, South Vietnam—103
TANG Krasang—111
TANGKOK—200
TANI—81
TASS (Soviet news agency)—29, 43, 134, 186
TAYNINH Province South Vietnam—100, 103
TEAMSTERS, Chauffeurs, Warehousemen & Helpers of America, International Brotherhood of (IBT)—147
TEOCHIU Dialect—5
TERRELL Jr., Col. Ernest—74
TEXAS, University of (Austin, Tex.)—147
THAI—5-6
THAI Communists—195
THAILAND—3, 6, 17, 21, 32, 43, 86, 107, 110, 129, 142, 175, 185. Cambodia (incursion)—181, 183; (Military assistance)—135, 137-9
THAILAND, Gulf of—3, 198
THANH, Maj. Gen. Nguyen Viet—73
THANT, U—51, 56, 66, 71, 75, 181, 183, 186, 190
THBENG Menachey—114
THE City, Binhlong Province (South Vietnam)—97
THERAVADA Buddhism—5
THIEU, Maj. Gen. Nguyen Van—41, 105-6, 121, 130, 136, 139, 207
THIOUNN Mumm—70
THLOK Trach Incident—34-5
THO, Nguyen Huu—25, 68
THOMPSON, William P.—168
THUY, Xuan—185
TITO (Josip Broz)—49
TODAY (NBC-TV program)—106

TOKYO—47
TONKIN Gulf Resolution (of 1964)—152. Repeal—178
TONLE Bet—104, 109, 114
TONLE Sap (Lake)—3, 5
TONLE Sap River—205
TOPEKA, Kan.—149
TOPOGRAPHY—3
TOWER, Sen. John G(oodwin) (R., Tex.)—150-1
TOWERY, Capt. Herman Y.—26-7
TRAD Province, Thailand—198
TRAM KHNAR—208
TRI, Lt. Gen. Do Cao—54, 85, 109
TRINH, Nguyen Duy—48
TRINH Heanh—82
TROEUNG—204
TRUCE (1954)—8
TRUMAN, Harry S.—155
TSEDENBAL, Yumzhagiin—32
TUKMEAS—75
TURNER, George—147
TY, Pham Huy—84-5

U

UNION Theological Seminary (New York, N.Y.)—157
UNION of Soviet Socialist Republics (USSR)—8, 15-6, 19, 21, 24, 29, 39, 42-3, 65, 75-6, 160, 190, 198. Cambodia (aid)—1, 30-1; (incursion)—47-9, 134, 181-3. Cambodian relations—69. International conferences—29, 32, 186, 188-9. International Control Commission—46-7
UNITED Church of Christ—168
UNITED Nations (UN)—23, 25, 41. Security Council—14, 23, 33, 36, 41, 54-6
UNITED Presbyterian Church—168
UNITED States—8, 190. Army (Special Forces)—97, 109, 192. Cambodia: air attacks—34-7, 72-3, 115-6, 191, 195-7; arms aid—135-7; border & border incidents—20, 33, 35, 76; 'hot pursuit' policy—33, 76; incursion—2, 47-9, 68, 76, 89, 108, 110, 113, 116, 119-34, 149-53, 181-90; relations with Cambodia—14-32, 35-8, 43-52, 54-8, 60, 64, 99-103,